100 American Soccer Legends

SHANE STAY

100 AMERICAN SOCCER LEGENDS

FROM THE U.S. MEN'S NATIONAL TEAM

Meyer & Meyer Sport

British Library Cataloguing in Publication Data
A catalogue record for this book is available from the British Library

100 American Soccer Legends
Maidenhead: Meyer & Meyer Sport (UK) Ltd., 2026
ISBN: 978-1-78255-288-8

Aachen, Auckland, Beirut, Cairo, Cape Town, Dubai, Hägendorf, Hong Kong, Indianapolis, Maidenhead, Manila, New Delhi, Singapore, Sydney, Tehran, Vienna

Member of the World Sport Publishers' Association (WSPA), www.w-s-p-a.org

Printed by King Printing Company, Inc., Lowell, MA
www.kingprinting.com
Printed in the United States of America

ISBN 978-1-78255-288-8
Email: info@m-m-sports.com
www.thesportspublisher.com

Manufacturer under the GPSR
Meyer & Meyer Fachverlag und Buchhandel GmbH
Von-Coels-Str. 390
52080 Aachen, Germany
www.dersportverlag.de

CONTENTS

PREFACE

The FIFA World Cup is the United States' final athletic frontier. Once the US wins the men's World Cup, it will be *There*. We'll get to that in a second. First, let's discuss aspects of this book.

This List Is Essentially In Chronological Order

With a few exceptions, the top 100 players are listed in chronological order, by birthday, as much as possible. For example, the "unbreakable group" of Tab Ramos (1966), John Harkes (1967), and Tony Meola (1969) were placed together because they made such a big splash, emerging from the same area in New Jersey.

Make No Mistake: US Soccer Players Are Among The Best In The World

Sometimes people get things wrong. Like the assumption, for all these years, that US soccer players aren't any good. Dead wrong. This book is to remind you that soccer greats—world soccer greats, that is—have existed and thrived on US soil.

I believe we could win the FIFA World Cup every time. Let's get that out of the way, right now. My first book is called *Why American Soccer Isn't There Yet*.

If you're wondering why the guy who wrote *Why American Soccer Isn't There Yet* is writing this, don't worry, I'm already anticipating the complaints. But I promise it's not a hate-fest. It's a reality check. The US—the all-time Olympic giant—hasn't won the World Cup yet. Get past it.

The *There* is when we win a FIFA World Cup. I believe the 1990, 1994 squads—and so on—all could've won the World Cup. The talent was there. It's the culture of soccer that was holding those players back. I was also raised in a culture of soccer that was similar. It was a "go forward now" mentality that was taught by virtually everyone involved with soccer. It was a strategy that emulated other American sports such as basketball, hockey, and football. Put points on the board quickly—score now. It created a rushed mentality.

I have nothing but respect for players of past years. They were great athletes and great soccer players. Take for example, Frank Borghi, who was keeper on the US team that defeated England 1-0 in the 1950 FIFA World Cup. An article from *The New York Times* pointed out, "He was a catcher in the St. Louis Cardinals' organization, playing two years in the minor leagues, before switching to soccer and playing for the Simpkins-Ford club in St. Louis."[1]

Then you get into modern times when players like Landon Donovan and Clint Dempsey proved they could compete with all nations on any given day.

Having said that, with all the great coaches and players over the years, we still have not won the FIFA World Cup. That's on paper, it's a fact. It's not my opinion, it's a real thing. Something has prevented the USMNT from an outright FIFA World Cup championship.

All the same, it's very true that American soccer is *there* in many respects: the growth of the game's popularity along with the MLS, and the national team improving greatly in its accomplishments and style of play. So, before you judge a book by its cover—or in this case, a previous book—be cautious to note that I believe the USMNT has had the talent to win every World Cup in history...and this will continue to be the case in the near and long-term future.

Now let's talk about some great players that have represented the USMNT. That's why we're here: the great US players that have come so far, of which there have been many! So many!

Time Out!

Games played and goals scored for players on the USMNT are *approximate* in some cases. Throughout the book, this type of information—along with related material—was cross-checked for verification. In some cases, the years of when players performed on the national team are inconsistent. Likewise, the same can be said of goals scored. At times, different sources have contradictory information. This may or may not be due to faulty research by the person or people that put it together. It might also have to do with the fact that games played in tournaments like the Olympics or the Pan

American games might not be viewed as authentic "international games on behalf of the USMNT." Essentially, recordkeeping has gotten a lot better post-2000 largely because the record-keepers—legitimate sources like ESPN, US Soccer, and FIFA—have had the ability to store information in digital form in real time. For older players, some information is harder to come by. Whatever the case may be, sources are not always consistent with one another.

One example: Ed Murphy. He played for the USMNT from 1955–69. On April 7, 2023, his *Wikipedia* page stated contradictory things. In one place it said he earned 17 caps. On the same page, it also stated he earned 18 caps. On April 7, 2023, online at the Society for American Soccer History, it stated that Murphy "played 18 full internationals."

Another example. When I spoke with Steve Trittschuh on the phone, he pointed out that over time his online stat of goals scored has varied because, apparently, some of his national team games were viewed as being part of the Olympic team category and not a true international game.

In short, if you go online and see a discrepancy in one or more of these things, believe me, it was likely cross-referenced over and over again. This is why these two areas, games played and goals scored, are *approximate*.

Don't Kill the Messenger! Or In This Case, the Author!

For a book like this, everyone has an opinion about who or who should not be on this list. Any such list evokes passion and emotion from fans that have followed the game. Trust me, I operated along the lines of commonsense, truth, and an open-mind while compiling these deserving players. It wasn't easy. There are many players not on this list that very well should be! Without doubt, it was very difficult to exclude some players.

However, this book isn't just one man's opinion. Far from it! For information on past players and the like, top experts in the country—former national team players and coaches of the highest regard—have been consulted. I leaned on the opinions of these types for great insight into the game. They recognized how vast talent is around the country.

Keep in mind, despite the USMNT not yet winning a World Cup, we are talking about the United States of America, the world's leading Olympic nation in gold medals. We have talented athletes, and, it goes without saying but should be pointed out nonetheless, we have talented soccer players. And, not to mention, the common American fan knows sports. So, considering all the talent the US has with respect to soccer, the act of putting this list together was challenging, to say the least.

One thing I kept in mind while researching and writing this was the following: At any given time, realistically speaking, a coach of the USMNT has over 150 center midfielders to choose from. He has over 150 outsider midfielders to choose from. He also has over 150 center defenders to choose from. And so on. But here's the problem: MLS doesn't have room for all these extra players. Only a few select ones get to that level. And from that level, only a few get a chance with the USMNT. And even at that point, not all players get a fair shake. So you have to remember, I'm going with who got to the highest levels based on decision-makers putting players at that level. As a prominent former member of the USMNT told me, (at any given time) essentially it's up to the powers that be to make up a team.

With that said, there are obvious salient talents—such as Tab Ramos and Landon Donovan—who will be easy choices. Then there are others that fill in the blanks. After many discussions with friends, who are fans of the game, I can go down a rolodex of players that I either played with or against that very well could've led the USMNT from their respective positions. But this is just my region of the country, where I grew up (St. Louis). You could just as easily go to Chicago and do the same.

At one point, so the story goes, Bruce Arena passed on his former Virginia standout, Mike Fisher, for a high level team. Mike Fisher—a very smart person—wound up going into the field of medicine. If you're wondering, "Who? What in the hell are you talking about this Mike Fisher for? Never heard of him!" Well, look up Hermann Trophy winners. You'll see. For that matter, why haven't you heard of Johnny Torres? The list goes on.

You can go around the country—Los Angeles, Dallas, Cincinnati, the Washington DC area—and form a list of players that didn't make it through the political system of soccer. You want someone who was crafty and good with possession? Jeff DiMaria—formerly with Scott Gallagher, CBC,

Colorado Rapids, St. Louis Steamers, and the United States national futsal team—is one of the best I've seen. Hell of a player. Point is, there are many players that either played with the USMNT or didn't play with the USMNT that deserve to be acknowledged. But we're not dealing with players that you may or may not have known. This list is the best *of the best* of those that represented the USMNT.

INTRODUCTION

A quick overview of the early history of the USMNT: The first US national soccer team formed in 1885 when they played Canada, the first international match to be held outside of the UK. The US played the match in Newark, New Jersey, and they were soundly defeated 1-0. The teams played a rematch the following year, also in Newark. Neither match, though, was officially recognized. The US earned silver and bronze medals in men's soccer at the 1904 Summer Olympics held in St. Louis, Missouri. FIFA, however, doesn't endorse tournaments that were held before 1908. The US played its first official international match as U.S. Soccer on August 20, 1916. The match was played in Stockholm and was against Sweden. The US won 3-2.[2]

A quick note. Throughout these pages, the following timeline will be referenced from time to time. In summary, soccer competed for a long time within mainstream America to be cool. By and large, throughout the 1900s, soccer was fighting against the Big 3: baseball, basketball, and football. So essentially, for many generations, there is a Pre-Cool phase for soccer and a current Cool phase. By mainstream standards, soccer only has become cool very recently in American history. This inflection point arrived circa 2010, when the USMNT had an exciting FIFA 2010 World Cup and MLS had been gaining in popularity, among other factors.* Right around 2010, it could be argued successfully that soccer finally became cool within the mainstream of the US.

* Also, the media had been covering soccer more often; MLS teams were thriving with soccer-specific stadiums; big name players, like David Beckham, were continuing to land in MLS; and fan support, such as the American Outlaws, was growing for the national team.

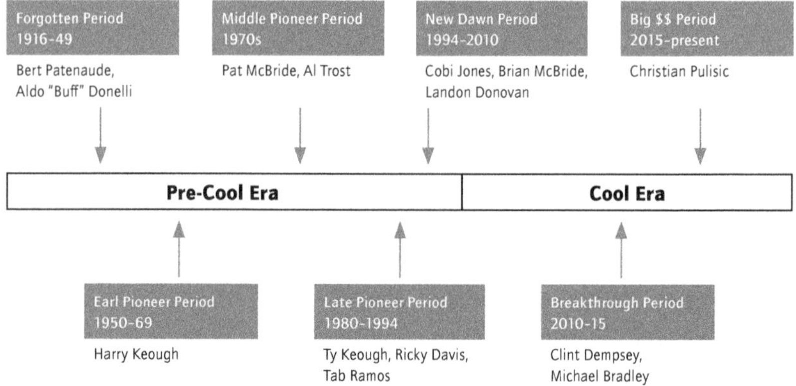

Additionally, throughout the book, the terms *period*, *phase*, and *zone* may be used interchangeably when describing these timelines. For example: the Forgotten period, the Forgotten phase, and so on.

There is obviously some crossover between periods; for example, Landon Donovan—who had a lengthy career—played long before 2010 and beyond it, thus being part of both the New Dawn period and the Breakthrough period. The players listed above provide a general idea of each epoch.

Additionally, throughout the book, the terms *period*, *phase*, and *zone* may be used interchangeably when describing these timelines. For example: the Forgotten period, the Forgotten phase, and so on.

THE TOP 100 USMNT PLAYERS OF ALL TIME

1 Bert Patenaude
USMNT: 1930

Bert Patenaude is one of the few players whose birthdate year is out of place, but I wanted to start out with a bang just as Bert did back in the 1930 FIFA World Cup. Let's look a little closer at this amazing, mythical, legend of the game.

Bert Patenaude–born in 1909 in Fall River, Massachusetts–played forward for Philadelphia Field Club, Fall River Marksmen, Newark Americans, St. Louis Central Breweries, Philadelphia Passon, and the USMNT (in 1930). For the national team, at a time when things were very different and games were far and few between, Patenaude earned four caps and knocked in six goals. In the 1930 FIFA World Cup, Patenaude allegedly scored a hat trick–thought to be the first in World Cup history–against Paraguay, though some thought the second goal was, perhaps, an own goal. Finally, many years later–in 2006–FIFA decided it *was* the first World Cup hat trick.

One could argue that it was a different era–guys had funny-looking long shorts on and everyone wore the same style shoes, the black Model T Ford look. But one could also point out that US soccer has been a prominent part of international soccer as far back as the very first World Cup! And Patenaude, by way of the USMNT, proved it. But that's not all.

He helped lead the USMNT to a third-place finish in the 1930 World Cup, where he won the Bronze Boot (with four goals in that tournament). Quite an accomplishment for the inaugural World Cup. Back then, did anyone really know how big the World Cup would become? Maybe, maybe not. But the US was front and center, as was Patenaude.

In 1970, he was inducted into the US Soccer Hall of Fame. This enigma–who went onto a life of carpentry and painting–died on his 65th birthday in 1974 back in Fall River, Massachusetts. What he left was a unique World Cup record, the unicorn of international soccer achievements: a hat trick in a World Cup. But not just any hat trick, the very first in FIFA World Cup history.

2 Aldo "Buff" Donelli USMNT: 1934

Aldo "Buff" Donelli. There's a lot to unpack here. Was he just a soccer player? Nope. Not even close. Donelli, a college football player for Duquesne University as a halfback and punter, eventually coached an assortment of teams. Between 1939–67, Donelli was a football coach for Duquesne University, Boston University, and Columbia University; he was even a coach in the NFL for the Pittsburgh Steelers (partially in 1941), and the Cleveland Rams (1944).†

Donelli also had the unique distinction of coaching college and NFL teams at the same time—one for the record books. During his stint with the Steelers, Donelli also coached Duquesne University. He administered Steelers practices in the morning and in the afternoon he'd run the Duquesne Dukes through some drills. How did he find time for soccer? Perhaps, back in a time when the sport, along with football, was working its way toward mainstream acceptance, he found merit in soccer when others turned their attention to baseball.

Ever wondered when the US-Mexico rivalry started? Donelli—who was born in 1907—had everything to do with it. Writing for US Soccer, Michael Lewis explains: "The rivalry started with a bang 87 years ago—a 4-2 US qualifying triumph in Rome, Italy on May 24, 1934. The neutral site qualifier was played just three days before the start of the 1934 FIFA World Cup and occurred that way because the USA had submitted its qualifying application late."[3]

It's interesting that this monumental game against Mexico occurred in Italy. "After a semifinal finish at the inaugural 1930 FIFA World Cup in Uruguay, the USA was given the opportunity to qualify via a one-game playoff against Mexico, who had booked its ticket to Italy after winning three qualifying matches against Cuba earlier that spring."[4] Waiting for Mexico was

† Over the years, the Rams have changed from the Cleveland Rams to the St. Louis Rams and again to the Los Angeles Rams.

a guy who just made the team. "Aldo 'Buff' Donelli, who forged a reputation as an American gridiron football star and coach, struck four times in a 4–2 triumph against *El Trí* to book a spot among the final 16 teams."[5] For a first impression, that's pretty amazing. "A late-minute addition to the squad on the insistence of star Billy Gonsalves, Donelli...put on a one-man show before 10,000 spectators and Italian dictator Benito Mussolini at Stadio Nazionale PNF in Rome."[6] As a member of the USMNT in the 1934 FIFA World Cup, he scored the lone goal against Italy in Rome during a Round of 16 defeat to the hosts and eventual champions.

So what happened to Donelli? Why only two caps? Long story short: it was a different era. It was 1934. Donelli—who eventually had a weight room named after him at Columbia University—was part of the Forgotten period (essentially, US soccer before 1950). To his credit, it was two caps with five goals. Not bad. But as part of a different era, he has turned into a symbolic figure in this lost time and his role in the original Mexico rivalry—the biggest rival for the US to this day—sets him apart as a special figure in USMNT history.

3 Billy Gonsalves USMNT: 1930-34

Billy Gonsalves—born in 1908 in Rhode Island—is said to be the Babe Ruth of US soccer. A versatile athlete who entertained boxing and baseball, Gonsalves—who was of Portuguese descent—grew up in Fall River, Massachusetts and played pro soccer in the US before pro soccer as we know it today existed. In fact, he spent over 20 years with different teams that included Boston Soccer Club, Fall River Marksmen, Fall River F.C., St. Louis Central Breweries, Stix, Baer & Fuller of St. Louis, and various other sides.

As soccer was taking off worldwide, the first ever FIFA World Cup took place in 1930, in Uruguay. Billy was front and center for the US in 1930 and 1934. He started every game in 1930, essentially as an attacking mid. As for 1934, despite the US exiting early after a defeat from Italy, Billy started for the team as well.

On eight occasions, Billy won the National Challenge Cup (aka the US Open Cup). That's a remarkable amount. Billy and Bert Patenaude, another member of the USMNT, won the tournament together on two occasions playing for the Fall River Marksmen in 1930 and the following year in 1931 with the Marksmen who changed names to the New York Yankees. After all was said and done, Billy played in the ASL (American Soccer League), St. Louis Soccer League, and National Soccer League of Chicago. He was inducted into the National Soccer Hall of Fame in 1950.

The place where he grew up, Fall River, Massachusetts, was a soccer hotbed. The place where he died, Kearny, New Jersey, was another. His playing career lasted from the 1920s to the 50s. A great talent from a time lost in history, he helped set the stage for the Pioneer periods (1950s-90s) that followed his path.

4 John Souza USMNT: 1947-54

John Souza—born in 1920 in Fall River, Massachusetts—played forward for Fall River Ponta Delgada and New York German-Hungarian. From *New England Soccer Today,* an article by Brian O'Connell points out "...Souza grew up in the Flint section of Fall River at a time in which it was impossible to escape the beautiful game. The city was a hotbed of soccer in the first half of the 20th century, and gave rise to the Fall River Marksmen, Fall River F.C., and Ponta Delgada."[7]

New England at large, and this area for sure, was big on soccer back in the early days. As such, it produced talents like the amazing Souza. Over the years, many soccer fans have forgotten about him and this era. Nonetheless, he's gone down as one of the greats in US soccer history.

"Although he was characterized as a shy personality off the field, he was far from bashful with the ball at his feet. He had sensational touch and dribbling skills, and was called a 'magician' by many who watched him play. But it wasn't the only reputation he'd earn during his playing career."[8] His nickname, incidentally, was "Clarkie." O'Connell wrote: "Many of his teammates and friends noticed that Souza had an uncanny resemblance to actor Clark Gable, who starred in *Gone with the Wind* in 1939. Thus, John Souza had a nickname he'd never shake: 'Clarkie.'"[9]

Quietly, hidden away in the archives of early US soccer history, Souza was part of a number of championships. "Toward the latter part of the 1940's, he helped steer Ponta Delgada to three straight Amateur Cups from 1946-48 and a double in 1947 when they also clinched the US Open Cup championship."[10] But he wasn't done there. "In 1951, he moved to New York to play for the German-Hungarians and, for the second time in his career, he was part of another club that won the Amateur Cup and Open Cup in the same year."[11]

With the USMNT "Clarkie" suited up for 14 games,‡ with two goals—a good number of games in his day. His time with the national team spanned from 1947–54 and included the 1948 and 1952 Olympics, along with the renowned 1950 FIFA World Cup.

In the 1–0 defeat over England in the 1950 FIFA World Cup, John was a starter in the middle of things with captain Ed McIlvenny (who had played for Wrexham, a Welsh team with a storied history that, in recent times, Hollywood stars Ryan Reynolds and Rob McElhenney administered as owners). Incidentally, John was on the field that important day with forward Ed Souza, who apparently is of no relation, yet both were from Fall River, Massachusetts, both played for Fall River Ponta Delgada and New York German-Hungarian, both were on the national team during the same time, and while John was born in 1920, Ed was born in 1921. Nonetheless, as non-relatives, they teamed up for perhaps the most famous game in USMNT history. When it was over, John Souza left Brazil with a unique accolade: "He was selected for a World Cup All-Star team by the Brazilian sports newspaper *Mundo Esportivo*, and remained the only US player ever selected to a World Cup All-Star team until Claudio Reyna in 2002."[12]

In addition, "Clarkie"—who earned the respect of Brazilian paper *Mundo Esportivo*—was inducted into the National Soccer Hall of Fame in 1976 and the New England Soccer Hall of Fame in 1983.

‡ This information was acquired at *Wikipedia* entitled "John Souza" on April 3, 2023. On the same date, at *New England Soccer Today* entitled "The Passing of a Legend" (updated in 2012), it stated that he earned 16 caps.

Charlie Colombo
USMNT: 1948-52

Charlie Colombo—born in 1920—grew up in the famous Italian neighborhood, The Hill, in St. Louis, Missouri. As you may or may not have heard, the tradition of soccer in the US pretty much revolves around St. Louis.§ The lore of this mythical soccer city is thanks, in part, to guys like Ralph Tracey,¶ Frank Vaughn, Harry Keough, Frank Borghi, and Charlie Colombo.

As a center mid, Colombo played for the powerhouse club St. Louis Simpkins-Ford, with which he won the National Challenge Cup (aka US Open Cup) in 1948 and 1950.

Colombo—referred to as "Gloves" because he was known for wearing a pair while playing—also played for the US in the 1948 and 1952 Olympics. As a member of the USMNT (1948-52), Colombo earned 11 caps and played in the 1950 FIFA World Cup, including the major 1-0 upset of England. Following the match, he even rejected a chance to stay in Brazil and play professionally.

He's a member of the St. Louis Soccer Hall of Fame. He was also inducted into the National Soccer Hall of Fame in 1976.

---

§ Save for a few areas, particularly on the Eastern Seaboard, like Massachusetts, New York, New Jersey, and Philadelphia, for example. However, despite the soccer prowess of these areas, St. Louis has long been considered the US' first soccer capitol.

¶ There seem to be variations of his name, such as: Raphael "Ralph" Tracy, found at Society for American Soccer History and *Wikipedia*, on March 31, 2023. Also, on this date, the St. Louis Soccer Hall of Fame spelled his last name "Tracey" which is the preferred spelling in this book.

Frank Wallace
USMNT: 1949-50

Frank Wallace—born in 1922 in St. Louis, Missouri—was a forward that played for the renowned St. Louis teams of his time: Raftery, Steamfitters, and Simpkins-Ford. With Simpkins-Ford, he won two US Open Cups in 1948 and 1950.

He served in WWII and ended up spending some 16 months in a German prisoner of war camp. Upon his release, he re-established himself in St. Louis—incidentally, a city with a heavy German background—and suited up for Raftery in 1945-46.

For the USMNT (1949-50), he earned seven caps and three goals. In the 1950 FIFA World Cup, Wallace—nicknamed "Pee Wee"—was one of the five St. Louis starters against the Three Lions in the 1-0 win. There he matched wits with England's renowned John Aston, Al Ramsey, Billy Wright, Jimmy Dickinson, Laurie Hughes, Stan Mortensen, Roy Bentley, Tom Finney, Wilf Mannion, and Jimmy Mullen. Famous English Coach Walter Winterbottom didn't know what hit him. Five starters from St. Louis that did England in? How could it be? Wallace, along with his St. Louis cohorts, carried a little secret the rest of the world may or may not have known then: St. Louis is the United States' first soccer capital.

In the following game, Wallace scored a goal against Chile, a game the US lost and subsequently was the last match for the team that tournament. All in all, despite not advancing from its group, the 1950 World Cup was chalked up as a monumental success, seeing as how the USMNT shook things up with an upset over tournament favorite England. If anything, it was a hint of things to come for US soccer.

Frank "Pee Wee" Wallace was inducted into the St. Louis Soccer Hall of Fame (1975) and the National Soccer Hall of Fame (1976).

7 Frank Borghi USMNT: 1949-54

Frank Borghi—born in 1925 in St. Louis, Missouri—represented the USMNT from 1949-54.** Aside from the USMNT, Borghi played for St. Louis Simpkins-Ford, a very successful team in its day.

Prior to the big game in 1950, Borghi was a medic for a United States infantry unit and, in World War II, involved in the Battle of the Bulge. Subsequently, he was given the Purple Heart and the Bronze Star.

In the FIFA 1950 World Cup he was guarding the net against England in, perhaps, the biggest World Cup upset in history, when the US held on for a 1-0 shocker. Borghi—the last man of defense—managed to keep things in order. Jim Leeker—the 1970 NASL Rookie of the Year and president of the St. Louis Soccer Hall of Fame—explained that Borghi was highly regarded in England thanks to his 1950 World Cup performance. After defeating the Three Lions in such a way, they couldn't help but take notice. The US, who was not supposed to win, shocked the world that day in 1950, down in Brazil. Certainly England was taken aback.

Years later, as 1976 came around, he was inducted into the United States National Soccer Hall of Fame.

In 2005, Borghi was portrayed by Gerard Butler in *The Game of Their Lives*—in reference to the 1-0 defeat of England. The film also involved Eric Wynalda as a consultant, certainly for moves and technique and what not. What's more, John Harkes can be seen in the movie. Some filming took place in St. Louis, Missouri (where, of course, five of the starters against England were from).

** On April 10, 2023, the Society for American Soccer History and *Wikipedia* listed his USMNT time from 1949-54. As mentioned in the preface, these dates sometimes vary. Another account—the St. Louis Sports Hall of Fame, April 10, 2023—has Borghi's USMNT career listed from 1949-53.

8 Harry Keough
USMNT: 1949-57

St. Louis-native, **Harry Keough**—born in 1927—was a prominent defender that competed for the US national team from 1949-57. The big game, the one that's still spoken of to this day, was the 1-0 defeat of England in the 1950 FIFA World Cup. Five starters on that USMNT were from St. Louis. Key in the mix was Harry Keough. It's been said that, after the US scored that goal in the 38th minute, England—stunned and bitter, with its top players Alf Ramsey, Billy Wright, Tom Finney, Roy Bentley, and Stanley Matthews as an option—unleashed an angry onslaught of attacks that never stopped. Somehow, with determination and resolve, Keough and the US held on.

Keough was born to Patrick John and Elizabeth (née Costley) Keough. He grew up in St. Louis, Missouri, and attended Cleveland High School. As a youth he played several sports, including track, swimming, and fast-pitch softball, particularly excelling at soccer. His soccer career began in 1945 as a member of the St. Louis Schumachers, who won the 1946 National Junior Challenge Cup. He joined the U.S. Navy in 1946. He was assigned to a naval base in San Francisco, California where he played for the San Francisco Barbarians, which had dominated west coast soccer in the first half of the 20th century."[13]

Keough made his way back to St. Louis after completing his military service. "In 1948, he played for Paul Schulte Motors. The next year the team came under the sponsorship of McMahon Pontiac and played in the lower division St. Louis Municipal League. He was with McMahon when selected for the US national team as it entered qualification for the 1950 World Cup. When he returned home from the cup, Keough rejoined his team, now known as the St. Louis Raiders of the first division St. Louis Major League. The Raiders won both the league and National Amateur Cup championships in 1952, giving Keough his first 'double.' Following the 1952 season, Tom Kutis took over sponsorship of the team, renaming it St. Louis Kutis S.C. The team continued its winning ways under its new name, winning the 1953 and 1954 league titles, and went to the 1954 National Challenge Cup final where it fell to New York Americans of the American Soccer League. The St. Louis Major League had folded in 1954 and Kutis continued to play both as an independent team and as a member of various lower division city leagues over the next decade. Despite this turbulence, it continued to dominate both the city and national soccer scene. Kutis would win the National Amateur Cup each year from 1956 to 1961. In 1957, it won the National Challenge Cup, giving Keough another double."[14]

Keough, a critical part of the Early Pioneer period, was trekking a course for US soccer at large, while also working for the US Postal Service. He was often said to have a good understanding of players and where to place them, and eventually, Keough took over as coach at St. Louis University and won, if you can believe it, another five NCAA championships! Often with assistant coach Val Pelizzaro by his side, Keough added to a ten-run championship grab started by Bob Guelker...the record of ten national titles still holds to this day (with Indiana and Virginia universities in close pursuit). A St. Louis legend, a Saint Louis University legend, and a US soccer legend, Keough helped put soccer on the map for St. Louis and the United States.

9 Gino Pariani USMNT: 1948-50

If you're interested in another St. Louis talent, one from a famous neighborhood, then look no further. **Gino Pariani**—born in 1928—grew up in St. Louis on The Hill (an Italian-American area regarded for its Italian restaurants to this day). By the age of 15, he played for a top St. Louis side at the time, Schumachers. As an inside right (essentially a midfielder), Pariani had success with Schumachers as the team won the St. Louis league title in 1943. After that, he became league MVP while playing for Raftery's S.C. and eventually switched again to St. Louis Simpkins-Ford.

With Simpkins-Ford—a powerhouse—he was part of two national championships, winning the US Open Cup in 1948 and 1950. A regular all-star in the St. Louis league system from 1946-53, Pariani was excelling in the US' top league at the time. St. Louis, Missouri, the US' first soccer capitol, was the place to be and Pariani was one of the best around. As such, Pariani—who was around 5'8"—made the USMNT for the 1948 Olympics.

In addition, Pariani was part of the 1950 FIFA World Cup team—one of five St. Louis natives that started against England in the famous 1-0 victory that shocked the world. Overall, Pariani played for the USMNT from 1948-50, with five caps and one goal, this during the Early Pioneer period, a time when international games were few and far between.

In 1975, he was inducted into the St. Louis Soccer Hall of Fame. Also inducted into the National Soccer Hall of Fame (1976), Pariani is a mythical figure in the lore of St. Louis and US soccer.

10 Bob Kehoe USMNT: 1965

There are legendary figures in American soccer. And certainly, there are legendary players from St. Louis, more so, it seems, than from anywhere else in the US. **Bob Kehoe**–born in 1928–grew up in St. Louis, the headquarters of US soccer, and entered elite territory. Kehoe, without a doubt, is a legend within St. Louis soccer circles. Aficionados know he is integral in the growth of the sport nationwide. For many, he's not just a pioneer for St. Louis soccer but also US soccer at large.

Few people in St. Louis, or around the nation, can equal the impressive list of achievements as Bob Kehoe. He was on SLUH's original soccer team in 1943. SLUH, of course, is St. Louis University High School which won the Missouri high school state championship in 1972, 1990, and 2003. A few other notable students that went there include Dan Flynn (former CEO of US Soccer Federation), Ty Keough (former USMNT player and broadcaster for US soccer games), and Taylor Twellman (former USMNT player, MLS MVP, and a broadcaster for US soccer games).

After his high school graduation in 1947, Kehoe–a multi-talented sportsman–found himself in the farm system of the Philadelphia Phillies for a time. However, he preferred soccer and the defender achieved success with Kutis and the St. Louis Stars (1968), coached the Stars (1969-70), was captain for the USMNT (1965), and eventually coached the USMNT (1972).

According to Jim Leeker (NASL Rookie of the Year, 1970), one of Kehoe's proudest moments was walking onto the field for the US as captain and fielding an all-St. Louis team as coach of the Stars. The group included Tom Bokern, Steve Frank, Larry Hausmann, Jim Leeker, Pat McBride, Jerry Mueller, John Pisani, Paul Pisani, Joe Right, Gary Rensing, and Chris Werstein, some of whom played for the USMNT at one time or another. The long history of St. Louis soccer is immense. St. Louis is known as the US' first soccer capitol and Kehoe was front and center. This move, starting an all-St. Louis lineup, only bolstered the reputation of St. Louis nationwide.

Following this, in 1972, Kehoe reached another milestone, this time as coach of the USMNT—thus establishing himself as a captain and coach of the team. Quite remarkable.

In later years, Kehoe coached Granite City North High School—a powerhouse soccer city in the Metro East of St. Louis—from 1973-83. He was also director of coaching for Busch Soccer Club (North America's best club team for a time) and served as a broadcaster for the original St. Louis Steamers of the MISL (in the 1980s).

He was inducted into the St. Louis Soccer Hall of Fame (1983) and National Soccer Hall of Fame (1989).

Kehoe, who was living in the south St. Louis area, passed away in 2017 at the age of 89 and was unable to see the formation of St. Louis City SC. However, he definitely had a critical role in the shaping of soccer in St. Louis and the US at large.

11 Ed Murphy USMNT: 1955-69

Ed Murphy—born in 1930 in Scotland—played as a forward in the US and became an integral part of the USMNT during the 1950s and 60s. From 1955-69, he played approximately 18 games for the national team, with five goals. During this time, the Early Pioneer period (1950s-60s), there weren't that many USMNT games. Some years there wasn't a game at all. For Murphy to play in 18 matches is quite astonishing.

Outside of the national team, he was knocking home goals in the competitive arena of Chicago soccer. He played for the Chicago Vikings, Chicago Maroons, Chicago Slovak, and, notably, the Chicago Mustangs (of the NASL in 1968).

During his time with the USMNT, he was part of the 1956 Olympics. Three years later, he had a good showing—with eight goals—in the 1959 Pan American Games, hosted by Chicago. Three of his eight goals came as a hat trick against Brazil. In that tournament, a big deal in those days, the USMNT earned the bronze medal. During an era when the USMNT had many ups and downs, Murphy's eight goals in the Pan American Games did not apply to his stats as these games "were considered less than full international matches."[15]

In 1998, he was inducted into the National Soccer Hall of Fame.

12 Bill Looby USMNT: 1954-59

Bill Looby—born in 1931—was raised in St. Louis, the nation's soccer capitol. One of many great players from St. Louis, Looby represented the national team back in the Early Pioneer period. Four years after the USMNT's huge 1-0 victory over England at the 1950 World Cup, Looby got his first cap with the team in 1954 and played with them until 1959 (nine caps, six goals).

In 1956, Looby was on the US team that competed in the Olympics.

Looby—a forward with club experience on the St. Louis Raiders and St. Louis Kutis—was an integral part of the Kutis' success in the later part of the 1950s, including the 1957 US Open Cup championship. "Looby played in the Kutis' six consecutive National Amateur Cup championships (1956-1961). He also scored goals in both games of the 1957 National Challenge Cup championship over New York Hakoah."[16] (The National Challenge Cup is also known as the US Open Cup. The next US Open Cup title for a St. Louis team after 1957 would be in 1988 when the Busch Seniors won—a group Steve Trittschuh was part of.)

The following year was very big for Looby. He was part of something that, most likely, will never happen again in the United States. "In 1958, the US Soccer Football Association used the Kutis team as the US national team in two World Cup qualifying games against Canada.

Another memorable event for Looby as a Kutis team member took place on May 5, 1955, when Kutis defeated 1. FC Nürnberg, 3-2. The Nürnberg team featured four players from the 1954 West German World Cup championship team."[17] No words can really describe that: A club team, from St. Louis, was asked to play as proxy for the USMNT. They didn't ask New York, Philadelphia, Chicago, or Los Angeles. They asked the St. Louis Kutis.

In 1959, Looby—along with teammates John Traina, Herman Wecke, Val Pelizzaro, Ed Murphy, and Al Perhusen, to name a few—scored multiple goals for the US at the Pan American Games hosted by Chicago, in which the US received the bronze medal.

He was inducted into the St. Louis Soccer Hall of Fame in 1984 and the National Soccer Hall of Fame in 2001.

13 Al Zerhusen
USMNT: 1957-65††

Al Zerhusen—born in 1931 in Brooklyn, New York—played midfield for the USMNT during the Early Pioneer period (1950s and 60s) where he acquired some 10 caps and two goals. However, allegedly, he played for the USMNT in 1954 in games that were not deemed worthy of international credit. He's one of those mysterious players that has both games played and goals scored shrouded in mystery. Nonetheless, when looking at Al, you realize that this guy, from a different era, when recordkeeping was a little less stringent, had one hell of a run.

Perhaps the best thing that occurred to him at a young age was moving to Germany where he gleaned the finer points of the game from one of the best in the world. Upon his return in 1950, he landed in Cincinnati, Ohio, was drafted into the US Army, went back to Europe, and then back to the US where he played soccer in Cincinnati with an Armed Forces team and the Kolping Soccer Club. Eventually, he moved to Los Angeles and played for the Kickers as captain.

The team had much success, winning the US Open Cup in 1958 and 1964. In 1964, *The New York Times* featured a report:

> "LOS ANGELES, June 21 (AP)—The Kicker-Victoria Soccer Club of Los Angeles"[18] beat "the Ukrainian Nationals of Philadelphia, 2-0, today to win the United States open championship."[19] Helping the team along was Al Zerhusen who "scored on a penalty kick at the 77th minute"[20] and the "victory qualified Los Angeles to tour South America for the State Department."[21]

†† Zerhusen's time with the USMNT varies. At *Wikipedia* entitled "Al Zerhusen," on April 11, 2023, it suggested his national team experience began in 1954, but his games that year weren't recognized by FIFA or USSF; the same page also stated he played on the national team from 1956-65 and from 1957-65. Also on April 11, 2023, at the Society for American Soccer History, it stated he played on the USMNT from 1957-65.

Overall, Zerhusen played for the Los Angeles Kickers and Scots. He was the Greater Los Angeles Soccer League scoring leader on 13 occasions. As a result, Zerhusen was the preeminent star—call him the king—of LA soccer at the time.

During his stints in club soccer, from Ohio to California, Zerhusen, talented player that he was, earned a place on the USMNT. One particular honor arrived when he was chosen for the 1956 Olympics in Australia. In the only game for the US—which was a lopsided knockout by Yugoslavia—Zerhusen scored the lone US goal in Melbourne at Olympic Park Stadium before a crowd of just over 5,250. It may have been a quick stop for the US that year and one goal might seem like not that big of a deal, but "in preparation for the games, the US had played several exhibition matches and Zerhusen scored seventeen goals in nine games leading up to the Olympics,"[22] according to a *Wikipedia* article.

Then there were the 1959 Pan American Games, held in Chicago. The US placed third, earning the bronze. Zerhusen scored 10 goals, tying Brazil's Jose Ricardo da Silva (aka China)[‡‡] for first place in scoring.

Unfortunately for Zerhusen, he was stuck in a time when the US didn't compete as much and some of the games he did play in weren't counted as a full international. Nonetheless, he flourished during his time as a scoring threat and in 1978 he was inducted into the National Soccer Hall of Fame.

‡‡ China was no slouch. (Most Brazilians aren't.) From 1962–65, he played over 70 games for Sampdoria in Italy, scoring 30 goals.

14 Willy Roy USMNT: 1965-73

Some legends get lost to time because facts get lost in the shuffle. Stories get foggy in a haze of online information that seems credible enough, but there's something behind it, something that is slightly off. As I looked into **Willy Roy**, it became clear, at first, that he arrived in the US at the age of six and that the goals he scored as an adult on the USMNT varied from source to source. Was all this correct? What was going on? Then I spoke with Roy personally.

When we spoke, he was in Chicago, where he had lived for many years; where he started his playing career; where, as a young man, he owned a German nightclub–Hansa Club and St. Pauli Bar–on Lincoln and Addison, near Wrigley Field, that featured European music and teammates would swing by after games (a joint that sounds reminiscent of Jackie Moon's The Kremlin bar in *Semi-Pro*); and where he eventually coached the famed Chicago Sting–owned by the notorious Lee Stern–to two NASL championships. Willy Roy is a "pure US soccer legend" in every sense of the word: an immigrant, a captain of the USMNT, a champion.

Roy–born in 1943 in Germany–played the accordion as a youth on the back of a bus that toured different castles for a travel agency and "I would deliver flowers on a part-time basis" to keep busy, as his dad wasn't in favor of him playing sports. He moved to the US at the age of 13. Upon arriving to New York, Roy and family took a train to the Second City–"we had relatives living in Chicago"–to settle in.

He and his brother joined the Wanderers. Eventually, the 6'0" forward, who was said to be "one of the most dangerous goal scorers in US soccer in the late 1960s and early 1970s,"[23] suited up for the Chicago Spurs (1967-68), Kansas City Spurs (1968), St. Louis Stars (1971-74), and Chicago Sting (1975).

He kicked things off well as the 1967 NPSL Rookie of the Year and made the NPSL All-Star selection. Not bad. After impressing many around the league, he wound up in soccer central with the St. Louis Stars, a team that at one point or another included Pat McBride (USMNT), John Carenza (US Olympic soccer team), Buzz Demling (USMNT), Tom Bokern, Gene Geimer (USMNT), Carl Gentile (USMNT), Jim Leeker (NASL Rookie of the Year, 1970), Al Trost (USMNT captain), Don Popovic, Milonja Kalicanin, Larry Hausmann (USMNT), John and Paul Pisani, Steve Frank (USMNT), Gary Rensing (USMNT), Denny Vaninger (USMNT), Chris Werstein, and the man, Tommy Howe. According to Roy, with the Stars he was a rental: when the team had money they'd fly him from Chicago to games where he'd be embraced by the welcoming committee; he maybe practiced with them two or three times. Roy said of his time there: "I have so much respect, you know, not only Pat but Al Trost, Steve Frank, Geimer." In 1972, the Stars found a path to the NASL championship game, losing out to the New York Cosmos.

When I interviewed him, we talked for a while and his jokes were accompanied with the German accent he still carries. Of the USMNT, Roy confirmed that he did play from 1965-73, earning 20 caps with nine goals, or ten, depending on who you ask. Even Roy was hazy on that memory. "I couldn't even give you an exact number and I don't know if the federation actually kept, you know, total numbers in those days." Just as quick as a joke could pop out, he'd get serious and added, "My only preference really was, all my life, is for the team to win. I really didn't care who scored the goals, who got the assists, as long as we won the game." Nine goals—from 1968-73—were against: Israel, Canada, Haiti, Bermuda, Bermuda, Canada, Canada, Mexico, Israel.

In Roy's time with the US team, there were different coaches and player turnover was frequent. He explained to me how George Meyer, a new coach at the helm in 1965, said to the guys "Okay, we're gonna start jogging" to which someone said "No, we're gonna start walking."

Another of his USMNT coaches was Phil Woosnam, a former member of West Ham, Aston Villa, Atlanta Chiefs, and the Wales national team. Roy seemed to appreciate him, said his approach was Sargent-like, and it was a good group for a brief time before Woosnam became the Commissioner of the NASL.

It wasn't as stringently organized as it is today. During this time, the Pioneer periods—in particular, from the 1950s-70s—you'd be called a couple weeks before a game or event, told to have your passport in order, and be in shape. As Roy said, you'd be hard-pressed to have two games with the same players.

Despite different coaches and teammates, during the early 70s, Roy went on a three-game scoring streak. This feat of Roy's—which stood for around 30 years—didn't occur again until Cobi Jones matched it in 2000. Roy also had a six-goal scoring record during World Cup qualifying games—these goals arrived in 1968, 1968, 1968, 1972, 1972, 1972. This was finally bested by Earnie Stewart, who scored seven during qualifiers in 2001. Roy's records lasted quite a while. Not bad for a German immigrant that arrived via boat.

After his playing days, Roy coached the legendary Chicago Sting (1977-86). In 1981, leading the formidable black and yellow Sting from the sidelines, he earned Coach of the Year honors in the NASL to which he quipped, "I voted for myself ten times." This honor arrived, likely, because of his 23-9 record combined with his tackling of the New York Cosmos on route to the Soccer Bowl trophy that was the championship game at the time. A key player in Roy's arsenal was captain Karl-Heinz Granitza. Upon returning from the title match, a throng of fans gathered at O'Hare airport, causing a stir. As Roy pointed out, that was a sign of the shift for soccer in the US.

Roy's championships weren't done yet. He and Karl-Heinz Granitza won the NASL championship again in 1984 with the Sting. This was a time when soccer culture was just that: a group of soccer aficionados. From coast to coast, there was a shift toward soccer but it was still working its way into the mainstream; it would take a decade or two.

With respect to soccer, this was an extremely interesting moment in US sports history. For the Sting, after ousting the Toronto Blizzard in 1984 for the title, it was bittersweet. As it turns out, it was right at the tail end of the NASL's existence. When the league folded, pro outdoor soccer faded as well, and there was a gap between the end of the NASL (circa 1984) and the beginning of MLS (1996).

In that gap, pro indoor would outshine any and all ephemeral pro outdoor exercises. Because of the NASL and people like Roy, the MISL got a boost and flourished. Even still, in the late 80s indoor reached a decline. Despite its continuation to this day, indoor has had a rough go of it. Nonetheless, just like the NASL, indoor played a critical role in the advent of MLS. In the lore of pro US soccer, the top leagues have been: NASL, MISL, and MLS. Roy—whose name means king in French—was a two-time champion while at the helm of the Chicago Sting in the NASL, a league that holds a mythical grip over US soccer.

Beginning in 1987, Roy coached the men's soccer team at Northern Illinois University and, as he said, the job lasted some 17 years after that. He is the co-author of *Coaching Winning Soccer* (Contemporary Books, 1979) and in Roy fashion he remarked, "I think we sold five copies; I have three, my mother bought the other two." In 1989 he was inducted into the National Soccer Hall of Fame.

He remained active in the Chicago soccer scene, overseeing his Willy Roy's Soccer Dome in Dolton, Illinois. For this champion that left Germany and landed in Chicago, played for Chicago, coached Chicago, captained the USMNT, and set a few records in his day, it was a remarkable journey...one fit for a king.

Pat McBride
USMNT: 1969-75

Pat McBride–born in 1943–is synonymous with St. Louis soccer. Period. In 1972, McBride used all of his versatile midfield talent and became a First Team All-Star in the NASL.

During 1969-75, he gathered five caps for the USMNT. This was an era when the US team played far fewer games. Players like Pat were pioneering soccer at the time. Back then things were different. The USMNT program wasn't the same as today. As Willy Roy has said, at times players would be called a couple weeks before a game and asked if they were in shape. Players met up. The game took place. I asked Pat about the process back then, how a team was put together. Essentially, players from different parts of the nation were chosen–typically the East Coast, Midwest, and West Coast–by coaches in those areas who knew the players.

As a leading talent, his presence in US soccer was impactful as he pushed the sport forward while playing with the St. Louis Stars (NASL) and the USMNT, and eventually as a coach.

Initially, in 1972, he assisted Bob Guelker at SIUE for the university's first national soccer championship. Subsequently, following his career with the Stars, McBride was head coach of the original St. Louis Steamers (1979-81), where he was named MISL Coach of the Year in 1979-80.

Eventually, McBride departed St. Louis to coach the Kansas City Comets. Then one day, by popular demand, McBride made his glorious comeback. In 1985, *Soccer Digest*[§§]–essentially *the* soccer publication for US fans in the 80s–featured his rebirth in the Budweiser-dominated soccer town. McBride "who was extremely popular when he first coached the Steamers four years ago"[24] returned to St. Louis, the Gateway to the West, where he took hold of the legendary team one last time. Sam Bick–a St. Louis native who played

§§ Previous pages featured MISL legends Steve Zungul, Branko Segota, Tatu, UCLA's Paul Caligiuri, and coach Jerry Yeagley of Indiana University, heralded as one of the all-time gurus in college soccer.

for the Steamers and had USMNT experience—stressed how important it was for McBride to return. As Bick said: "Everybody in St. Louis who ever kicked a soccer ball knows who he is. Wherever he goes, he brings a positive attitude."[25]

McBride had a remarkable career, first in the college game as a national champion with SLU, followed by the Stars in the emerging NASL, then the USMNT at a time when soccer was finding its way in the US. Subsequently, he continued setting trends as an assistant coach with SIUE (under the auspices of Bob Guelker) and as head coach of the Steamers in the *rock-and-roll experimental project* known as the MISL. Not to mention, he earned a Master's degree from SIUE.

McBride was one of those players that was ultra-talented at a time when soccer was working its way up the cool ladder in US sports. When he returned for part two as coach of the St. Louis Steamers, Dan Caesar's article in *Soccer Digest* pointed out how "Steamers midfielder Ty Keough said McBride's return may be the spark needed to fuel the interest of marginal fans."[26] This was 1985, just under ten years before MLS launched in 1996.

For a time, the early-to-mid 80s,[¶¶] soccer on the indoor scene was thunderous, thanks in large part to Tim Leiweke—ahead of his time—who orchestrated the rock-and-roll atmosphere equipped with fog and laser lights for pre-game intros and the like. Then indoor fell off, but not completely.[***] Indoor, along with other efforts, was responsible for the birth of MLS and the increased popularity of the USMNT.

McBride forged a path for future stars such as Christian Pulisic. Incidentally, Pulisic's dad Mark played pro indoor in the 1990s. It's interesting how the progress of US soccer over the years leads back to players like McBride, who were putting the pieces in place well before Christian Pulisic came along. Because of standouts like McBride, the stars of today are able to flourish.

¶¶ The Golden era of pro indoor soccer. Food, fights, goals, fans going crazy in packed houses. What more could you ask for?

*** Pro indoor is still out there as a viable league. It's undergone name changes over the years. As of April 16, 2023, the MASL's commissioner was Keith Tozer, a former indoor player that eventually coached the Milwaukee Wave—where he won multiple championships—and the United States national futsal team.

On December 21, 2024, I attended Pat McBride's Funeral at Saint Francis Xavier College Church in St. Louis, Missouri. McBride was a true leader and was such a presence in St. Louis soccer.

In 2020, I interviewed McBride for my book, *This Is Our CITY,* which is about St. Louis City Soccer Club. When I spoke to him on the phone for the first time, it was like talking to the Frank Sinatra of soccer. It was a fascinating conversation about his contributions to St. Louis, and, more importantly, American soccer. Only a few moments after we had hung up, my phone rang. It was McBride. He said, "Shane, I just realized I didn't ask you more about your background! Tell me more about you!"

He was a class act, and he had such a desire for others to do good. When you look at American soccer, McBride was one of the best ever.

16 Al Trost
USMNT: 1973-78

Al Trost—the great one—is one of the best you'll ever come across. As a national champion with Saint Louis University (during its heyday), Al—who was born in 1949—accomplished something very unique. Most players are lucky to win the Hermann Trophy—an elite award for the best player in college—once. Al won it twice (1969, 1970).[†††]

From massive success with SLU, to the St. Louis Stars of the NASL, then the USMNT, Al was in the Middle Pioneer period (1970s) of US soccer. Like Pat McBride, Trost is a name from the past that fell in line with the greater powers of the universe that decreed, for one reason or another, their time would be now—now being the 1960s and 70s. If, in fact, they had been born later in life, you certainly would have seen them on TV alongside Landon Donovan, Clint Dempsey, or Christian Pulisic.

As things were, Trost and McBride—who grew up near one another—paired up in midfield for the Stars. Blazing a path forward for US soccer, despite being a few years apart, the two offered the NASL a one-two punch that was fierce. And both played for the USMNT.

Trost's time with the national team was essentially from 1973-78. Back in those days, Trost told me the USMNT offered a simple *luxury* for the players: hand-me-down uniforms and wash em' yourselves! Oh yeah, then at the end of your time with the team, please return them. You wanna talk about a different era—that was it!

Among his accolades, with the national team he scored the game winner—a smashing half-volley into the far upper-corner off an assist from a fellow St. Louisan, Gene Geimer—against Poland circa 1973 in Connecticut. In the 70s and 80s, Poland's national team was surging forward with talent,

††† Alongside Al Trost, only a small handful of players have won the Hermann Trophy more than once: Mike Seerey, Saint Louis University (1971, 1972); Kenny Snow, Indiana University (1988, 1990); Mike Fisher, University of Virginia (1995, 1996); and Patrick Mullins, University of Maryland (2012, 2013).

and this win was a badge of honor for US soccer, which, at that point, was still auditioning to be cool in US mainstream sports circles. Yet again, it was a hint of good things to come for the USMNT program.

Outside of being captain for the national team, Trost had a storied journey in pro soccer. When the St. Louis Stars concluded its run in the late 70s, he joined the expansion franchise known as the California Surf (greater Los Angeles). Then he bounced up the coast to play for the Seattle Sounders. This was followed by some time with the immensely talented New York Arrows of the MISL.

By this time, circa 1980, Trost traded his cleats for a whistle. He soon began coaching the St. Louis Steamers (1981–83), where these games were the second most popular tickets in the whole damn country—second only to the Edmonton Oilers of the NHL![‡‡‡] Go figure! That's how big soccer was in the Golden era of pro indoor. (Here's another tidbit: around this time, the Chicago Sting were outselling the revered Chicago Bulls for a time! That actually happened!) Trost had taken the reins of the Steamers during what was considered a star-spangled rock-and-roll era of indoor soccer, and as with McBride, Trost was part of this wave of soccer pioneers that were leading the sport nationwide.

Trost was guiding not just the Steamers proper but essentially a walking USMNT: Sam Bick, Dan Counce, Don Droege, Tony Bellinger, Denny Vaninger, Larry Hulcer, Ty Keough, Greg Villa, Greg Makowski, Angelo DiBernardo, Ricky Davis, and Steve Pecher—that's a lot. Trost's direct and indirect influence over this Golden era of indoor soccer was also part of the bigger picture of the US "moving forward, in a positive direction, with soccer." Trost's involvement had positive results for that era and what we see today—a true legend of the sport.

---

‡‡‡ Why the Edmonton Oilers, of all teams? For hockey buffs, you'd know this was the era of Wayne Gretzky, the greatest hockey player of all time.

17 Steve Pecher USMNT: 1976-80

The one and only **Steve Pecher**—a sturdily built 6'0" defender, mean and ready to tackle, coupled with the ability to distribute effectively—has accomplished basically everything you can in US soccer.

Early on, Pecher—who was born in 1956—played for the Florissant Cougars, a feared club team from north St. Louis. With Normandy High School he won the Missouri soccer state championship in 1974, and was All-American. At Florissant Valley Community College, he won the NJCAA national title, in addition to becoming a collegiate All-American. He was drafted into the NASL, and signed with the Dallas Tornado, which happened to be right in the middle of Pelé's New York Cosmos fame—1975-77—and Pecher made an immediate impact as the 1976 NASL Rookie of the Year. Perhaps most notably, Pecher became known for his years with the St. Louis Steamers, where he was a captain and MISL All-Star.

Equipped with a large frame, a pep in his step that always seemed to bounce on the balls of his slightly outward pointing feet, Pecher had a propensity for hard tackles, slide tackles—any kind of tackle—and he stopped at nothing to dominate his area of the field. Like a one-man wrecking crew, he'd go after anyone. He's not one to vacillate too much on his physical prowess: "I always tell people when I put a uniform on it was like Dr. Jekyll and Mr. Hyde. I never went on the field to lose the game. I would do whatever I could in the legal limits to win a game."[27] He added, "I played physical soccer."[28] Add to this, his ability to read the field with distribution for counters and getting teammates in good positions to make a play and it's pretty clear: you want him on your side.

Along with being a well-known member of the Steamers (1979-84 and 1985-87), he also made appearances with the talented Kansas City Comets and Los Angeles Lazers.

As for the USMNT, Pecher, who played 1976-80, had an eventful time. During his stint, he was fortunate enough to go mano a mano with the

Mexican national team in Mexico City, the high-altitude, intimidating, daunting fortress that it is. Every US player's dream, whether they know it or not, is to represent the United States in front of a packed house in Mexico City–it doesn't get any better than that. Pecher had that opportunity.

He also lived out another dream of most US players that have tinkered with a soccer ball: he was captain of the USMNT (1978-80). The natural leader, whose tough play was inevitable, earned a couple red cards over the course of time. Not bad. Not bad at all. (In fact, we need a little more of that today. Nonetheless, Pecher got it done for the rest of us!)

Cocky, arrogant, and full of self-assured confidence with a slight touch of Midwest politeness, Pecher rightfully earned his way into the St. Louis Soccer Hall of Fame (2007), and the St. Louis Sports Hall of Fame.

18 Ty Keough USMNT: 1979-80

The St. Louis Steamers, overflowing with stars, were lucky to have another team leader. The versatile, resilient, and soccer-savvy **Ty Keough** led the way from 1979–85. As a midfielder and defender with great touch, accuracy, field awareness, vision, and soccer IQ, his services were also sought by the Cincinnati Kids, San Diego Sockers, and Kansas City Comets—all top teams in their day.

If you're a coach and you're looking for someone, a true talent, with soccer in his DNA, Ty would be the one. He's the son of Harry Keough, another USMNT legend, that led the US national team to the famous 1-0 win over England in the 1950 FIFA World Cup and who also coached SLU to five NCAA national championships.

Ty chose to play for SLU in the mid-to-late 70s. SLU, to this day, is still the all-time leader in NCAA national championships for soccer, with ten. During his stint, Ty shared the field with many ultra-talented players, including but not limited to Dave Brcic, Gary Brcic, Pete Collico, Don Doran, Don Droege, Dan Flynn, Kevin Handlan, Don Huber, and Larry Hulcer—top-notch "don't mess with these guys" Billikens.

During Ty's time with the USMNT (1979–80) he earned eight caps and shared the field with fellow St. Louis native, Steve Pecher, a dynamic duo. This was still during an era when games weren't as common for the US men's team.

With limited games, there was another hurdle that got in the way. Ty was a member of the US Olympic soccer team that qualified for the 1980 Olympics, to be hosted by Moscow that year. But because of the Soviet Union's invasion of Afghanistan, President Jimmy Carter supported the subsequent boycott of the Olympics. As a result, Keough missed out on the grand opportunity to represent his nation at the Olympics (a much bigger deal in those days for US soccer).

Taylor Twellman, a USMNT legend and broadcaster for many international soccer games, went to St. Louis University High School. Ty, his elder, went to the same. Are you seeing a correlation? It's been a few years but Ty was *Taylor before Taylor*, in that, from approximately 1990-2002, Ty was *the* voice of US soccer as a broadcaster for four World Cups and numerous international games for ABC, ESPN, and TNT—a mega-force in broadcasting. This was before TV channels got out of control with so many options so if you saw a game in those days it was likely called by Ty Keough.

He's a one-of-a-kind soccer legend, one that has practically done it all. During much of his broadcasting career, he was also the head soccer coach of Washington University (St. Louis). Much more recently in time, presumably out of boredom and a love for the game, Ty took a different approach to soccer and he began refereeing local games in the St. Louis area. Many of the players, certainly younger ones, might not be aware that their ref was a legendary driving force in the sport nationwide.

19 Greg Villa USMNT: 1977-80

Greg Villa was a straight up thunder forward. Thighs the size of large downtown buildings; a strong upper body; a beard or mustache; a look that says "get out of the way, I'm coming through."

Villa—born in 1956—came out of St. Louis, Missouri, and played for Mehlville High School. After graduating, he took his talents to Busch Soccer Club, one of North America's best club teams during its run.

From 1975-76, Villa joined legendary coach Bob Guelker at SIUE where Villa gained notoriety and subsequently jumped into the NASL. Pro teams he played with include the Minnesota Kicks, Tulsa Roughnecks, Fort Lauderdale Strikers, St. Louis Steamers, Kansas City Comets, and toward the end of the NASL's run, Team America (a super-team experiment in 1983 out of Washington DC that was short-lived). During the heyday of pro indoor soccer, Villa became an MISL All-Star and was a member of the St. Louis Steamers during two second-place finishes in 1980-81 (coached by Pat McBride) and 1981-82 (coached by Al Trost).

Back in the days when St. Louis talent reigned supreme over the USMNT, there's a 1979 team photo with the squad—red uniforms for field players, black and yellow jerseys for goalies, and blue track suits for coaches—that includes a large number of players with St. Louis roots: Greg Villa, Ty Keough, Tony Bellinger, Perry Van der Beck, Steve Pecher, and Greg Makowski. For St. Louis, the original soccer capitol of the US, that's pretty impressive. Villa was part of that bunch—that was his era. In all, from 1977-80, he earned 18 caps with five goals. To open things up, he scored in his first game against El Salvador in 1977. He was also a member of the US Olympic team that qualified for the boycotted 1980 Moscow Olympics.

Villa was inducted into the St. Louis Soccer Hall of Fame in 2016.

20 Greg Makowski USMNT: 1978-82§§§

Greg Makowski—a product of St. Louis, Missouri—was a devastatingly good defender that could shut down oncoming dribblers, with a shift of the hips, a little body contact, and guide them like a horse to water to cough up the ball. Many defenders end their charm there, back on defense. Makowski had an added element of danger in his arsenal whereby he could unleash technically sound shots on goal from distance. If you play indoor soccer, which he did, this is pretty much a prerequisite for the position. As such, Makowski was a well-rounded defender, renowned for his time.

From the Golden era of pro indoor soccer, a St. Louis Steamers brochure from 1981-82 highlighted Makowski's background as "a three-time 1st team All-American"[29] at SIUE during the 70s. At SIUE, from 1974-77, he was under the tutelage of coaching guru Bob Guelker. Shortly thereafter, Makowski—who had a substantial journey in pro US soccer from 1978-86—was drafted number one overall in the 1978 NASL College Draft. A few other names in the draft included Perry Van der Beck (eventual winner of US Soccer Player of the Year in 1985), Dan Flynn (Saint Louis University; the future CEO of US Soccer), and Pete Collico (Saint Louis University, St. Louis Steamers) in a field of over 90 players nationwide. Makowski subsequently suited up for the Colorado Caribous, Atlanta Chiefs, St. Louis Steamers, Seattle Sounders, Kansas City Comets, and Los Angeles Lazers. On multiple occasions he was an MISL All-Star.

According to the SIUE Hall of Fame website, Makowski "was the team captain of the US Olympic Soccer team from 1977 to 1981 and a member of the US national team from 1978 to 1982." In the late 70s and early 80s, during a time when USMNT games were typically less than today, Makowski registered twelve caps with one goal. Part of the discrepancy of Makowski's

§§§ As of April 22, 2023, online records of Makowski's time with the USMNT varied. SIUE's Hall of Fame website "Greg Makowski" listed it from 1978-82. The St. Louis Soccer Hall of Fame listed it from 1978-81. The *Wikipedia* page "Greg Makowski" listed it from 1978-80.

time with the USMNT is because he played on the US Olympic soccer team, and, depending who you ask, some of these games aren't considered true internationals. Though, back in these days, the US Olympic soccer team was essentially interchangeable with the national team. Like his teammates Ty Keough and Greg Villa (to name a few), Makowski was unable to compete in the 1980 Olympics, hosted by Moscow, after President Carter's administration boycotted the games as a result of the USSR invading Afghanistan.

Makowski was inducted into SIUE's Hall of Fame in 2005 and into the St. Louis Soccer Hall of Fame in 2013.

21 Angelo DiBernardo USMNT: 1979-85

Angelo DiBernardo—born in 1956 in Buenos Aires, Argentina—was an attacking midfielder that arrived in Chicago-land in his teens. Noticed quickly by coach Jerry Yeagley, DiBernardo was lured to the illustrious Indiana University (1976-78) soccer program and had great success, earning All-American honors and winning the Hermann Trophy (1978). In 1976 and 1978, DiBernardo and Indiana were inches away from winning the NCAA championship, but came in second to the University of San Francisco both times. After the 1978 season, as the top collegiate soccer player, DiBernardo turned pro soon thereafter.

In 1979, he spent a year with the Los Angeles Aztecs before making a big signing with the New York Cosmos, with whom he played outdoor and indoor from 1980-85. For the tail end of his pro career, he joined the Kansas City Comets and St. Louis Steamers.

From 1979-85, DiBernardo amassed 20 caps with the USMNT, capturing three goals. Lost in the archives of US Soccer, 1979 marked the first cap for DiBernardo in a match against Cold War rival the Soviet Union. DiBernardo entered the game as a sub, replacing Ty Keough. Like Keough, DiBernardo was on the 1980 United States Olympic team that has become well known for not competing in the 1980 Olympics, hosted by Moscow, because of President Jimmy Carter's boycott.

As for the 1984 Olympics, hosted in the United States, DiBernardo made the starting roster with a squad that included Ricky Davis and Hugo Perez. Despite the US placing third in Group D (that included Italy, Egypt, and Costa Rica), this was a massive opportunity to represent the nation, on a global stage, at one of the highest levels of soccer at the time.

Upon the completion of his pro career, DiBernardo was inducted into the Indiana University Athletic Hall of Fame in 1991. In addition, he made the elite Soccer America College Team of the Century. Incidentally, that starting XI selection included:

- Brad Friedel, UCLA (goalie)
- Erik Imler, Virginia (defender)
- Paul Caligiuri, UCLA (defender)
- Adubarie Otorubio, Clemson (defender)
- Andy Atuegbu, San Francisco (mid)
- Claudio Reyna, Virginia (mid)
- Mike Fisher, Virginia (mid)
- Bruce Murray, Clemson (mid)
- Angelo DiBernardo, Indiana (forward)
- Kenny Snow, Indiana (forward)
- Armando Betancourt, Indiana (forward)

As the years have gone by, the name *DiBernardo* has become somewhat forgotten, replaced with Landon Donovan, Clint Dempsey, Michael Bradley, and Christian Pulisic. Yet, when one looks back into the 1970s and 80s, DiBernardo was a player that flourished, somewhat under the radar (by no fault of his own), and made way for future talents to emerge.

22 Fernando Clavijo USMNT: 1990-94

Born in 1956 in Uruguay, **Fernando Clavijo** was faster than fast. Typically, the speedster was an outside defender, with the ability to play outside mid. But sometimes there would be this burst of speed down the line—usually closing down a forward who had delusions of grandeur—and it was Clavijo soaring alongside the dribbler and inevitably shepherding him away from danger areas. Like Landon Donovan, Steve Cherundolo, Jimmy Banks, and Cobi Jones, Clavijo ranks among the fastest players to ever step foot on a field.

Professionally, he started out early, at the age of 16, with Atenas in Uruguay. In the late 70s he found his way to the United States, initially working at a restaurant in New Jersey, before eventually impressing locals enough with his soccer prowess to earn a spot on New York Apollo—which later became New York United—of the American Soccer League. Following this, he bounced around with a few teams and spent a lot of time in the legendary MISL.

In the early 80s, he joined the multitalented New York Arrows, followed by the Golden Bay Earthquakes. Biggest of all, he was with the powerhouse San Diego Sockers during its heyday in the 80s. With this group, he was part of three championships. It's somewhat mindboggling how many stud-players landed with the Sockers. A few are: Steve Zungul (Yugoslavian national team), Branko Segota (Canadian national team), Hugo Perez (USMNT), Kevin Crow (USMNT), Juli Veee (USMNT), Brian Quinn (USMNT), Brian Schmetzer, Alan Mayer (USMNT), and Mark Chung (USMNT). That's a tiny fraction of high-level talent that went through those Southern Californian doors. Clavijo was a prominent member, from 1984-88, playing in over 185 games with close to 50 goals. After departing San Diego, he made a stop with the Los Angeles Lazers (1988-89) before landing with the St. Louis Storm for his last professional hurrah (1989-92).

The early 90s were shaping up to be the last days for Clavijo's playing career. He was part of an impressive US squad—along with Paul Caligiuri, Peter Vermes, and Eric Wynalda—that won the 1991 CONCACAF Gold Cup. That was the men's first title in the Gold Cup, an important regional tournament.

Interestingly, Clavijo played his last professional games with the Storm in 1992 and suited up that year for the United States futsal team (eight games in all with two goals). A lessor known fact: the United States earned second at the 1992 FIFA Futsal World Championship in Hong Kong, losing in the final to Brazil. Under the guidance of coach John Kowalski, Clavijo was joined by Jimmy Gabarra, Chico Borja, Mike Windischmann, and Jeff Agoos, to name a few.

Oddly enough, toward the end of his career, Fernando played 61 games for the USMNT, from 1990-94.

Two years after the 1992 FIFA Futsal World Championship, Clavijo was front and center for the ultimate prize, the 1994 FIFA World Cup extravaganza. That tournament, still to this day, holds records for World Cup attendance. Talk about capping off a career with a splash! Coach Bora Milutinovic—who previously played for Nice and UNAM, and coached Mexico in the 1986 World Cup—certainly had a vision and Clavijo was a piece of the puzzle.

At the age of 38, Clavijo was called up for one last go around and was a crucial presence in the games against Colombia and Brazil. It was in the round of 16 as the USMNT lost dramatically 1-0 to Brazil at a packed house in Stanford Stadium—over 84,000 strong. This game and tournament were pivotal for US soccer at large. Excitement had been brewing in the US for years. The NASL was given a boost from Pelé. The MISL, which Clavijo was a large part of, was a shot of adrenaline.

Lastly, the 1994 FIFA World Cup sent things over the top as soccer was rocketing forward in popularity around the nation, like never before. Only two years later, in 1996, MLS finally launched. By that time, Clavijo had retired from playing yet his presence in the game was a piece of the larger puzzle of soccer gaining momentum in the US.

In lieu of playing, Clavijo continued to influence the game from the sidelines. Given his indoor experience, eventually Clavijo was coach of the US national futsal team in 1998. In fact, he coached and assisted an assortment of teams: St. Louis Storm, Seattle SeaDogs, Florida ThunderCats, Nigeria, MetroStars, New England Revolution, Haiti, Colorado Rapids, and Miami FC.

In 2005, he was inducted into the National Soccer Hall of Fame. One of those guys that caught your eye with speed and was always a part of the game, Clavijo was a prevalent force in US soccer.

23 Ricky Davis USMNT: 1977-88

If you're looking for the Tom Cruise of soccer, someone straight off an F-18, look no further: **Ricky Davis**—a product of the greater Los Angeles area—was a high-flying stud of the USMNT, fully equipped with statesmen-like qualities as the team's captain for many years. Low to the ground, with thighs like tree trunks, he would explode past defenders with deafening quickness, a ruthless—right to the point—"I'm challenging you one-on-one right here" kind of approach. He was like a feisty sparkplug with tenacity. He was also smart, with thoughtful passing from the midfield, a player all too willing to get others involved and to make them look good.

Davis arrived in an era before MLS. He was a high school soccer All-American (Damien High School, La Verne, California) where he also lettered in, believe it or not, baseball, football, golf, tennis, track, and volleyball. The *Salina Journal* pointed out that in soccer "Davis became so accomplished that, by his senior year, he was an All-American who played on the US Soccer National Youth Team. At age 16, he had been recruited by three professional soccer teams."[30] He played briefly at Santa Clara University before he was drafted by the New York Cosmos of the NASL and seen in pictures with Pelé and Franz Beckenbauer as the chosen one of US soccer at the time. Davis flourished with the Cosmos in the late 70s and early 80s, earning North American Player of the Year in 1979. While there, he was part of three NASL championships: 1978, 1980, and 1982.

Then he transitioned to the MISL, where he spent a bulk of his time with the legendary St. Louis Steamers (1983-86), where he tallied up 89 goals. In the late 80s, getting back to his New York Cosmos roots, he made a brief switch to the New York Express, an indoor team. This ephemeral venture was trying, at its most optimistic, to relive the glory days of the original New York Arrows and New York Cosmos. On this team, according to a piece from *Soccer Digest* in 1987, Davis was said to be "probably the most recognized player"[31] in a city that's one of the biggest sports markets in the US. However, the Express, just like its name, came and went. Many attempts at pro soccer in the 80s met a similar demise: a poor record and troubled finances fueled the end of the road. On a personal note, this move back to New York was just a pit stop before Davis signed with the Tacoma Stars, the famed indoor side from greater Seattle.

Davis was a member of the US team that qualified for the 1980 Olympics, only to be boycotted by President Carter's administration. Nonetheless, Davis represented the USMNT in the Olympics of 1984 (held in the United States) and 1988 (held in South Korea).

In 1984, he won the very first US Soccer Player of the Year award, thus setting a trend for many other greats to follow, such as Clint Dempsey and Christian Pulisic. In the late 80s, Davis suffered a knee injury, slowing down his playing career and keeping him from joining the 1990 FIFA World Cup squad.

After hanging up his cleats, he became a color commentator for TV games and represented ABC for the 1990 and 1994 World Cups. Rick would expound on short sprints, passing the ball correctly, using the inside and outside of the feet, what a proper throw-in is, essentially citing rules and regulations of the game manual-style as he went in a very endearing way.

From 2004–10, Davis took on a leadership role with the American Youth Soccer Organization (AYSO). It was founded in 1964, south of LA proper in Torrance, California. Today, it's comprised of approximately 50,000 teams with over 625,000 players. As a non-profit, its revenue is a bit over $72 million.

Davis switched gears in 2011 and opened a steak restaurant in Kansas: Ellsworth Steakhouse. The *Salina Journal* notes how Rick—who once led some of the biggest studs in the country—will be back in the kitchen, standing over steaks, giving them the proper attention they need: "Steakhouse patrons who wonder what happened to Davis need only look in the restaurant's kitchen. There, Davis often can be found grilling a New York strip steak or frying a hamburger for a bustling lunch or dinner crowd."[32]

He was inducted into the National Soccer Hall of Fame in 2001. Davis is regarded by many as the best player of his generation and perhaps the best in the history of US soccer. A class act, he was one of the top captains in the history of US soccer and ranks among the very best to wear a US jersey. He *is* the Soccer Hall of Fame—a California expat quietly running a kitchen in the middle of Kansas, likely wearing a pair of glasses and posting a soccer video every once in a while of him kicking a ball against a wall, demonstrating how to use the inside and outside of the feet. Pure legend.

24 Perry Van der Beck USMNT: 1979-85

After winning a Missouri high school state championship under the guidance of legendary coach Vince Drake at St. Thomas Aquinas in St. Louis, the one and only **Perry Van der Beck**—born in 1959—went straight to the Tampa Bay Rowdies of the NASL in 1978.¶¶¶

Unheard of. The league hadn't seen that from a US player before. It was a first. In a sense, it wasn't too surprising. Hailing from the northside of St. Louis, the US' first soccer capitol, Perry followed in the footsteps of St. Louis juggernauts: Harry Keough, a key member of the USMNT that defeated England 1-0 in the 1950 FIFA World Cup; Bob Kehoe, captain and eventual coach of the USMNT; Pat McBride, USMNT and NASL All-Star in 1972; Carl Gentile, USMNT; Gene Geimer, USMNT; Al Trost, captain of the USMNT; Jim Leeker, NASL Rookie of the Year in 1970; and Denny Vaninger, USMNT, just to name a few.

The groundwork had been laid out. Perry was just the first to make serious history as a high school kid transitioning straight to the NASL. The gifted 6'0" skinny-legged midfielder from Florissant, Missouri, was exploding onto the scene in the late 70s as soccer in the US was beginning to take off like never before. It was a simpler time: back when players rolled down their socks and didn't have to wear shin-guards to prevent injury. Perry was one of those guys—often seen with his socks rolled down, which was very fashionable in those days with players from Argentina, Brazil, Denmark, Germany, and elsewhere. An article from *Soccer America* pointed out:

> "Van Der Beck played through the glory years of the Rowdies, leaving in 1983 for a one-year stint with Team America, the U.S. national team in training that played in

¶¶¶ The same year Argentina hosted and won the 1978 FIFA World Cup, led by Mario Kempes, Leopoldo Luque, Daniel Passarella, and Osvaldo Ardiles.

> the NASL. He returned to the Rowdies in 1984, the NASL's last year of operation. One of the most popular players ever to don the Rowdies green-and-gold, Van Der Beck played in 144 career games. He totaled 17 goals and 20 assists for 54 points playing mostly in the defensive midfield. The Rowdies were two-time Soccer Bowl finalists during his career (1978 and 1979), and won the 1979 NASL Indoor Championship."[33]

Perry also spent a good portion of his prime in the MISL—the league that rocked the US soccer mic in the 80s—with the Dallas Sidekicks, St. Louis Steamers, Wichita Wings (173 games, with 58 goals), and eventually with the St. Louis Ambush in 1997.

From 1979-85, Van der Beck earned 23 caps and two goals for the USMNT. At the 1979 Pan American Games, Van der Beck got on the board with two goals. It was thought that in 1980 "he would have been the captain of the US soccer team at the 1980 Summer Olympics"[34] that eventually were boycotted by the Carter Administration. Certainly, it was a disappointment for him and the other players. In addition, the USMNT had not qualified for a World Cup since 1950, so this Olympic appearance would've been a much-needed boost for the US program. The US team—with players available like Van der Beck, Ricky Davis, and Ty Keough—had qualified but it wasn't meant to be.

In 1985, he became the second player to win the US Soccer Player of the Year award. By this time, soccer was becoming a much more serious sport in the United States, yet it was still lingering in part of the Late Pioneer period (1980s-90s). Players like Van der Beck and Ricky Davis were essentially household names in the soccer community but not the mainstream.

By 1985, the NASL had folded. This renowned league, a revolution of sorts, was given a huge spark by Pelé. When he retired from the New York Cosmos in 1977, the league slowly ran out of gas. Yet, in its place, the magnificent and exciting MISL took off with a blaze in 1978. Soon this league would lose popularity as well. Yet pro indoor continues to this day.

And, notably, it was the efforts of the original NASL and MISL that, in part, led to the creation of MLS in 1996.

By the late 90s, Van der Beck had reached the end of the road as a player. Between 1998 and 2001, he served as assistant coach for the Tampa Bay Mutiny (MLS). In 2001, he became head coach for the team at the tail end of the season.

Van der Beck was one of a kind. He was following a path laid down by others while creating a new one for future stars to follow. In 2011, he was inducted into the St. Louis Soccer Hall of Fame. Van der Beck switched from St. Louis, Missouri, to Tampa, Florida, and remained there as a critical piece of the local soccer scene and eventually helped lead the USL (United Soccer League, a tier below MLS) where he served as a league executive. He's a noteworthy midfielder lingering in the archives of the USMNT from the mysterious time of the late 70s through the mid-80s that had a crucial role to play in the development of US soccer.

25 Thomas Dooley USMNT: 1992-99

Thomas Dooley was a player with vision, positional awareness, deft touch, accuracy with his passes, and one thing that is hard to define: intentional passes. Like Clint Dempsey, Dooley's simplest passes connected with a teammate and sent them to the next move—whatever that was—in a productive way. It could be just a five-yard pass. Or it was a dangerous ball into the box. That's an innate quality that only a few players have. Carlos Valderrama was one, or Platini, Pirlo, and a few others.

Another quality of Dooley's was that he made things happen; things clicked; things were in motion; chances on goal were often quality chances (as opposed to half-chances). As a 6'2" defensive-mid, he joined the attack—he was always in the mix, stirring things up. Bottom line: He was a thinker and made games interesting to watch.

How did this come about? Perhaps because he wasn't the fastest, he had to compensate by out-thinking the others. Dooley maneuvered around guys with skill, craft, guile, and thinking. Just as the United States has fostered an environment for top-tier basketball players to emerge, Germany has done much the same in the realm of soccer.

Dooley—born in 1961 in West Germany—spent almost the entirety of his pro career in Germany. He gained much of his insight during the early 80s and 90s with German sides FK Pirmasens, FC Homburg, 1. FC Kaiserslautern, Bayer Leverkusen, and Schalke 04, and eventually rounded out the late 90s and early 2000s with MLS franchises Columbus Crew and MetroStars.

As for the USMNT, he dominated the 90s. Over time, he earned 81 caps and seven goals, leading the team with experience, providing quality touches on the ball, bright ideas during the flow of play, and results. A personal result came in the form of the US Soccer Player of the Year award in 1993.

Although the US came second in the 1993 CONCACAF Gold Cup, Dooley's role helped cement the US program as a growing power within CONCACAF. The results since, in part thanks to a seed planted by Dooley, have proven as much. The US won the CONCACAF Gold Cup in 1991, 2002, 2005, 2007, 2013, 2017, and 2021. That's a lot of Gold Cups. A second place finish in 1993 might be a tough price to pay for future successes, but sometimes it's a necessary part of the process.

In 1994, playing for the US in the FIFA World Cup amidst huge crowds and electricity in the air, Dooley and the squad turned heads in the round of 16, losing 1-0 to the eventual champions that year, Brazil.

Following in the footsteps of captain John Harkes, Dooley was named captain of the team during the 1998 FIFA World Cup, an awkward phase for US uniforms. Yet, whatever the uniforms were, Dooley and the others made the most of it. He had a fresh, thoughtful way of playing and each move was in accordance with how the game should be played. It's as though he was bestowed with a certain amount of wisdom that others around the world, perhaps, lacked. There was a vibe about him, a pleasant demeanor that gave comfort to everyone else, a certain glowing confidence that reassured teammates that his way was, indeed, the right way and it was infectious, with ball movement and positive action.

His last game for the USMNT in 1999, against Chile, saw the end of an era. One could argue that his constructive passing from deep in the midfield was carried on by Claudio Reyna and Michael Bradley. All the same, Dooley was a little different. In his early days, Dooley was a forward though he became known as a defensive mid. All in all, Dooley had a little of Harry Kane in him. They each have that schoolyard way, in which they might not dazzle you with dribbling moves (like Denilson), overwhelm you with speed (like Andriy Shevchenko), or keep you guessing with quickness (like Raheem Sterling), but they both have an inner quality that revolves around using their bodies, creating space, seeing the field, knowing a moment, deft touch, positional awareness, creating danger with simple plays, and the ability to guide the game as needed—which is very hard to teach.

26 John Stollmeyer USMNT: 1986-1990

John Stollmeyer–born in 1962 in Pittsburgh, Pennsylvania–stood about 5'9" with legs cloned from Arnold Schwarzenegger. His strong build was intimidating to any pesky attacker meddling in the middle of the field thinking he might make some ground in Stollmeyer's territory.

After attending Thomas Jefferson High School in Virginia he was viewed as an elite player–the National Amateur Soccer Athlete of the Year in 1981–and sought after by Indiana University, where he eventually landed. At IU he was All-American.

Let's let IU do the talking for a second. According to Indiana University's Honors & Awards section:

> "John won soccer letters in 1982, 1983, 1984 and 1985. He is a member of NCAA championship teams in 1982 and 1983, NCAA Defensive MVP 1982, and was second team All-American in 1982 and third team All-American in 1984 and 1985. He was a member of the East Regional Team for the Olympic Sports Festival in 1982, 1983 & 1985, and a member of Youth World Cup team 1981 and National Amateur Soccer Athlete of the Year. He played professionally with the Cleveland Force 1986-87 & 1987-88 and was rookie of the year 1986-87. John was a member of the Pan American Games team and the World University Games team in 1987 and the 1988 US Olympic team and the 1990 US World Cup Team. He is a member of the Soccer America All-Decade '80s team. John set IU career assist record and currently ranks third on IU career list."

In addition, Stollmeyer won the NCAA Division I Men's Soccer Tournament Most Outstanding Player Award for Offense in 1983.

Back in a time when MLS didn't exist, players like Stollmeyer didn't have an academy team to start out with. He was subjected to the ODP program as it was back then and represented the East Coast regional team before he eventually suited up for the nation with other elite players shrewdly chosen by coaches across the country.

For the US in the 80s, he represented multiple national teams: at both youth and adult levels. During that era, the Olympic team was huge; the nation of soccer-going fans looked to the Olympics as a means to make a name for our soccer-playing aspirations. Part of the USMNT program back then was to do well in the Olympics and strive for a place in World Cup action as well.

Stollmeyer was a relied-upon figure for various national teams—a go-to guy. He competed in the 1981 FIFA World Youth Championship; the 1983 Pan American Games; the 1987 Pan American Games; and the 1987 Sumer Universiade (a tournament in Croatia). From 1986–88, he competed in the famed MISL for the Cleveland Force. He was the league Rookie of the Year. At a time when the MISL was losing steam, he played in just over 100 games, with over 25 goals.

It was a peculiar time for US soccer. In the late 70s and early 80s, the MISL was rocking, but over time, the finances for teams were not what they used to be. Despite indoor soccer continuing in the US to this day, it was a time of flux when Stollmeyer played as the Force folded, thus causing Stollmeyer to take up shop with the Arizona Condors and Washington Stars, who both had issues of their own and folded.

By the time 1996 came around, thus introducing the lucrative MLS to the world, Stollmeyer was tapped out. Yet he had pursued the game during a crucial time in US soccer history. He was laying down the groundwork in the 80s for future generations. When Stollmeyer played NCAA DI soccer, it was essentially a pro league because of the absence of a viable pro outdoor league. US players that competed in college were in one of the highest leagues in the nation. In the post-college world,

Stollmeyer and his cohorts were often players without teams, as the US was a soccer nation trying to find itself in the aftermath of the NASL and the dawn of MLS.

One big milestone for Stollmeyer was the "Shot Heard Round the World" game in Trinidad in which Caligiuri struck a famous volley that won the game and sent the US to the World Cup in 1990 for the first time since 1950. Stollmeyer joined the action that historic day as a sub.

He subsequently joined the USMNT in the 1990 FIFA World Cup. Upon his completion, he registered 31 games for the USMNT. Then after a stint with the coaching staff at Notre Dame, he settled into a financial job in Indianapolis, not too far from Indiana University where he took flight once upon a time.

27 Hugo Perez
USMNT: 1984-94

If you were to look at **Hugo Perez** circa 1988, full curly afro and all, you might think: "That's the coolest guy ever from El Salvador!" Given the classic 70s look, you'd probably mistake him for an El Salvadorian Diego Maradona: the hair, the gaze, the build, the ball skills. There's a shot of him, posing for a picture with Gary Lineker, each wearing the other side's jersey, with Perez looking like a 70s soccer genius.

His soccer prowess is partly in his DNA. His dad and grandpa played professionally in El Salvador. This background, this structure he received being around the game at a high level, most certainly gave him an edge. Similar to Chicharito, of Mexico, whose dad and grandpa played at high levels, it's often just a matter of time for the new generation to reach great heights. Just as Chicharito became the most famous Hernandez in his family, so too did Perez.

Born in 1963 in El Salvador, he moved to the US and became a citizen in his youth, and subsequently joined the national team in 1984 after impressing those around him with dazzling displays of skill and energetic impulses during the early 80s.

He joined the Tampa Bay Rowdies in 1982, transitioned to the San Diego Sockers, and found much success in Southern California where he was a salient element of the early MISL days. As it turns out, the bulk of his pro career was spent in San Diego as the Sockers flourished in the 80s.

In all, Perez flourished with the Sockers from 1983-90, the heyday of the franchise. Playing alongside many greats, such as Branko Segota (Canadian national team), Steve Zungul (Yugoslavian national team), Fernando Clavijo (USMNT), Brian Quinn (USMNT), Kevin Crow (USMNT), and Juli Veee (USMNT), the team stormed through the competition in the 80s, earning the lion's share of championships, with Perez taking center stage on a number of occasions. In 1988, he was named MISL championship player of the finals.

Perez was in the thick of things leading into the 1990 FIFA World Cup but thanks to an injury he was left off the final squad for Italy. With setbacks come motivation. And often you have comebacks. For Perez, in a crowded field of talent, that comeback arrived in 1991.

1991 was a big year as the Chicago Bulls won the NBA championship, Michael Jordan won the league MVP, Jimmy Connors had an epic US Open comeback run, MTV was still playing music videos, Nirvana was soaring high, the FIFA World Player of the Year was Lothar Matthaus, and Hugo Perez joined an elite list of US players in 1991 as he earned the US Soccer Player of the Year award.

Then came 1994. The biggest World Cup to date, at least by the standards of actual attendance; the US was rocking and Perez was along for the ride. Though the US lost in the round of 16 to Brazil, Perez, not just in this game alone, was part of that long process that had roots in the MISL that so many US players helped along. As it turns out, the NASL, MISL, and the 1994 FIFA World Cup were laying down a foundation for the inevitable formation of MLS which is exactly what the US needed to rejoin the global soccer landscape.

When Perez finished things up for the USMNT, he had gathered some 73 caps and 13 goals. As of 2021, Perez took over as head coach of El Salvador's national team. Almost overnight the team began playing with a certain aplomb: the overall technique–from player to player–is better, passing combinations are crisp, and there's a group cohesiveness that is present that was lacking in previous years. One coach can make all the difference and Perez began proving as much for his home team.

28 Preki
USMNT: 1996-2001

Preki, whose US career started with the Tacoma Stars, kicked things off with a bang. Born in 1963, Preki was one of many hopeful players in Eastern Europe. In his early 20s, the Yugoslavian native was spotted in Europe by a Tacoma Stars coach and former player for the English national team, Bob McNab. McNab–a defender in his day–must've instinctively seen the challenge Preki presented to any and all opposition. In Tacoma, a Seattle suburb: "It took approximately 15 games, by Preki's own recollection, before he started to feel comfortable with the new team in the new country in the new league. Then he started scoring goals, lots of them,"[35] said a 1987 *Soccer Digest* piece.

If you think, for a second, indoor's a joke: you're sorely mistaken. Sometimes, in outdoor, players get only a few touches per half and there are often long intervals between touches. With indoor, there's none of that. There's nowhere to run and hide like in outdoor; it's all on display, right there. In fact, indoor puts an exclamation point on all your weaknesses as a player. Very soon after Preki's arrival in Tacoma, the left-footed dynamo was an MISL All-Star selection. What got him there was the scoring and dribbling that set it all up.

Soccer Digest elaborated on what everyone was seeing: "What Preki has that others don't is an uncannily coordinated left foot. A strong left foot for a soccer player boggles defenders in the same way a natural left-handed boxer messes up a righty. Everything comes at you backwards and therefore forces you to move in opposition to your strengths."[36] His lethal left foot egged on cheers from massive crowds. What's more, he had great movement on the ball.

Preki, akin to creative mids like Hagi and Ronaldinho, was a phenomenal dribbler. Great dribblers have a way of toying with opponents, no matter the opposition. A classic Preki moment: He's dribbling nonchalantly, for the time being, at a defender near the top of the box; he sets up a little dribble with the outside of his left foot then with the left he does a scissors fake to the left, then pushes the ball with his outside left to the left, then—very quickly—with his left he cuts it back across his body to the right foot (his weaker of the two) for a shot. The sneaky thing here is that defenders are apt to think that a scissors fake will result in the ball going the other way after the fake. In other words, a scissors fake with the left foot *to the left* is often followed by the outside of the right foot pushing the ball *to the right*. But Preki would often catch you off guard; he was a true artist.

Additionally, he would mesmerize you with a flurry of movement. He was able to stop and go left to right, right to left, fake on the dribble with a little hesitation, cut back with frightening effectiveness, and chop the ball past players with a fake shot that inevitably set up a blast on goal. How did goalies handle it? They were often dumbstruck at the ball zipping by with amplified volume by way of a nasty line drive that could strain anyone's wrist.

While he was grinding it out on the indoor scene, an impressive future was in store for this scoring stud: EPL stardom, a FIFA World Cup, MLS MVP. Yet back in the days of US indoor soccer, during the Late Pioneer period, when soccer was catching hold in the US, Preki was thought of as "a bit of a team clown, 'an imp,' according to president John Best."[37]

Preki, who was full of surprises, likely was a mischievous imp. The left-footed jokester was getting used to life in the US: one step, one kick at a time, mid-80s style. "Since he moved out of an apartment he shared with teammate Gary Heale and two Seattle Seahawks cheerleaders and into a room of Zungul's suite in a downtown hotel, Preki's been learning about the finer things in life."[38] *Zungul* is none other than Steve Zungul: MISL MVP in 1978-79, 1979-80, 1980-81, 1981-82, 1984-85, 1985-86, an MISL champion on multiple occasions, NASL MVP in 1984, a former player with the Yugoslavian national team, and, a non-USMNT player that earned his way into the US National Soccer Hall of Fame (class of 2023).

Preki was a sensation. In 1988-89, he was the MISL MVP and league scoring champion, assist leader, and the 1989 All-Star Game MVP. It was only a matter of time before he got official paperwork in order and joined the USMNT.

A few players in this book are not completely represented by their stats. In Preki's case, his USMNT goals are underwhelming, which is odd considering his pro stats. Without a doubt, Preki is one of those statistical enigmas as he scored four goals for the US in 28 games. On the upside:

- Tacoma Stars (indoor): 209 goals
- St. Louis Storm (indoor): 113 goals
- Everton: 4 goals
- San Jose Grizzlies (indoor): 67 goals
- Portsmouth: 5 goals
- Kansas City Wizards: 50 goals
- Miami Fusion: 8 goals
- Kansas City Wizards (Part II): 21 goals

When it comes to indoor, where you get plenty of touches, Preki was king. He didn't just score: he scored with authority.

It seems that, like Everton and Portsmouth, Preki's style as a dribbler—one who needs the ball at his feet with time to work magic—wasn't in line with the EPL's style of play. Like it or not, the EPL in the 90s was very direct and followed a "get the ball to the end-line and cross it into the mixer" kind of approach. It's a brisk pace, up-tempo and demanding which is just not Preki's style. He'd be better suited in La Liga, where possession tends to dominate the flow of play and allows someone like Preki time to establish his game—dribbling like an artist—around the top of the box.

Around the mid-90s, Preki found a brief home in indoor again, playing for the San Jose Grizzlies in the CISL (Continental Indoor Soccer League). In 1995, he was the CISL MVP.

Then from 1996-2005, he resided in MLS, and with the Kansas City Wizards, he flourished. There he was able to be free, play his game, and take players on with fortitude.

Preki is still the only player in MLS history to win the MVP award twice: 1997 and 2003. Amazingly, he won the awards in his mid-30s and early 40s. Despite some criticism of MLS over the years, it's a league of athletes, young ones at that. So for an "old man" to put them all in their place is really saying something. Like Roger Milla at the end of his career in 1990 at the FIFA World Cup, Preki was at the top of his game for one last hurrah.

And what about the MLS Scoring Champion, aka the MLS Golden Boot? Preki won that twice as well: 1997 and 2003.

Titles? Preki, a featured player with the Kansas City Wizards, was part of the 2000 MLS Cup championship squad coached by Bob Gansler (USMNT), with elite teammates Tony Meola (USMNT), Peter Vermes (USMNT), Chris Klein (USMNT), Matt McKeon (USMNT), Nick Garcia (USMNT), Kerry Zavagnin (USMNT), and Chris Henderson (USMNT). This group also won the 2000 Supporters' Shield.

For most players, that's an overwhelming amount of success.

Although his scoring stats at the national level might label him an underperformer, his contributions came in other forms. To opposing defenders, he was always a menace, a persistent threat, cutting left and right with the ball, creating avenues for teammates and danger on offense.

However, a big goal came against Brazil in the 1998 Gold Cup semifinals. After receiving a pass outside the top of the box, Preki sidestepped a Brazilian defender, going to his much-preferred left, then unleashed a left-footed line drive from outside the box that eluded the outreached arms of the keeper at the near post. With a little help from everyone else, the US held onto one of those games that turned into a classic for US soccer.

His pro career took him to Red Star Belgrade, Tacoma Stars, St. Louis Storm, Everton, San Jose Grizzlies, Portsmouth, Kansas City Wizards, Miami Fusion, and Kansas City Wizards (Part II).

As a coach, Preki has served with Chivas USA, Toronto FC, Sacramento Republic, Saint Louis FC, and Seattle Sounders FC.

He was inducted into the National Soccer Hall of Fame in 2010 and the Indoor Soccer Hall of Fame in 2013. A well-deserved salute for one of the best in the history of US soccer.

29 Paul Caligiuri USMNT: 1984-97

The Shot Heard Round the World happened in 1989. The US was in a final showdown against Trinidad to earn a place in FIFA World Cup 1990. The US had to win. A tie or loss would've advanced the other team. In a moment of brilliance, with a chest trap and a juggle past an opponent, **Paul Caligiuri**—a former standout with the UCLA Bruins that won the US Soccer Player of the Year in 1986—struck a miraculous volley from deep that went into the right corner. It's the kind of shot every player dreams about; the biggest stage, the biggest moment and a goal that was out of this world—and the US qualified for the World Cup for the first time since 1950. It certainly had to be Caligiuri's biggest moment on a soccer field.

That goal essentially was the starting point of the modern era of US soccer in that World Cup appearances have regularly followed. This was, believe it or not, about six years before MLS arrived (1996) and there was still a lot of work to be done for US soccer to earn the respect it was earnestly looking for on the international stage. This moment in 1989, this shot heard round the world in Trinidad, was a huge step in that direction.

The US moved onto the World Cup in Italy and, despite the team not advancing out of its group, Caligiuri scored on Italian soil. Perhaps Caligiuri was meant for that stage.

An article from *Soccer Digest* in 1986 pointed out: "When the globe's greatest stars took to the Rose Bowl field in July for the FIFA World All-Star Game one US player was included among the elite. The man honored wasn't the highly regarded Rick Davis—who'd acquitted himself so well in the 1982 World All-Star match at Giants Stadium—or other well-known pro stars such as Kevin Crow, Mark Peterson, Bruce Savage, David Brcic, Chico Borja, and Hugo Perez. The man chosen was a collegian, a central defender from UCLA named Paul Caligiuri."[39]

Some may forget that in 1988, during the Olympics in South Korea, Caligiuri was part of the team that included Ricky Davis, Tab Ramos, Bruce Murray, John Harkes, John Stollmeyer, Peter Vermes, and others. The Olympics was huge for US players. It helped bolster the value of these players overseas. As did the 1990 FIFA World Cup appearance.

During this transitional time of the late 80s and early 90s—when youth soccer in the US was exploding in popularity like never before and kids had adult stars to emulate such as Ricky Davis, Peter Vermes, and Caligiuri—more and more US players were quietly getting signed to European clubs. To be a US player and get signed to a European deal, when Europe was considered to be the mecca of the sport, was practically mythical. At that time, in the 80s and 90s, the gravitational pull of European clubs—especially but not only England, Spain, Italy, Germany—had gathered the likes of Diego Maradona, Careca, and Romario. These players, from primetime countries Argentina and Brazil, would arrive in Europe and were legends before you knew it. At the time, US players were making strides. You'd hear about Bruce Murray in Switzerland and England or John Harkes in England and so on. These were players forging a path for others to follow.

Caligiuri spent time in Germany with SV Meppen, Hansa Rostock, SC Freiburg, and FC St. Pauli. He was a solid two-way midfielder that was versatile; he was good with both feet; a team player; a good athlete. From Germany to the 1990 and 1994 World Cups, his talents were being appreciated. And perhaps you saw a few of his Pert shampoo commercials following his newly found acclaim during the decade that also saw the explosion of the internet.

As the late 90s came around, he rounded things out with MLS teams Columbus Crew and LA Galaxy. Not without a little controversy, Caligiuri had to sue MLS in order to play for LA Galaxy, his hometown. He had been placed by the league—through complicated measures—on the Columbus Crew. When he got his way, his final LA Galaxy game in 2001 was a US Open Cup championship over the New England Revolution.

In 2000, *Soccer America* included Caligiuri—an NCAA champion with UCLA in 1985—in its College Team of the Century. This was followed by his eventual induction into the 2004 National Soccer Hall of Fame.

For an unassuming guy that attended Walnut High School in the LA area, Caligiuri played 110 games for the USMNT and caught the imagination of fans around the nation. Perhaps most significant of all, he and others of this time were quietly opening doors in Europe for future US stars to enjoy.

30 Brent Goulet USMNT: 1986-90

The US Soccer Player of the Year in 1987? **Brent Goulet**. Perhaps his name has gotten lost in the ever-expanding pantheon of US soccer talk, but Goulet was—once upon a time—a lethal weapon, with good posture, that finished with skill and technique; in a Peter Vermes-esque way, he had a way of jabbing at the ball with the outside of his foot from around the box, straight to the back of the net. Pure forward. Pure finisher.

Goulet represented the USMNT in the 1988 Olympics. Of these Olympic games, *Soccer Digest*—a top US soccer publication in the day—noted that, "Brent Goulet is one of three US team members with European soccer experience."[40]

Goulet, who hails from Tacoma, Washington (by way of Cavalier, North Dakota), ended up navigating through the treacherous waters of soccer in the 1980s—back when a viable pro outdoor league in the US just plain didn't exist. Goulet—like many players of his generation—surged forward anyway, playing for the Seattle Storm, Tacoma Stars, Tennis Borussia Berlin (43 games, 21 goals), SV Elversberg (who he eventually coached), and represented the US national team from 1986-90.

As a member of the United States futsal team, Goulet added up over 10 caps in the late 80s and also earned a 1989 bronze medal in the World Championships held in Netherlands.

If there's a silent winner on this board of USMNT legends, Goulet's definitely one of them. His era, one that featured fewer games than today's, was one that got lost on TV, literally, as games in the 80s were hard to come by in the United States. Back when Copas were practically the only shoes worn, Goulet's brown curly hair—with just a hint of a mullet—was supported by that good posture, a confident demeanor, along with an arrogant glimmer in his eyes that stood out proudly against a USMNT uniform that often times was simply all white with blue trim. A genuine stud from the Northwest, Goulet didn't make a household name for himself, such as Donovan and Dempsey, but he helped guide the way for younger generations to come along.

Though his time with the USMNT may have been short, his name and recognition as the 1987 US Soccer Player of the Year conjures up the idea of what a soccer star in the 80s was. And for a brief time, it was Goulet.

31 Mike Windischmann USMNT: 1984-90

Mike Windischmann—born in 1965 in West Germany—grew up in the New York City area and played for clubs there, including but not limited to Queens United, before attending Adelphi University in 1983. Soon thereafter, he was honored in the school's Athletic Hall of Fame in 1986.

He had previously played for the U16 US national team and participated in the World Cup for the age group. As for pro soccer, he took a different route. At first, to the surprise of many, he opted for the Cosmopolitan League of New York City, representing the Brooklyn Italians. From roughly 1986-88 he stationed himself there until he switched gears and landed with the Los Angeles Lazers of the MISL from 1988-89. As the team disbanded, he jumped over to the Albany Capitals of the American Soccer League. As this was going on, he found more of a name for himself with the USMNT.

In the 80s, he was a key piece of the puzzle for the national team, leading things from central defense with skill, vision, and soccer IQ. In 1984, he made his debut for the senior national team which led to appearances in the 1987 Pan American Games, the 1988 Olympics (where he scored against Argentina), and the 1990 FIFA World Cup. Prior to the World Cup, the first the US had competed in since 1950, he was honored with the US Soccer Player of the Year award in 1989. For the 1990 World Cup, Windischmann was captain as the team took on Czechoslovakia, Italy, and Austria in the group stage. By this time, he'd been a regular starter for the team. By the time of his retirement in 1990, he hit the 50-cap mark.

In 1989 he played for the US futsal team in the FIFA Futsal World Championship in which the US defeated Italy, Argentina, and Brazil on its way to a third place finish. In 1992 he again played for the US futsal team in the FIFA Futsal World Championship, hosted by Hong Kong. This time around, the US beat Russia, China, Argentina, and Iran on a path to the final where they lost to Brazil. A few teammates on this ride were Jeff Agoos, Andy Schmetzer, Chico Borja, Ted Eck, Jim Gabarra, and Fernando Clavijo. This, for Windischmann, was the end of the road.

At the end of a short—but interesting—career, Windischmann has the unique claim to fame of being captain at a FIFA World Cup. Also part of that journey was the big game in Trinidad and Tobago—a 1-0 thriller—that got the USMNT to the 1990 World Cup, a monumental moment for US soccer. Windischmann, the captain that game, helped guide the team to victory as it was the first time the US made the World Cup in 40 years.

32 Christopher Sullivan USMNT: 1987-92

Sulli! This guy, **Christopher Sullivan**, is the epitome of a player who was slowing down right as MLS began but transitioned smoothly to media afterwards.

Sullivan—a 6'0" midfielder-forward—and his cohorts paved the way for future players to land in Europe. Grinding away were players like Sullivan, getting what they could out of Europe before it was somewhat en vogue to bring US players over the pond. Sullivan went to the University of Tampa (in Florida) in the mid-80s then tried his luck with European soccer in the late 80s, including ETO FC Gyor (Hungary; some spellings list it as Gyori), Landskrona BoIS (Sweden), and Hertha BSC (Germany) all while working his way up through the labor years of US soccer—in his case, 1987-92—that were mired in difficulty.

Sullivan got quite far, 19 caps and two goals, and was even included on the squad for the 1990 FIFA World Cup. His calling in life required perseverance and determination at a time when it was not super-cool to be a US soccer player.

The USMNT at that point was trying to earn respect around CONCACAF and the world while being ignored regarding TV exposure. It was treated like a professional team, which in one sense was good—it allowed players to be active—but at the same time it was clear that the US was a nation without a viable pro outdoor league. The players were essentially viewed as toy pieces that were not allowed to play significantly in Europe based on a longstanding belief system that the US didn't understand soccer, while the USMNT was busy building a stone monument on the hill, bit by bit, that said, "We've arrived." Except it hadn't quite arrived yet, but each outing was another chance to put US soccer on the map.

Eventually Sullivan joined the fledgling MLS in 1997, with the San Jose Clash. Sullivan's listed as being born in 1965 in San Jose and for him to return, it was full circle.

After playing, Sullivan made interesting moves in media that led him to cover five World Cups, as of 2022. He's worked with various outlets as a soccer analyst, including that of Fox Sports Bay Area, the MLS Wrap on Fox Soccer Channel, the Soccer Night in America (that focused on a MLS game of the week), and with Fox Soccer Channel he's contributed his talents with respect to the FIFA World Cup, UEFA Champions League, CONCACAF Champions League, and others. He also worked with Yahoo Sports and beIN Sports. For the 2022 FIFA World Cup in Qatar, beIN Sports had an impressive list of pundits, led by former World Cup champion, Kaka; Sullivan was listed as one of the North American reps alongside Jermaine Jones (USMNT) and Kaylyn Kyle (of Canada).

Despite coming up during a difficult era of US soccer, Sullivan kept going. He persevered. As a result, his soccer IQ is on full display around the world as a representative of US soccer.

33 Bruce Murray
USMNT: 1985-93

Bruce Murray—born in 1966 in Germantown, Maryland—played for the Montgomery United Ponies and won the U16 national championship (1981) and the U19 national championship (1983). In addition, while attending Clemson University, he was part of the 1984 and 1987 NCAA championships. Not bad, that's a lot of national championships! In addition, he won the Hermann Trophy in 1987, and as an All-American in college, Murray also made the *Soccer America* College Team of the Century as compiled in 2000.

With the national team, Murray's accolades accumulated over the years as he suited up in the 1988 Olympics, in South Korea, and was a member of the US futsal team that placed third in the 1989 FIFA Futsal World Championship.

On the biggest stage, one of his goals arrived at the 1990 FIFA World Cup against Austria. In the 1991 Gold Cup, which the US won for the first time, Murray tallied up two more goals. Murray and teammate Peter Vermes (who also had two goals) helped put the US over the top with a strong tournament. After sliding past a strong Mexican side in the semis, Murray was among the starters in a final that culminated against Honduras in the Los Angeles Memorial Coliseum. It went to penalty kicks as the US completed its first-place claim. Murray, along with teammates Marcelo Balboa, Hugo Perez, Paul Caligiuri, and others, made history with the United States' first Gold Cup title.

Coach Jerry Yeagley of Indiana University, long considered one of the greats in NCAA history, essentially said he recruited winners—as in players that had a history of winning tournaments. Murray, who had won two national youth titles, two NCAA titles, and the Hermann Trophy, is a strong indication of what you get when you place winners on a field.****

**** Of course, chemistry and coaching have a lot to do with it. Certainly, the competition is also fielding winners so someone has to lose. But the notion of starting a team from scratch with proven winners and going from there is the idea.

Certainly his teammates on this 1991 team had winning backgrounds of their own. Murray and his cohorts brought the US a much-needed Gold Cup title. Hence, to this day and long into the future, it will stand as a prominent moment for the US in the region of North America.

Overall, be it in friendlies, the Gold Cup, or World Cup, Murray gathered 21 goals as a forward in 85 appearances from 1985–93. A stellar career for one of the US' greatest talents.

34 Frank Klopas USMNT: 1987-95††††

To date, in the history of the men's soccer program, the top 10 goal scorers range between 57 and 17 goals. Not far from that mark is **Frank Klopas**, with 12. His goals, over time, came against Jamaica, Turkey, Moldova, Iceland, Estonia, Armenia, Greece, Saudi Arabia, and Argentina.

Professionally, Klopas—a 5'9" attacking threat—distinguished himself by winning the Greek Super Cup (1989) and Greek League Cup (1990). In addition, he won the MLS Cup and US Open Cup with Chicago Fire in 1998. However, he got his pro start with the Chicago Sting in the indoor days of the 1980s. This undoubtedly fine-tuned his skill and quick decision-making which he was known for. In all, he played for the Sting (1983-88), AEK Athens (1988-94), Apollon Athens (1994-96), Kansas City Wizards (1996-97), and Chicago Fire (1998-99).

For the US, Klopas played in the 1987 Pan American Games where he scored a goal against Trinidad and Tobago. He also played for the US in the 1988 Olympics, under coach Lothar Osiander. When it comes to full internationals, things get tricky for players that competed with the Olympic team or at the Pan American games. FIFA hasn't always recognized those as full internationals.

At one point, the Oakland As and San Francisco Giants had a precocious pitcher, one that received a lot of well-deserved hype, Barry Zito. Klopas is the Barry Zito of US soccer. At first, you were wowed by the guy. Then things kind of tapered off. But that didn't take away the existing talent, waiting to be unleashed. Later in his career, it turned into: "Oh, not quite the same, but good to have around." Klopas—who had hype in the beginning and then

†††† There are discrepancies with the years Klopas played for the USMNT. As of January 14, 2024, US National Soccer Players (ussoccerplayers.com) listed it from 1987-98; olympics.com listed it from 1987-98; *Wikipedia* listed it from 1987-95; and chicagofirefc.com listed it from 1987-95. Based on his extensive experience coaching the Chicago Fire, it would be logical to assume that source is correct.

things faded a bit—fell into a similar category. In the 80s, he was with the exciting Chicago Sting, then in the late 80s he joined AEK Athens in Greece. Things were rocking. Klopas was on the move.

Leading into the 1990 FIFA World Cup, Klopas was a factor going so far as to score against Jamaica in 1988. Yet, in 1989, because of claims of fitness or lack thereof, coach Bob Gansler—an ardent fitness guru—didn't include Klopas in the epic Trinidad and Tobago match—which the US won 1-0 to launch into the 1990 World Cup—and he was subsequently not brought along to Italy.

Despite an injury Klopas suffered circa 1991, he bounced back in 1994. In fact, Kopas was part of the squad at the FIFA 1994 World Cup, coached by Bora Milutinovic, but didn't get in. After much time spent in indoor, one would assume his injury-status in the early 90s hampered his ability to perform for a couple years. This was the tail end of his national team run.

However, with the US, 1995 was significant for Klopas as he scored a big goal against Argentina in a 3-0 victory in group C, in the 1995 Copa America. He scored a crucial PK in the shootout against Mexico in the quarters. Subsequently, the team lost to Brazil in the semis and placed fourth overall. Klopas, a part of that run, helped the US find success in the mid-90s as the New Dawn of the USMNT was underway. All the same, Klopas was part of the Late Pioneer period (1980s-90s) and the New Dawn period (1994-2010).

Shuffling in-between eras, Klopas was part of the USMNT during an interesting time—1987-95—when MLS hadn't formed yet and US soccer was emerging. There was a boom in the 80s; youth soccer was soaring like never before; and the youth players were gaining more knowledge about the USMNT as games were periodically on TV. Yet US soccer was still something of an enigma to many people in the US. It was fighting for TV time and in the process of earning respect around the nation.

After retiring from play in 1999, Klopas eventually entered the coaching ranks as he ran the Chicago Storm (2004-06), Chicago Fire (2011-13), and Montreal Impact (2013-15), and then from 2020-23 he returned to the Chicago Fire as an assistant and subsequently took the head coach position in 2023.

While he's also done some color commentating (providing interesting information alongside the play-by-play announcer) for the Chicago powerhouse MLS side, he'll probably be best known for his attacking play during much of his life, including the infamous MISL and the mystical Greek league, an injury in the early 90s that sidelined his true potential, and a 1994 World Cup that he never saw action in, even though he scored a ton of goals in 1994.

Even after that, as *Wikipedia* said: "Klopas would go on to score five goals in the eight international friendlies the US played immediately prior to the start of the World Cup, tallying against Iceland, Estonia, Armenia and his native Greece. He also scored a brace in a pre-World Cup friendly against Bundesliga champions Bayern Munich on May 22, 1994 and went on to make the U.S. roster."[41]

As so many interesting stories go, he never quite got to the pinnacle of playing in a World Cup. *Wikipedia* summarized his situation: "Despite the suspension of starting midfielder John Harkes for the Brazil game and Tab Ramos leaving the game in the first half after catching an elbow from left back Leonardo, Klopas was not used in the match as Hugo Perez replaced Harkes in the starting lineup and Eric Wynalda came on for Ramos. The U.S. held well defensively but were undone by Bebeto's 72nd-minute strike and fell 1–0 to the eventual champions at Stanford Stadium."[42]

Yet there's more. If you thought, perhaps, he was just some has-been Milutinovic overlooked, he reminded everyone after the 1994 World Cup that he was still around. "Despite not playing in the team's four biggest matches of the year, Klopas played in the team's remaining four friendlies in 1994 and scored three more goals to finish as the US team's top goal scorer that year, tallying eight goals in 15 appearances."[43]

35 Peter Vermes USMNT: 1988-97

Peter Vermes—born in 1966 in Willingboro, New Jersey—was a versatile forward and defender, an uncanny mix. The 6'1" talent scored 109 goals in high school and eventually landed with Rutgers University where he became All-American.

Professionally, Vermes encompassed the Late Pioneer period—1980s and 90s—just before the arrival of MLS (1996), spent some time in Europe (Gyor in Hungary, Volendam in Holland, and Figueres in Spain), and finished his career with the MetroStars, Colorado Rapids, and Kansas City Wizards. Like many of his compatriots of this period (such as Harkes, Ramos, and Caligiuri), Vermes was dispersed throughout Europe, establishing a foothold for future US talent, and returned home to bolster the launch of MLS.

Toward the end of the 80s, Vermes joined the squad in the 1988 Olympics. In 1988 he won the US Soccer Player of the Year award. Like Brent Goulet, who also won the award, Vermes had a similar way of jabbing the ball into the net, with a quick nudge from the outside of the foot—shooting the ball past the keeper. It was the act of the shooting itself but also the timing of the shot, the uncanny awareness of when to strike the ball past the keeper that set Vermes apart.

Vermes was a standout in the 1989 FIFA Futsal World Championship as he represented the US team with six goals on route to a third place finish.

From 1988-97, Vermes was a critical component of the USMNT. As such, he tallied up just over 65 caps for his country, with 11 goals, participating in the devastatingly epic qualifier win against Trinidad in 1989 (which sent shock waves around the world), each of the three matches at the 1990 FIFA World Cup in Italy, and a strong contribution during the 1991 CONCACAF Gold Cup championship run in which he scored two goals in the tournament.

A milestone for Vermes was scoring a critical goal in the 2-0 victory over archrival Mexico in the semifinals of the 1991 CONCACAF Gold Cup in Los Angeles. The USMNT won the Gold Cup that year (defeating Honduras in the final), its first title for the competition. The top scorer that tournament was Benjamin Galindo of Mexico, with four. Vermes had two goals overall (a team leader, tied with Bruce Murray who also had two). This was, to say the least, a big result. As the first Gold Cup title for the US, it was one for the record books. But to get a goal in the semis against Mexico was something special on a personal note, an achievement not many players can claim.

Towards the end of his time on the field as a transformed forward-turned-defender, Vermes proved just how valuable his acumen was by winning the MLS Defender of the Year Award in 2000. As an added bonus, with the Kansas City Wizards he won the MLS Cup in 2000.

He followed his playing career with an exemplary job as coach of Sporting Kansas City beginning in 2009 where he won the 2013 MLS Cup, along with the 2012 US Open Cup, 2015 US Open Cup, 2017 US Open Cup. Why is this worth pointing out? Many players, who reach the high levels as he did, do not transition very well to coaching. But Vermes and staff at Sporting KC have solidified a prominent place in the lore of MLS history, with championship teams that might keep going. He recently signed a new deal with Sporting KC in 2023 that should extend into 2028.

His teams play with a distinct confidence, combined with fluid passing skill. For the most part, Vermes has an uncanny ability to find the right players and coach them the right way. The result is a particular rhythm on the field—combining offensive and defensive prowess, his signature traits as a player—that any coach should emulate.

36 Tab Ramos USMNT: 1988-2000

For a time there, with his spry nature, fully-chiseled legs with extreme definition from hours of ball skills, **Tab Ramos**—born in 1966 in Montevideo, Uruguay, and all of 5'7"—was encroaching on the heels of Ricky Davis for the title of greatest player in the US. With the national team, from 1988-2000, he acquired 81 caps and eight goals, one of which was a half-volley that rocketed into the net at over 70 mph! Ramos was a shifty player behind the scoring, who broke through the channels and created dangerous opportunities that led to scoring chances for others.

Originally, before going pro, Ramos represented North Carolina State in college. Perhaps one of the best players to never win the Hermann Trophy, Ramos excelled and quickly moved into the ranks of the USMNT with skill, flair, exquisite dribbling, immaculate technique, and phenomenal quickness; Ramos could stop on a dime, with perfect control of the ball. This ability earned him a spot on the 1988 US Olympic squad, alongside Ricky Davis, John Harkes, and Peter Vermes, to name a few. From there, during that transition period of US soccer, after the NASL and before the arrival of MLS, Ramos played for the New Jersey Eagles, Miami Sharks, Figueres, Real Betis, and, eventually from the mid-90s through 2002, he suited up for the MetroStars. He also spent time, on loan, with Tigres UANL in Mexico.

Ramos also played on the US futsal team that earned third place at the 1989 FIFA Futsal World Championship. Along the way, the US team defeated Italy, Argentina, and the eventual champs, Brazil. By tournament's end, Ramos gathered three goals alongside teammates Peter Vermes (six goals) and Jimmy Gabarra (five goals).

In 1990 Ramos became the seventh player to earn the US Soccer Player of the Year award, and started in that historic match, whereby Caligiuri hit the miraculous game-winning, World Cup-entering volley. Ramos had a solid match—as did others—and it was the first time in 40 years that the USMNT competed in the FIFA World Cup.

Fast forward to 1994 and you have the US hosting the FIFA World Cup, with sellout crowds for each US game—another stepping stone for the US to establish itself on the international scene. The atmosphere was insane as Ramos, Meola and the gang were becoming household names. This was a turning point, in a big way, for US soccer. Ramos was front and center in more ways than one. After earning a spot in the round of 16, Ramos took an unforgiving elbow to the temple from Leonardo of Brazil—who was subsequently given a red card by referee Joel Quiniou of France in front of over 84,000 spectators at Stanford Stadium. Ramos went down and left the game. The US, unfortunately, lost that match 1-0 to the eventual champions. However, it was a great step forward for US soccer at large, seeing as MLS arrived two years later in 1996 (in part, due to the momentum from the 1994 World Cup). Ramos played a huge part in that growth.

That ends part one of the New Jersey connection. The one-two-three punch of New Jersey: Ramos-Harkes-Meola!

37 John Harkes USMNT: 1987-2000

John Harkes. If you're looking for a good player–one who played with passion, to win–then Harkes is an easy candidate...a noteworthy player in the history of US soccer.

Harkes–born in 1967 in Kearney, New Jersey–is of Scottish descent and became the 1984 *Parade* High School Player of the Year. He subsequently went onto play for the University of Virginia, a soccer powerhouse.

Harkes earned a distinct honor as he was on the USMNT for the 1988 Olympics.

Professionally, he became the first US player to compete in the English Premier League; at the time his team was Sheffield Wednesday. Overall, he played with a number of teams, including Albany Capitals, Derby County, West Ham United, DC United, Nottingham Forest, New England Revolution, and Columbus Crew. He was part of two MLS Cup championships, with DC United.

Overall, Harkes played for the USMNT from 1987-2000, with 90 caps and six goals. He competed in the 1990 and 1994 World Cups but didn't make the 1998 squad.

Despite not holding a World Cup championship trophy, Harkes excelled on and off the field as a broadcaster and coach. He was an assistant with New York Redbulls and then coached FC Cincinnati, along with Greenville Triumph.

As a player, Harkes was definitely in the middle of the hurricane that was the Late Pioneer period of US soccer (1980s-90s). Following in the footsteps of Pat McBride, Al Trost, and Ty Keough, Harkes led the team at a critical time in USMNT history, right when soccer was about to be cool in the mainstream of the US, during the 1990 and 1994 World Cups, and the advent of MLS (1996). It's as if Harkes–and his cohorts–pushed US soccer over the inflection point. A critical player for a monumental moment in US soccer history.

38 Tony Meola USMNT: 1988-2006

Outside of **Tony Meola**, not many goalies are on this list, save for Frank Borghi and a few others. Meola—who was born in 1969 in New Jersey—was a great talent that happened to land in a time that was worthy of unique legendary status.

Meola excelled at Kearny High school in the 80s as goalie and forward, was captain of the basketball squad, an All-State baseball player that was drafted by the New York Yankees, the 1989 Hermann Trophy recipient while at University of Virginia, and down the road he would attempt to kick field goals for the New York Jets.‡‡‡‡ He wasn't just a niche soccer guy: he was Mr. Everything. In his nonchalant way, combined with athletic drive, he was very relatable to a mainstream, beer-drinking, hard-working, US public that was used to kicking back over a baseball game to cap off a long day at work. Meola was the perfect player to push US soccer forward to the masses. Therefore, the top elite players were chosen to win, be ambassadors, and, if you will, pitch the game as they went.

In 1989, Meola was part of the team that defeated Peru for the Marlboro Cup title in the New York City area; celebrating ensued, and he almost lost the actual trophy when dropping it off at a hotel where the team was staying before heading home to prepare for the coming schedule.

He was one of the elite starters against Trinidad, in perhaps *the* most critical game in US soccer history, on the road in Trinidad, for all the marbles to reach the 1990 World Cup. With everything on the line, and with Caligiuri's huge goal, Meola held his own with a chill-inducing performance from his frontline of defenders that sent the US to Italy as a representative of CONCACAF.

Meola, who is of Italian descent, had the unique opportunity to not only play in Italy, on Italian turf for the World Cup of a lifetime, but to start

‡‡‡‡ It was an audacious move, but in the end it didn't work out.

against the Azzurri, his homeland. Would he have liked to win? Of course. But the odds were highly stacked against the US playing against a world great, the hosts in Italy, a favorite that year, in Rome in front of the home crowd. It just wasn't looking too auspicious. On paper, a 1-0 loss was very respectable.

Then, four years later, Meola—ponytail and all—guarded the net in the FIFA World Cup of 1994, hosted in the United States. Soccer mania was off the charts that year, with record attendance for any World Cup. The US was booming; stadiums were filling up; there was a frenzy. While hopes for the USMNT had a limited scope, there was optimism as the team was turning a few heads. In group A, Meola and company tied Switzerland 1-1, defeated Colombia 2-1, and took a 1-0 loss to Romania. Despite the loss, it was practically mass hysteria wherever the team went. For the first match against Switzerland, at the Pontiac Silverdome in Michigan, over 73,000 were in attendance. Games two and three against Colombia and then Romania were held at the Rose Bowl in Pasadena, California, in front of over 93,000.

The US got to the round of 16, where captain Meola exchanged pre-game pleasantries with Dunga, only to be toppled by Bebeto and Brazil, 1-0, but, when it was all said and done, it was a part of the biggest show on earth and the US had a place in primetime...finally.

As the late 90s came around, after Meola sought to kick for the New York Jets, Kasey Keller and Brad Friedel gained favor as the next top goalies for the team. As it turns out, the late 80s and early 90s were Meola's prime with the team. He still suited up as the late 90s turned into the early 2000s, and played his last game in 2006. In all, he gained 100 caps.

As a goalie, Meola broke barriers by winning the Hermann Trophy in 1989. (Brad Friedel followed suit in 1992, playing for UCLA.) His pro career, an interesting one at that, took him to Brighton & Hove Albion, Fort Lauderdale Strikers, Buffalo Blizzard, Long Island Rough Riders, New York/New Jersey MetroStars, Kansas City Wizards (his longest venture with 125 appearances), New York Red Bulls, and New Jersey Ironmen.

In his post-playing days, Meola has had a number of broadcasting gigs.[44] Maybe you've heard him calling MLS games or perhaps his SiriusXM show with former USMNT standout, Eric Wynalda. Meola has that East Coast Italian-American laidback calmness about his demeanor, speech, and disposition. Millions of fans will always have a seat available for Meola. Likewise, Meola will have a seat waiting for them.

39 Marcelo Balboa USMNT: 1988-2000

Marcelo Balboa—born in 1967—experienced national success early on. He was born in Chicago but eventually moved to Cerritos, California, a suburb of LA. As part of the club team Fram-Culver, Balboa won the 1986 McGuire Cup (U19), a big tournament back then, and became a national champion. At that time, those who won that competition were typically elite talent bound for top college programs.

Balboa attended Cerritos High School—class of 1984—which is in the south Los Angeles area. Interestingly, a few years after Balboa attended CHS, a few other players walked through its halls, including Jorge Salcedo (USMNT and UCLA coach), Eddie Soto (a member of US beach soccer and coach of the US beach soccer team),[§§§§] and Eddie Lewis (USMNT). As it turns out, Balboa is the elder statesman of Cerritos High—the OG.

He first attended Cerritos College, then San Diego State, where, predictably, he became an All American. In the late 80s and early 90s, Balboa played for the San Diego Nomads, San Francisco Bay Blackhawks, and the Colorado Foxes. In the mid-90s, he joined Leon in Mexico. Following this excursion, he played the bulk of his career with the Colorado Rapids (MLS), even going so far as to get the MLS Goal of the Year in 2000 in a match versus the Columbus Crew—a smashing bicycle kick off a cross with authority.

During his pro journey, Balboa won the US Soccer Player of the Year award in 1992 and 1994, becoming the first player to win it twice. During that time, he was largely known for his contributions on defense with the USMNT in the 90s. For a central defender to receive so much acclaim was odd. Usually it's the midfielders and forwards! For Balboa, who was front and center, it seemed like he was unstoppable. It wasn't just his mullet and mustache that were garnering attention—it was his standout play.

§§§§ Soto was also a member of the North Huntington Beach club team that won the 1991 McGuire Cup national title.

He became one of only a few US players to be part of three FIFA World Cups: the 1990 World Cup, 1994 World Cup, and 1998 World Cup. In 1994 Balboa showed off his acrobatic ability–as a defender, no less–with a near-miss bicycle kick off a corner. And it wasn't just a bicycle kick, as you sometimes see, where a player takes a miss-kick in the box and leaps up for a bike (or maybe a half-bike in which they just sort of flop backwards and swat at the ball with one leg). No, this was a ball from distance, straight off a corner kick that he struck–with perfect technique–in full flight on the far side of the box. If there's a non-goal in a FIFA World Cup that needs to be considered among the actual goals: count this one in. The effort alone was phenomenal and the fact that it just missed the post added to the electricity he brought in that moment.

As for the '98 World Cup, it was a tough year that saw three consecutive losses for the US against Germany, Iran, and Yugoslavia. Just two years later in 2000, Balboa played his last game for the USMNT versus Iran in a friendly, giving him over 125 caps and 13 goals.

In his post playing career you might have heard him calling a few games, including the 2006 FIFA World Cup final that saw France paired up against the eventual champion Italy. It was the historic game that saw Zidane notoriously headbutt an opponent, followed by an ejection. Balboa was there, live in the booth, covering the action as the color commentator for millions of US fans. In addition to this benchmark experience, his contributions to the world of soccer media have been carried out with ABC, ESPN, NBC Sports, Univision.

After playing over 150 games for the Colorado Rapids, this son of Argentine immigrants now resides in Colorado, coaching and staying active in media. He's a one-of-a-kind defender for the US that marked out a unique place in soccer history both on and off the field.

40 Dominic Kinnear USMNT: 1990-93

Dominic Kinnear—born 1967 in Scotland—played as a versatile defender for a number of teams: SF Bay Blackhawks, San Jose Hawks, Fort Lauderdale Strikers, Necaxa, Seattle Sounders, Colorado Rapids, San Jose Clash, Tampa Bay Mutiny, and the USMNT.

At a young age, his family moved to Fremont, California, just a short drive from San Jose, where he'd eventually have much experience as a player—with SF Bay Blackhawks, San Jose Hawks, and San Jose Clash—and later as a coach.

In 1995, as a player with Necaxa, it was an honor—at the time and now—to be part of the Mexican top division. During his stint, he was part of the squad that won the league title that year. For the United States, he compiled 54 caps, nine goals. That's quite a few caps for anyone. But, considering the brief spell of brilliance from Kinnear that came in 1990-93, it's even more impressive. As a valuable member of the team, his services were called upon as long as he could provide substance on the field. His nine goals arrived against Costa Rica, Chile, Romania, Canada, Venezuela, Cayman Islands, and El Salvador.

In his post-playing career, Kinnear entered the coaching ranks and had immediate success. As an assistant with the San Jose Earthquakes, Kinnear was part of two MLS Cups: 2001 and 2003. Things progressed in his career to the Houston Dynamo, where he became head coach, and so too did his winning ways. In east Texas, Kinnear won the MLS Cup in 2006 and 2007 with the Dynamo. His stint in Houston was quite lengthy, 2005-14, until he left to take on the head coaching position with San Jose Earthquakes, from 2014-17.

Kinnear was a top-level talent that brought exquisite play, with deft touch, to the field, along with athletic flair. He was a special player, one that definitely made his mark in the halls of the USMNT, albeit under the radar just a bit.

41 Jeff Agoos USMNT: 1988-2003

Jeff "Goose" Agoos played 134 games for the USMNT and scored four goals in that time. In that respect, he's currently ranked fifth all time. That list is:

1. Cobi Jones: 164
2. Landon Donovan: 157
3. Michael Bradley: 151
4. Clint Dempsey: 141
5. Jeff Agoos: 134

Agoos—born in 1968 in Geneva, Switzerland—was actually raised in Texas where he attended high school in Richardson. While there, he was a *Parade* All-American twice.

He took his defending talents to the University of Virginia where he was coached by Bruce Arena. At the college level, he was named All American as well.

He played for a number of teams after college that included Maryland Bays, Dallas Sidekicks, Los Angeles Salsa, SV Wehen (Germany), DC United, San Jose Earthquakes, and MetroStars.

In the earliest stage of MLS, Agoos was allocated to DC United. He won the league's first title, as coached by Bruce Arena, and also the US Open Cup. Then in 1998, DC United defeated Vasco de Gama to take the Interamerican Cup, and Agoos won his second MLS Championship, followed by his third with DC United in 1999. From 2001 to 2004 he played with the San Jose Earthquakes, winning his fourth and fifth MLS Championships. He earned a place in the MLS Best XI in 1997, 1999, and 2001, when he was also named MLS Defender of the Year. In 2005, he was named as the league's All-Time Best XI. He was traded to the Metro Stars in a fourth-round draft pick after the 2004 season. In his ten years playing in MLS, Agoos scored 11 regular-season goals, and had 25 assists in 244 matches.[45]

Basically, Agoos was a giant gobbling up titles in a league that had barely taken shape. But rather than a goal-scoring highlight reel, he was a lonely outside back that got little of the credit when his team put the ball in the goal. He was a workhorse, a rock, a steady force that gave his teammates confidence to do their thing. His experience, savvy, and athletic wisdom was on full display when forwards would go at him, tapping the ball down the wing, trying desperately to get an edge, a jump on him, and Agoos would turn his hips, body the player off the ball and ride it out.

His time with the USMNT dominated the 90s yet he was not included in the US roster for the 1990 and 1994 FIFA World Cup tournaments. Although he was part of the 1998 FIFA World Cup, there was a rivalry, as implemented by Coach Steve Sampson, with David Regis, and Agoos didn't play that tournament.

In the following 2002 FIFA World Cup, as coached by Bruce Arena, the Virginia connection came through as Agoos—in his 30s at the time—started the group matches and got an injury. Also at the 2002 CONCACAF Gold Cup, Agoos was part of the squad that won its second title. Agoos started in the semifinal match against Canada that went to a penalty shootout and he was one of the US players that converted a penalty. He also started in the final against Costa Rica and scored a goal, along with Josh Wolff, to win the championship 2-0.

He also played for the US national futsal team. The team placed second in the 1992 FIFA Futsal World Championship, held in Hong Kong.

He was the MLS Defender of the Year (2001) and became a member of the National Soccer Hall of Fame in 2009.

42 Kasey Keller
USMNT: 1990-2007

Kasey Keller—born in 1969 in Olympia, Washington—had an interesting pro career as a goalie that landed him with Portland Timbers, Millwall, Leicester City, Rayo Vallecano (Spain), Tottenham Hotspur, Southampton, Borussia Monchengladbach, Fulham, and the Seattle Sounders. The quiet 6'2" sensation, that was a trusted choice abroad, got his start at North Thurston High School in Lacey, a south suburb of Seattle.

According to ESPN *Press Room,* following high school:

> "Keller began his goalkeeping career in 1989 with the Portland Timbers of the Western Soccer Alliance while still a student at the University of Portland. That same year, he split time between the Timbers and the U.S. U-20 Men's National Team, which finished fourth in the 1989 FIFA U-20 World Cup in Saudi Arabia. Keller was awarded the tournament's silver ball as the competition's second best player. As a college senior in 1991, he earned first team All-America honors and was named the 1991 Adidas Goalkeeper of the Year."

Some players seemingly emerge out of nowhere: one second they're in college and then all of a sudden they've turned into the top player in their respective position in the nation. In 1990, Keller got his debut for the national team against Colombia. He also made the squad for FIFA World Cup 1990, as Meola's protégé.

In the 1996 Olympics, on the squad coached by Bruce Arena, Keller was front and center for the team, starting in every game.

He later racked up games in the 1998 FIFA World Cup, a doomed experiment so to speak. Not so much for Keller, but for the squad as a whole in which nothing seemed to go right for the Steve Sampson-led group that year.

Perhaps his biggest accolade came in the 1998 Gold Cup game against Brazil in which the US won 1-0 off the foot of Preki. As the match progressed, Brazil unleashed an arsenal of attacks on the US goal whereby Keller's stellar play received high compliments from former Barcelona superstar and World Cup champ, Romario.

His play wasn't just noticed by one of Brazil's greatest stars. Keller won the US Soccer Player of the Year award in outstanding fashion, a remarkable three times: 1997, 1999, and 2005.

What's more, in the 2005 CONCACAF Gold Cup Keller oversaw the net in the final against Panama as the US won its third title in a penalty-kick shootout.

He also added to his resume with time on the field—notably the semifinal win against Canada—during the 2007 CONCACAF Gold Cup. The USMNT won the title, making it the fourth in its history. Tim Howard was the main keeper that time around, yet Keller's vast experience was a key component to the team's success.

As good as Keller was, there came a guy named Brad Friedel. Pretty much throughout Keller's time with the USMNT, he and Friedel "were engaged in a head-to-head battle for the US goalkeeper's jersey. Keller got the nod in 1998 but was second choice to Friedel in the 2002 FIFA World Cup. In spite of this stiff competition he has the second most caps and wins of any men's goalkeeper in US soccer history with 102 and 53, respectively, behind Tim Howard. Keller remains the team's all-time leader in keeping clean sheets with 47."[46]

What's more, Keller oversaw the USMNT's run in the 2005 CONCACAF Gold Cup tournament—a clean sheet in the final match against Panama and two saves in the penalty shootout to win the trophy. Keller started the first seven games of the final round of World Cup qualifying in 2005, recording five consecutive clean sheets and 507 consecutive goalless minutes to lead the US to qualification for the 2006 FIFA World Cup Finals in Germany. He then became the first male player in US history to win his third Athlete of the Year award. On May 2, 2006, Keller and teammate Claudio Reyna became the first two US men named to four World Cup Rosters. In that World Cup,

Keller played in all three games and was named Man of the Match in the 1-1 draw with Italy in Kaiserslautern on June 17, 2006. Keller is the only US player to participate in both the 1990 and 2006 World Cups."[47]

Keller has remained in media since his playing days where he's been seen and heard as a color commentator for the Seattle Sounders and as an analyst for ESPN.

Keller and goalie Marcus Hahnemann, a former USMNT member, became coaches for Newport High School in the Seattle area. Nowadays, far removed from his central role with the USMNT and overseas professional gigs, Keller isn't the starting keeper. Yet given all his experience it still feels like there's something going on, just on a different level.

43 Earnie Stewart USMNT: 1990-2004

Earnie Stewart—born in 1969 in Netherlands—stood at 5'9" and played striker and midfield for the majority of a career that included stops at VVV-Venlo (Netherlands), Willem II (Netherlands), NAC Breda (Netherlands), DC United, and, of course, the USMNT.

Stewart's father was a member of the US Air Force, based in Netherlands. Earnie grew up in Netherlands and found early success in soccer where he suited up for VVV-Venlo in 1988. The Netherlands was a proving ground for him as he attracted US attention rather quickly. All in all, his goal tally abroad was quite impressive. He found the back of the net a number of times with VVV-Venlo (over 10 goals), Willem II (over 45 goals), and NAC Breda (over 45 goals). This scoring prowess made him the predominate-scoring US player in pro club competition abroad.

In 2004, playing for DC United, Stewart was part of the MLS Cup championship in which United defeated the Kansas City Wizards 3-2 in the final. United—featuring Nick Rimando, Ben Olsen, Dema Kovalenko, and Jaime Moreno—was stacked with talent and saw Stewart join the starting lineup for, what turns out to be, a great send off for his MLS experience. The 2004 season wound up being the end of his brief MLS stint (2003-04). What better way to end things than to gather a championship? His overall pro career came to a close a year later in 2005 where he began, VVV-Venlo.

During this general timespan, Stewart was known more in the United States for his contributions to the national team than his Dutch experiences. For over a decade, he was a mainstay with the USMNT, particularly in the 90s. This trickled into the 2000s as he gained the honor of US Soccer Player of the Year in 2001. With the national team, he played from 1990-2004, a lengthy run that included 101 caps, with 17 goals. What's more, he represented the US in the 1994, 1998, and 2002 FIFA World Cups. As *Wikipedia* pointed out, this made him "one of only five US men to play at three World Cups."[48]

In the 1994 World Cup—the first World Cup for the US since 1950—Stewart scored the game winner in a 2-1 thriller against Colombia at the Rose Bowl before over 93,000 live fans.

After assuming the role of director for NAC Breda, AZ Alkmaar, and Philadelphia Union, Stewart took on the directing role of a lifetime with the USMNT as he became GM in 2018 and eventually sporting director for the US Soccer Federation in 2019.

He somewhat quietly achieved that position, held it for a few years, and in 2023 made a major shift to become the director of PSV Eindhoven, as he vacated his role with US Soccer.

44 Eric Wynalda USMNT: 1990-2000

He speaks with an air of authority, one might say. **Eric Wynalda**—born in 1969 in Fullerton, California—was a forward listed at 5'10 ½" that sped downfield with a strong stride, like that of a stud racehorse, with an eye for goal. Wynalda grew up in the Westlake, California, area alongside future USMNT star Cobi Jones. A youth soccer standout and a scoring phenom, Wynalda won the AYSO state championship and attended Westlake High School where he was honored as an All-State player.

During his freshman year at San Diego State University, where he turned a lot of heads, Wynalda led the team to a second-place finish in the 1987 NCAA Division I tournament against Clemson (which featured Bruce Murray). By this time, Wynalda was ready for action, which he'd see—quite quickly, in fact—in the 1990 FIFA World Cup as he catapulted to the top of the soccer pyramid in stunning fashion.

Wynalda, like many players immersed in the Late Pioneer period, found himself entering his early prime just before MLS launched in 1996. From 1988-2008, he played for the San Diego Nomads, San Francisco Bay Blackhawks, 1. FC Saarbrucken (in Germany, where he scored over 30 goals), VfL Bochum (Germany), San Jose Clash, Leon (Mexico), Miami Fusion, New England Revolution, Chicago Fire, and he wound things up in 2007-08 with Bakersfield Brigade.

In 1990 soccer was still taking off in the US and Wynalda was front and center as one of the stars on the rise. He wasn't just a player on the field: he was creating something grand for US soccer. Whether they liked it or not, he and his teammates were tasked with building the sport, game by game, as ambassadors for the world's game in a country that was still pessimistically dismissing it as a sport for foreigners. So to make soccer cool in the US was still very much a real thing for Wynalda's generation and who better to lead the charge? He had the look, the swagger, and a scoring touch.

"An excellent run of warm-up matches helped the Fullerton, Calif. native secure a Starting XI spot against the Czechs in the opening match of Italia '90, but he never set a foot on the field after that match,"[49] said Michael Lewis, writing for US Soccer Federation. But that's not quite the end of his 1990 World Cup story. Wynalda, whether he likes it or not, is the first USMNT player to "receive a red card in a World Cup match, which occurred in the 53rd minute of the 5-1 loss."[50]

After the Italy experience, the US team moved onward with a little more swagger in its step. There was a feeling in the air that it wouldn't take another 40 years to reach the next World Cup. US soccer had arrived, albeit one step at a time. Each team in the way presented a challenge, as per usual. However, there was a vibe that tough opponents could be taken down with more consistency.

The 1991 Gold Cup proved as much. This tournament, which the US won, was a trendsetter. From here on out, CONCACAF would be dominated by Mexico, the US, Costa Rica, and whoever had the team of the month—be it Honduras, Panama, Canada, Jamaica, or Trinidad—for fourth place. This was the USMNT's first Gold Cup championship. On route to this historic title, Wynalda got a goal against Guatemala in group B action. In the final, a penalty kick shootout victory over Honduras, Wynalda got the start alongside Balboa, Caligiuri, Clavijo, Vermes, Henderson, Doyle, Perez, Quinn, Murray, and the ever-talented Meola.

As it turns out, 1991 was a big year as the US was proving itself time and time again. Wynalda scored the United States' much-needed goal in a 1-1 friendly with Ireland, a raucous affair held in Massachusetts. The US—far from a World Cup semifinals appearance—was still proving itself on the world stage, and teams like Ireland were viewed as better than the US, so the tie was a strong result. Wynalda finished it off in style with a chip over experienced keeper Pat Bonner for his goal.

The 1993 Gold Cup proved to be interesting. Wynalda, who got two goals, was in the mix as the USMNT earned second place overall. In the final, held at Estadio Azteca in Mexico City, around 120,000-ish people were there.

After his World Cup debut in 1990, Wynalda hit the ground running in Germany, playing for 1. FC Saarbrucken (1992-94) and then VfL Bochum (1994-96). He was a trailblazer for US soccer players abroad. This trend, of Yanks in Europe, was quite new. Thanks to guys like Wynalda, Murray, Trittschuh, Harkes, Preki, and Joe-Max Moore, the floodgates were slowly opening up for players—such as Dempsey, Donovan, and Pulisic—to find open arms in European clubs.

Wynalda's European experience overlapped the 1994 FIFA World Cup, hosted by the US. This time around, Wynalda had cemented his presence with the squad, more than ever, and was a starter in every group match. For the first game against Switzerland, Wynalda cracked in an electric free kick. Claudio Reyna, another free kick taker, had suffered an injury. Nonetheless, "Eric Wynalda scored one of the most dramatic goals in domestic soccer history."[51] There it went zooming over the wall, with textbook loft, and into the upper corner area. The huge crowd—over 73,000 strong—at the Pontiac Silverdome in Michigan went wild.

The US eventually lost to Brazil in the round of 16, but for Wynalda and the team it was a monumental showing. The World Cup itself had record attendance. Everything was booming. Two years later, MLS began. There was a wave of US soccer popularity and Wynalda was riding it like Laird Hamilton—balancing atop a monster 5AM Hawaiian breaker—at his best.

"Twenty years ago today, a league was born. On April 6, 1996, the San Jose Clash and DC United converged at Spartan Stadium in San Jose, Calif. for the inaugural fixture of an embryonic league. Little did we know that two decades later, it would grow and persist as the United States' top tier of professional soccer,"[52] said *Foxsports.com* in 2016, marking the league's anniversary. Who scored the first goal in MLS history? Wynalda sent in a "curling finish for the league's first goal in the 87th minute in a 1-0 victory over DC. It sent a sell-out crowd of 31,683 into delirium and created many, many fans."[53] This curling finish came from the left side of the six-yard box, a sneaky inside of the right foot curling shot to the far post, right past the keeper...the type of placement you'd see from Messi. In addition,

Eric Wynalda led the 1996 CONCACAF Gold Cup tournament with four goals, an impressive feat; overall, the US placed third that year.

In the 1998 Gold Cup, during the historic 1-0 semifinal defeat over Brazil, Wynalda was a starter alongside his childhood cohort, Cobi Jones. The same two were starters in the final, a narrow 1-0 loss to Mexico—off a goal from Hernandez, "El Matador"—in front of over 91,000 fans at Los Angeles Memorial Coliseum. Wynalda finished the tournament with one goal.

The 1998 FIFA World Cup would be Wynalda's last World Cup appearance, and third overall. He finished with the team a short time later, in 2000, as the all-time leading men's scorer. At the time it was 34 goals. This was equaled in 2007 by a fellow LA-native, Landon Donovan, who then bested it in 2008. But, for a time, Wynalda was commander-in-chief of goals scored.

And that's not all: The 1996 US Soccer Player of the Year award? Wynalda. The Honda US Player of the Decade for the 1990s? Wynalda. A member of the CONCACAF All-Decade Team of the 1990s? Wynalda. Inducted into the National Soccer Hall of Fame? Wynalda, in 2004.

In his post-playing days, he's been a media analyst for ESPN, ABC, Fox Soccer Channel, and Yahoo Sports!, and he's also been heard on SiriusXM alongside Tony Meola.

45 Cobi Jones USMNT: 1992-2004

A walk-on at UCLA became the most capped member of the USMNT ever? How'd that happen?!

Cobi Jones—born in 1970 in Detroit, Michigan—has a bright attitude, optimism, and high-octane quickness. Similar to Roberto Carlos, who was all over opponents that dared enter his realm, Jones was relentless in his pursuit of the ball. He never quit and the person being guarded by him was in for a long game.

There was a moment in the 1994 FIFA World Cup round of 16 game against Brazil that was quintessential Cobi Jones. Near the corner flag there was a scrum between he and Jorginho—one of the best outside defenders of all time, who was quick, feisty, relentless, and whose legs never stopped moving. The two contested the ball, and somehow Jones emerged with the ball. Victorious, he gets bumped by Jorginho—but to no avail. Jones was just too feisty, too full of energy, too low to the ground, too hungry to win the ball. Jones was the best *of the best* when it came to those 1v1 showdowns. Much like Zenden from the Netherlands, Jones was ready for a fight, and more often than not, he was going to win. And, by the way, this is all on defense. When he gets the ball it's much of the same.

Jones grew up in Southern California where he attended Westlake High School, just north of Malibu in Westlake Village (near Thousand Oaks), and in the same neck of the woods as future USMNT star Eric Wynalda.

While Jones (born in 1970) landed at UCLA and Wynalda (born in 1969) went to San Diego State, the two pioneers were charting a course for US soccer that, most likely, was far bigger than they ever could've imagined. They hold the distinction of being part of the Late Pioneer period (1980s-90s) and the New Dawn period (1994-2010). The New Dawn period was the rise of US soccer on the international stage.

First, with respect to the USMNT, things were on the move as the US hosted the 1994 FIFA World Cup, where the team showed that it belonged.

The team fought through CONCACAF and qualified for the 1998, 2002, 2006, 2010, 2014, and 2022 FIFA World Cups. The New Dawn period ushered in a new swagger for the USMNT. Part of this was regular qualification in FIFA World Cups, and a bona fide confidence in individual players, such as Wynalda, Jones, Brian McBride, Landon Donovan, and others.

Jones played in the 1992 Olympics, along with UCLA standouts Joe-Max Moore and Chris Henderson. However, with a win, draw, and loss the team didn't advance out of its group.

The US placed second in the 1993 Gold Cup. Jones was a starter in the final against Mexico, in Mexico City, in front of around 120,000-ish fans. Games like this were formative experiences for USMNT players. In the US, the team might have moderate turnouts. Then they'd travel just a bit south to Mexico City—where soccer is like a religion—and have an awakening experience of sorts within the realm of international competition. A few of his teammates on this occasion were Thomas Dooley, John Harkes, and Eric Wynalda, along with UCLA stars Chris Henderson and Joe-Max Moore.

Next up: the 1994 FIFA World Cup. For Jones, this was a massive experience on an individual level (as he was on the biggest stage). For the USMNT, this was a huge step in the right direction.

At this time, he joined Coventry City (1994-95) and Vasco da Gama (1995-96).

In the 1995 Copa America, Jones had "impressive performances"[54] in which the US placed fourth.

Then came 1998. After a disappointing run in the 1998 FIFA World Cup, the US placed second in the 1998 Gold Cup and won an important—and historic—semifinal contest over Brazil (led by Romario at the time). Jones was on the field for that match, a 1-0 win, helping to keep a clean sheet for Kasey Keller. In the final, which Jones started in, the US squared off against Mexico—led by Luis Hernandez and Cuauhtemoc Blanco—inside a rocking Los Angeles Memorial Coliseum that hosted a little over 91,000 on that occasion. The final score was 1-0, as Hernandez—aka "El Matador"—got the goal.

Four years later, the USMNT got some redemption and won the 2002 Gold Cup, which Jones was part of. He started the majority of matches, including the final against Costa Rica—a 2-0 victory. In the same year, Brazil won the 2002 FIFA World Cup for the fifth time. You may ask, "Why are we comparing the US to Brazil?" Because Brazil—where Jones played professionally—is the king of soccer and the US is the king of sports. Many think it's high time the US step up its game and take over men's soccer. Many think that time will inevitably come. With anything, there needs to be a start, a spark. It could be argued that Jones, Wynalda, and others, have been responsible for that spark, one step at a time.

Speaking of the 2002 FIFA World Cup: Jones made the trip though this would be his last World Cup. In all, he was in three: 1994, 1998, and 2002. In 2002, the US—coached by Bruce Arena—advanced to the round of 16 to defeat rival Mexico. In the quarterfinals, the US lost in a narrow 1-0 defeat to Germany. Jones, at this point a veteran, was a valuable part of the mix that saw the US into the quarters, a place that's been just out of reach since.

His USMNT run ended in 2004. But his legacy has lived on. The USMNT won the 2005 and 2007 Gold Cups. Jones was not with the team but it could be persuasively argued that his presence over the years—his approach that was ready for any team—created groundwork for this to occur. In fact, the swagger and confidence that players like Donovan and Dempsey brought to the fold is in direct alignment with the attitude Jones had: cocky, arrogant, and humbly aware that the US can consistently beat any opponent on any given day.

His professional career took him to Coventry City (1994-95), Vasco da Gama (1995-96), and LA Galaxy (1996-2007). He catapulted from Vasco da Gama, a Brazilian experience he cherished, to what turned out to be a massive move for the Galaxy. Jones, who grew up nearby in Westlake Village and starred at UCLA, was joining his hometown team. With the Galaxy, he played in just over 305 games. His presence there cannot, in any way, be understated. With LA, he was a starter and captain in the 2002 MLS Cup championship game, in which LA defeated New England Revolution 1-0 for the title. In 2005, yet again, the Galaxy defeated the Revolution 1-0 for the MLS Cup championship; Jones was a starter in that game. Jones then retired in 2007.

At the time of writing, Jones is the all-time USMNT leader in caps: 164. During that span, he scored 15 goals. Along the way, he earned the 1998 US Soccer Player of the Year award and in 2011 he became part of the National Soccer Hall of Fame.

46 Chris Henderson USMNT: 1990-2001

Chris Henderson—a 5'9" outside mid, born in 1970—originated in the Seattle area and made a big splash early on in his career: "Henderson secured the 1988 National High School Player of the Year award at Cascade H.S. while serving as student body president. More success followed him at UCLA, helping the Bruins capture the NCAA Division I crown as a sophomore,"[55] wrote Michael Lewis at ussoccer.com. Henderson was so renowned, in fact, that he played briefly for the Seattle Storm—in the Western Soccer League—in 1989 and attended UCLA from 1989-90 where he was part of the aforementioned national title in 1990, the school's second at the time. This wasn't just a blip on the screen for the Bruins. UCLA is one of those schools—like Saint Louis, Indiana, Maryland, and Virginia—that attracts elite talent. Henderson can attest to that. Down the road, in 2016, he entered the UCLA Athletics Hall of Fame. As a player at UCLA, Henderson was called to the USMNT.

Henderson's overall stint with the USMNT lasted from 1990-2001 where he attained 79 caps and three goals. His contributions came in the form of dashing runs down the line, with step overs, maneuverability, pace, speed, relentless ambition, determination, resolute defiance, and extreme confidence that left opponents bewildered in their tracks. Trying to keep up with Henderson was a task that most probably wanted to avoid. In the world of outside mids, he was the best *of the best.* This, in part, is why he was called upon so many times to represent the United States.

In the 1991 Gold Cup, the first one the US won, Henderson was part of the equation on the wing. The coach on this occasion was Bora Milutinovic. During the final against Honduras, Henderson started alongside Tony Meola, Paul Caligiuri, Fernando Clavijo, Peter Vermes, Eric Wynalda, and others. This was a huge step in the right direction for US soccer. From here the team firmly began to establish its iron grip over the region, which exists to this day. Prior to this, consistent dominance over CONCACAF foes hadn't quite come to fruition. Previous US teams were usually equal to or better than such opponents, yet a consistent stroke of dominance was an idea floating around that was just out of reach. Therefore, 1991—the first year the USMNT captured the Gold Cup—was a vital component for the progression of the men's national team.

For the 1992 Olympics, Henderson joined the ride as the team consisted of a star-studded UCLA group that included Cobi Jones, Joe-Max Moore, Zak Ibsen, and Brad Friedel, along with non-UCLA standouts Claudio Reyna (Virginia) and Steve Snow (Indiana). Overall it was an ill-fated journey as the US placed third in group A against Poland, Italy, and Kuwait and failed to escape its group.

Henderson played an important role in the 1993 Gold Cup and started in the final, an unfortunate loss to Mexico in Mexico City. Other teammates that game included fellow UCLA standouts Cobi Jones and Joe-Max Moore and distinguished players Tony Meola, Thomas Dooley, John Harkes, and Eric Wynalda. Always a tough venue for the US, Estadio Azteca was rocking on that occasion for another side. The US earned second, however. Not bad for a squad earning its place as a leader in the CONCACAF region.

Henderson's time with the USMNT is somewhat of a phenomenon: As one of the top players during the 90s, one of the most relied upon, he didn't enter a World Cup. He was the youngest player at FIFA World Cup 1990, yet, on this list of the top 100 USMNT players, he earns a spot as one of the few—in the modern era—that didn't have a direct impact in a World Cup. It goes to show that, depending on the coach, sometimes things aren't guaranteed.

All the same, this former high school Player of the Year, NCAA champion, and USMNT mainstay—on most occasions—wasn't going to be derailed. His pro career took him to FSV Frankfurt (1994-95), Stabaek (circa 1995-96), Colorado Rapids (1996-98), Kansas City Wizards (1999-2000), Miami Fusion (2001), Colorado Rapids again (2002-05), Columbus Crew (2005), and the New York Red Bulls (2006).

In 2000, the Kansas City Wizards made MLS Cup history. The trusted touch of Henderson was front and center among the starters—along with Tony Meola, Peter Vermes, Chris Klein, Matt McKeon, and Preki—that defeated the Chicago Fire for the championship. (Chicago's team included Jesse Marsch, Carlos Bocanegra, Dema Kovalenko, Chris Armas, and Hristo Stoichkov.) This was the first MLS Cup title for Kansas City, a 1-0 victory that took place in Washington DC, at RFK stadium in front of just over 39,000.

Henderson's retirement in 2006 was a sign of the times. He'd finished his career, for the most part, with Colorado as a leader in games played. His final march with Columbus Crew and New York Red Bulls was an older version of a once great, flashy, dynamic winger that was better than most in the world.

The Mexican national team puts out, as it has for generations, superstars that are everything you'd expect: movie star looks, confidence, swagger, cool. Henderson had a presence all the same. He was a guy whose rival players would likely scan over before kickoff and think: we're gettin' the best they got.

47 Alexi Lalas USMNT: 1991-98

Alexi Lalas—born in 1970—became Michigan High School Player of the Year in 1987. But wait...if you can believe it, he began playing at age 11. Go figure. He was also a talented hockey player who captained his high school team and won the state championship.

While attending Rutgers University, Lalas—who stands around 6'3"—won the 1991 Hermann Trophy and MAC[¶¶¶¶] Player of the Year.

In the 1992 Olympics, Lalas played against Poland. The team was coached by Lothar Osiander and featured players including Steve Snow, Chris Henderson, Cobi Jones, Joe-Max Moore, Brad Friedel, and Claudio Reyna. In group A, against Poland, Italy, and Kuwait, the squad finished third and did not advance further.

In soccer, as with other sports, there are ups and downs. Sometimes a particular moment can lead one to zealous determination. "After college and the 1992 Summer Olympics, Lalas trained with former Arsenal player Bob McNab in California. This led to a trial with Arsenal during the winter of 1992. It was quickly determined that Lalas did not have the quality for a first team spot. As a result, Lalas only had a few training sessions with the Reserve team before being cut shortly after his arrival in North London. Lalas then returned home in Detroit and spent a month reluctant about his future in soccer before coach Bora Milutinovic invited him for the United States tryouts in Mission Viejo, California," said the *Wikipedia* page "Alexi Lalas" on July 18, 2023. Lalas made that squad and turned out to be one of the featured players in the 1994 World Cup.

The 1994 World Cup was a turning point for US soccer. The USMNT program was getting better, attendance for the World Cup was record-setting, and enthusiasm around the nation was growing each day. In front of huge crowds, the team was creating a stir. Lalas started in every match. With a

---

¶¶¶¶ Missouri Athletic Club.

large orange afro meets dreds (it wasn't easy to discern) and a long goatee (that appeared to be something ZZ Top created in a lab), Lalas surged forward all the way to the round of 16 where the US lost, in a tight game, to Brazil.

Following the 1994 World Cup, his talents were acquired by Italian club, Padova. From 1994-96, he played there and eventually joined the New England Revolution of MLS (1996-97). In 1997, a sojourn took him to Emelec (Ecuador) before he joined the MetroStars (1998), Kansas City Wizards (1999), and LA Galaxy (2001-03).

In the 1995 US Cup, which featured the US, Colombia, Mexico, and Nigeria, Lalas—who flew in after obligations with Padova—was part of the equation as the USMNT emerged as champions and in that same year he won the US Soccer Player of the Year award.

As with the 1992 Olympics, Lalas appeared in the 1996 Olympics.

When people think of the 1994 World Cup, often times Lalas, Cobi Jones, Marcelo Balboa, Valderrama, Romario, and Roberto Baggio come to mind. In that window, the mid-90s, Lalas made his presence known.

Lalas won the awards US Soccer Player of the Year and the Honda Player of the Year in 1995; he was an MLS All-Star in 1996, the league's inaugural year; he was placed on the unique MLS Best XI in 2002; with the LA Galaxy, he was part of the 2002 MLS Supporters' Shield and MLS Cup championship side.

His time with the USMNT ended in 1998 with 96 caps and ten goals. His pro career ended in 1999 when he first retired, and then after a return to the game shortly after that he again retired following the 2003 MLS season in 2004. After his playing career, Lalas served behind the scenes—in leadership roles—with the San Jose Earthquakes (2004-05), New York Red Bulls after that, and Los Angeles Galaxy (2006-08).

Today Lalas's look is much more refined—with a short, parted, haircut, shaved beard—as he is featured on Fox Soccer Channel with plenty of opinions about set pieces (which he's become known for).

Over the years, Lalas has fancied a side gig in the realm of music. In 1998, in a group called The Gypsies, he opened for Hootie & The Blowfish. In between his playing career, team management jobs, and media obligations, he's released eight albums from 1996-2022. Perhaps more are on the way.

48 Chad Deering
USMNT: 1993-2000

There are many great players from Texas, particularly the Dallas area. One, who may just be the most talented, is **Chad Deering**. His soccer-playing ability was, for a center mid, as good as you get.

The Dallas Tornados—of the original NASL—brought in many international players who eventually would coach soccer in the area. As such, from the 70s onward to now, experienced players—with the Tornados and Sidekicks—spread their knowledge of the game. One result of soccer taking off in Dallas was the formation of the Dallas Cup soccer tournament in 1980. Something of a calling card for Dallas soccer, the Dallas Cup tournament—which has featured international, domestic, and local Dallas clubs—is arguably one of the top tournaments in North America. From the tournament's website,***** on November 23, 2023, it stated: "The long list of players that have gone on to have professional and international careers is an impressive one. A partial alumni list includes the likes of David Beckham, Clint Dempsey, Chicharito, Landon Donovan, Raul, Andrea Pirlo, Michael Bradley, and Wayne Rooney, as well as rising stars like Alphonso Davies, Bukayo Saka, Weston McKennie, and Mason Greenwood. In fact, Dallas Cup alumni have gone on to play in over 500 World Cup matches." If anything pointed toward soccer being huge in Dallas, that tournament has certainly been part of the equation.

If you made a list of the top five players to emerge from Dallas, Deering would probably be number one. It's not often you find a center mid with such skill, technique, touch on the ball, insight, ability, confidence, soccer IQ, and something special that only a few players, who aren't overwhelmingly fast, truly carry. Such talent would be Franz Beckenbauer, Franco Baresi, Michel Platini, a lesser-known Paulo Henrique Chagas de Lima, aka "Ganso"—all technicians on the ball, like creative magicians. The thing about the

*****The website address was dallascup.org.

aforementioned talent—and Chad Deering—is that none of them were ever accused of being outright fast. Instead, what set them apart was ingenuity, skill, and that intangible genius that some players possess.

Deering—born in 1970—was the 1988 high school Player of the Year in Texas. In addition, according to *Parade*, he was All-American on two occasions. Deering was a dazzling midfielder who emerged as one of the best Texas has produced. When a player of such regard gets noticed, US universities—elite universities—start sending letters. Phone calls are made. The recruiting process begins.

For Deering, this led to Indiana University—the best *of the best*, one of the US elite soccer destinations. That was before MLS, when D1 college soccer essentially was a pro league in the United States. Under the auspices of college-coaching legend Jerry Yeagley, Deering turned heads all around the nation becoming an NCAA First-Team All-American selection. At the time, he was teammates with Kenny Snow (USMNT) and Juergen Sommer (USMNT), a formidable team.

Following his departure from the Midwest, Deering began a European pro journey in the 90s—at a time when US players were fighting hard for respect in Europe—with Werder Bremen, Werder Bremen II, Schalke 04, Kickers Emden, and VfL Wolfsburg. In 1998, he transitioned to MLS side Dallas Burn where he spent a good amount of time (163 games) until 2003.

By 2004, a little over 15 years after arriving at Indiana University, things were winding down: He played for the Dallas Sidekicks, DFW Tornados, and again with the Dallas Sidekicks, which is fitting as all those years ago, before he set out on his journey to Indiana, a player he undoubtedly looked up to and learned from, the one and only Tatu of Brazil, was the focal point of the Sidekicks.

As a US player attempting to earn respect in Europe, during a time when European soccer minds had a pre-conceived notion that US players weren't up to the task, he was a trailblazer. Deering had 18 caps and one goal for the USMNT. Maybe, in a far off universe, you could call him the Dan Auerbach of soccer: a great talent that many don't directly know of, and a few other names overshadow his.

Perhaps you can sum up Deering this way: He got into the illustrious 1998 FIFA World Cup. Deering played against Germany in the loss suffered by the US. When all is said and done, he is arguably the most technically-gifted, pure soccer-playing, center mid the US has ever produced. A one-of-a-kind technician that was far ahead of his time.

49 Joe-Max Moore
USMNT: 1992-2002

Joe-Max Moore was born in Tulsa, Oklahoma in 1971. His dad—well-to-do—was in the oil business and part of the ownership of a North American Soccer League team, the Tulsa Roughnecks. Moore was a gifted talent that, with craft and guile, stood out quickly to any soccer passerby. From Tulsa, the family moved to Irvine, California, where Moore excelled further in soccer and landed collegiately with UCLA where he played with standouts Cobi Jones, Chris Henderson, and Brad Friedel. He quickly found success with the Bruins as a national champion in 1990. He earned the 1990 NCAA Men's Division I Offensive MOP††††† award. Before he left UCLA, he earned All-American honors.

"After the 1992 college season ended, Moore signed with the US national team. Beginning in 1988, the United States Soccer Federation (USSF) had begun to sign top US players to contracts, making the US national team a de facto professional club. USSF would then loan out US players"[56] to another team, likely a pro club team, and "recall them for national team games. Moore chose to not return to UCLA for his senior year and joined USSF as a full-time national team player."[57]

As 1994–95 came and went, Moore played for 1. FC Saarbrucken (Germany) and then in 1995–96 he joined 1. FC Nurnberg (Germany). These are interesting footnotes as this was a time that US players, after many years of work, were starting to make big noise by joining European clubs. He was a trailblazer, setting the stage for future stars such as Christian Pulisic and Josh Sargent.

As 1996 was the groundbreaking opening year for MLS, Moore was lured back and started his first stint with the New England Revolution, which lasted from 1996–99. During this time, he played in 90 games with 49 goals.

Big news arrived in 1999, as he shifted gears and flew back across the pond for his biggest gig yet: a deal with Everton that would last until 2002.

††††† Most Outstanding Player.

During this English tour, he gathered over 50 appearances and scored on eight occasions. Moore represented the United States as a whole, juggling a ball upon his Everton introduction, showing off his highly technical skill as if to ward off naysayers. At a time when US soccer was waking up to the fact that it was better than expected, this 5'7" attacking mid, with technique, a hard work ethic, and the ability to mix it up on tackles, was performing at the highest level of pro soccer in one of the most intimidating venues: EPL. However, as things were winding down, he suffered a knee injury in the 2002 FIFA World Cup and his time at Everton came to an end.

That marked his comeback tour with the Revolution. Moore registered his last MLS games with the New England Revolution during his second stint there, from 2003-04. Upon his return, he scored four goals in 19 games. During all that time, he was matching pro strides with the USMNT and recorded 100 caps and 24 goals for the United States.

During a 1991 championship game in the Pan American Games, Moore scored the game winner against Mexico. To say it meant a lot to the guys on that team should be a vast understatement. That's one of those moments in time, a grand achievement, that should not be forgotten. The United States—which featured Kasey Keller, Claudio Reyna, Cobi Jones, Steve Snow, Brad Friedel, and Alexi Lalas—squared off against Honduras, Suriname, and Canada in group B. The US and Honduras advanced. In the semis, the US got past Cuba by 2-1. Then, for the final against Mexico, thanks to goals from Reyna and Moore, the US flaunted its prowess, 2-1, for its first Pan American Games championship. To date, this has been the only Pan American Games soccer title by the USMNT.[58] Moore's big-time moment, the game-winner in the championship, against none other than Mexico, is one to be cherished. Not only that, but in the 95th minute—does it get any better than that?

As for the 1992 Olympics, Moore was there. The team didn't triumph as it previously did at the Pan American Games just a short year or so earlier, but, nonetheless, it was a great opportunity to represent the US.

In the 1993 Gold Cup, Moore appeared in the group match against Honduras and in the final against Mexico which turned out to be a 4-0 loss for the US.

The 1995 Copa America came and went as the USMNT placed fourth. In 2016 the squad also placed fourth. These two instances are the best results—to date—for the USMNT in that tournament. In 1995, Uruguay took first, Brazil got second, and Colombia grabbed third from the US. In the quarters against Mexico, it went to a penalty kick shootout and Moore put one in. As for the consolation match against Colombia, a 4-1 loss, Moore scored the lone PK.

The 90s were busy for Moore and the growing US soccer program. The US placed third overall in the 1996 Gold Cup where Moore got a goal against Trinidad and Tobago early on, then started in the consolation match against Guatemala, a 3-0 victory. The third place finish for the US wasn't ideal, but it was still a medal in the history books of Gold Cups.

The 1998 Gold Cup was big for a few reasons: It was hosted by the United States, the US placed second, and Preki went down in history for scoring a big one that defeated Brazil 1-0 in the semis; Moore, a starter that game, was a crucial part of the lineup. Things kicked off with a 3-0 win over Cuba—Moore started and got a goal. Moore carried over his skillful ways as a starter against Costa Rica, a 2-1 win. Then, as a fixture in the starting lineup, Moore helped topple Brazil in that semifinal thriller that saw Preki's shot blast into the net, a complete upset. Though the final was a 1-0 loss to Mexico, it was an honor to take the field, an electric setting that sent the town into euphoria, despite the runner-up finish.

In total, Moore was a member of three USMNT squads in the FIFA World Cup: 1994, 1998, and 2002. In the 2002 extravaganza (in which the US eventually reached the quarters), Moore earned his 100th cap against Poland.

He received the honor of entering the Oklahoma Soccer Hall of Fame in 2006. A few years later, he entered the UCLA Athletics Hall of Fame, in 2014 (joining previous inductees such as Jimmy Connors, John Wooden, and Kareem Abdul-Jabbar).

To date, Moore's 24 goals place him seventh all-time for the USMNT. Tied for first are Landon Donovan and Clint Dempsey, each with 57.

Moore's long playing career as a regular for the USMNT in the 90s, his goals, leadership, and ability on the ball set him apart as one of the premier midfield-forward threats the US has put forth.

50 Mike Sorber USMNT: 1992-98

Mike Sorber—born in 1971—represents the Gateway to the West, the home of soccer in the US. Coming out of Florissant, a notorious northside soccer town, Mike had soccer in his DNA. His dad, Pete Sorber, an accomplished coach at Florissant Valley College—in the St. Louis area—won some ten national championships as coach of the program. Pete passed on his knowledge to Mike and it showed quite quickly.

In high school, playing for another legendary coach, Vince Drake, Mike won the Missouri state championship for soccer representing St. Thomas Aquinas-Mercy in the mid-80s. In the case of St. Thomas Aquinas-Mercy, it was, and still is, the best *of the best* with a record 11 state titles (1975, 1977, 1985, 1988, 1989, 1990, 1992, 1993, 1996, 1997, 1998). It was a school that sat atop the throne of greatness—with top-level players such as Steve Sullivan, Bob Bozada, Perry Van der Beck, Dan King, and Mike Sorber—that was largely overseen by the mastermind, a coach of extraordinary talents, Vince Drake. Everything that Drake—the great one—accomplished makes him the all-time leader in that category. Ipso facto, that makes him one of the best coaches in the nation. (To date, the closest teams to overtake this magical run of titles would be Rockhurst and powerhouse CBC. Don't mess with CBC.)

Sorber transitioned to the Saint Louis University Billikens soccer team, which still has the highest number of NCAA national championships: 10. With a strong unit, Sorber helped lead the team to the Final Four in 1991. His time there ended in 1992, however he remained steadfast in receiving his academic degree which he attained in 1994 by getting a BA in Communications.

Shortly after his time in college, he suited up professionally for a few teams that included: UNAM (1994-96), Kansas City Wizards (1996), MetroStars (1997-99), and Chicago Fire (2000). His most pro games came with the MetroStars, 74, where he tallied up four goals along the way. Never known as a scorer, Mike was a defensive midfield presence that helped keep things steady on the backline and opened up smart passes to unleash teammates in times of transition. His professional accolades include being a Mexican league All-Star (the first US player to achieve that honor), and as his career wound down he was part of the Chicago Fire season that earned the team a runner-up finish in the MLS Cup 2000.

He was a steady—and somewhat quiet—force for the USMNT that earned the nickname "Team MVP" in the 1994 FIFA World Cup. After taking in much respect from Coach Bora Milutinovic as a smart, relied upon player, he would be gone from the squad four years later in 1998. By that time he'd done a lot to push US soccer into the forefront of the international scene. During his time with the national team, 1992–98, he gathered 67 caps and two goals.

As a coach, he assisted numerous teams including Saint Louis University, the USMNT with Bob Bradley (2007–11), Montreal Impact, Los Angeles FC, and Toronto FC.

51 Brad Friedel
USMNT: 1992-2005

Over the years, the US has been known for producing top-quality keepers, including Tony Meola, Kasey Keller, Tim Howard, and the great **Brad Friedel**.

Born in 1971 in Lakewood, Ohio, Friedel eventually attended Bay High School—near Cleveland—and became All-State in basketball. Also a talented keeper, obviously, he was named Bay High's Outstanding Athlete of the Year in 1989. The accolades kept rolling in, as Friedel was part of UCLA's 1990 NCAA championship, he was All-American in 1991 and 1992, and won the 1993 Hermann Trophy. For a keeper to win the Hermann Trophy is quite significant as it's typically reserved for field players. He was also named to the Soccer America College Team of the Century. A few others on that list include Paul Caligiuri (UCLA), Claudio Reyna (Virginia), Bruce Murray (Clemson), Angelo DiBernardo (Indiana), Ken Snow (Indiana), Armando Betancourt (Indiana).

Friedel's pro career spanned 1995-2015 as he played for Galatasaray, Columbus Crew (where he won MLS Goalkeeper of the Year in 1997), Liverpool, Blackburn Rovers, Aston Villa, and Tottenham Hotspur.

With the USMNT—over an immense run, typically jockeying for position against Kasey Keller—he earned 82 caps. Early on, following his UCLA triumph, Friedel signed with the USSF (United States Soccer Federation) leading up to the 1994 FIFA World Cup. A member of the 1992 Olympic squad, Friedel did not beat out Tony Meola for the 1994 FIFA World Cup gig.

For the 1995 US Cup, Friedel was part of the team as it won the tournament for the second time. "The **1995 US Cup** was a four nation invitational tournament organized by the United States Soccer Federation (USSF) in June 1995. USSF began the US Cup in 1992 and it was played annually until 2000, except for the World Cup years of 1994 and 1998. The cup used a round-robin format in which the team with the highest number of points took the title. The four teams included the host United States, along with Mexico, Colombia, and Nigeria. This was the first year that these three invited teams participated in a US Cup. The US won the title for the second time this year."[59] The titles went as follows: United States won it three times: 1992, 1995, 2000; Mexico won it three times: 1996, 1997, 1999; and Germany won it once: 1993.

In 1998, Friedel joined the US squad for a second-place finish at the 1998 Gold Cup. As for the 2000 Nike U.S. Cup, Friedel was there as well, alongside Kasey Keller, for the third championship for the US.

Despite not getting the nod in the 1994 FIFA World Cup, Friedel's World Cup action came in 1998 and then again in 2002. In 2002, which is the best result the US has achieved (reaching the quarterfinals) since the third place finish in the 1930 FIFA World Cup, Friedel was the engine in defense that helped push the team forward. As a result, he was referred to as the human wall thanks to his remarkable abilities in front of the net.

In 2005, Friedel called it quits from the USMNT but kept going another 10-odd years in pro soccer as he ended his run with Tottenham in 2015.

In his post-playing years, Friedel was coach of the United States U19 team, and the New England Revolution. He's also called games for media outlets including the 2014 FIFA World Cup as an expert for BBC and with an Irish public service broadcaster, RTE.

The best goalie in USMNT history? Hard to say. Tim Howard, Kasey Keller, Tony Meola, and Friedel are right there with the best of them.

52 Brian McBride USMNT: 1993-2006

Brian McBride is probably the best forward in the history of the United States. Born in 1972 in Arlington Heights, Illinois, a suburb of Chicago, McBride was part of a state championship in 1988 and earned All-American honors in *Parade* magazine, a big deal at the time (long before social media). He chose Saint Louis University, the renowned college soccer king that still is number one all-time in NCAA Division I men's soccer championships (10 to date). While there, with the Billikens, he got 72 goals and became All-American and Great Midwest Conference MVP recipient three years in a row (quite remarkable).

Upon his departure from SLU in 1993 he debuted with the USMNT in the same year. Although McBride played his first game for the USMNT in 1993, he got his first taste of scoring in 1996 against Guatemala. In this early part of his national team tenure he didn't make the 1994 FIFA World Cup squad, though, he was subsequently part of the 1998, 2002, and 2006 World Cups. McBride became the very first US player to have scored in two World Cups (1998 and 2002). Since then Donovan and Dempsey have also scored in multiple World Cups.

At the 1998 Gold Cup, where the US defeated Brazil 1-0 in the semis, McBride contributed to that run that saw the US place second overall. By the 2002 World Cup things had shifted: Wynalda out, McBride in, and it was clear that McBride—who had been making noise with the USMNT since 1993—was the next guy up, a US sensation. When all was said and done, McBride had knocked in 30 goals for the USMNT.

As for the 2000 Gold Cup, under Bruce Arena, he started against Peru, and scored against Colombia in the underwhelming quarterfinal loss for the US. McBride was part of the 2000 Nike US Cup championship side. During that adventure, he scored a goal to help the team get the title. His teammates included Cobi Jones (two goals), Ante Razov (two goals), Claudio Reyna (one goal), Earnie Stewart (one goal), and Frankie Hejduk (one goal).

The 2002 CONCACAF Gold Cup was something different altogether in which McBride was named the tournament MVP. The US first got a 2-1 victory over South Korea, with goals from Donovan and Beasley. Then, in game two, the US defeated Cuba 1-0 with a critical goal from McBride. In the quarterfinals, the US trounced El Salvador by 4-0, with a goal from Razov and a hat trick by McBride. In the semis, McBride was a successful penalty-kick taker in the penalty shootout against Canada that put the US in the final. Although McBride didn't score in the 2-0 championship victory over Costa Rica, he was a starter–with Kasey Keller, Carlos Bocanegra, Eddie Lewis, Cobi Jones, Landon Donovan, along with Josh Wolff–and added to the win. Getting the hat trick was a pretty good indication of who the MVP would be. (In 1970, when Jim Leeker–a fellow SLU forward, similar in stature to McBride–won the NASL Rookie of the Year award, it was partly due to a hat trick he attained against Atlanta. Hat tricks tend to be telling.) As McBride walked away with the '02 Gold Cup MVP honor, a nice individual accomplishment, it was a team effort as the US won its second overall Gold Cup title–a big step in the right direction of dominating CONCACAF.

Not only was McBride the face of the team but in the early 2000s he was coupled with another up-and-comer, an attacking force that added speed up top that kept defenses off-balance: Landon Donovan. Josh Wolff and Clint Mathis were also important pieces to the puzzle as newer players on the scene. With veterans like Joe Max-Moore, it was a competent group that was setting a new precedent for US soccer: that being, CONCACAF no longer belonged solely to Mexico and Costa Rica.

According to Bruce Arena, the playing scheme (so it would seem) was to have McBride be a target in the box, to lay off passes to oncoming teammates, to drive home headers and gather rebounds and piercing shots around the box. While this was going on, Donovan–the fastest player you might have seen–would create danger around him in open spaces that–theoretically and practically speaking–would puncture the heart of defenses. McBride–around 6'0" tall–had the classic head-ball ability; a wonder in the air, he was fearless and extremely good. Brazil is a team that has produced smaller forwards—who were the antithesis of head-ball giants—over the years with great success: Pele, Garrincha, Romario, Bebeto, and Ronaldo (a slight hybrid) for instance. So what Arena was doing happened to be a classic US line-up: a strong, largely built, target forward with speedier roadsters nearby. Be that as it may, the combo—which was taking CONCACAF by storm—was turning into McBride and Donovan.

The team escaped its group at the 2002 FIFA World Cup among topsy-turvy results from basically everyone in the group. Nonetheless, with a goal from McBride against Portugal, the US escaped to the round of 16. As for the match-up against CONCACAF foe, Mexico, the 2-0 US victory was thanks, in part, to a goal from McBride.

In the 2003 Gold Cup, McBride was front and center with goals in the opening games. First, he got a goal in the 2-0 victory over El Salvador. Then he struck twice for a 2-0 defeat of Martinique. The team eventually got defeated by Brazil in the semis and this led to the consolation match against Costa Rica in which the US won 3-2 for a third-place finish. By the tournament's end, McBride was among the lead scorers: Landon Donovan (4), Walter Centeno (4); Brian McBride (3), Kaka (3), and Jared Borgetti (3).

McBride was part of the group for the 2006 FIFA World Cup. In a 1-1 draw with Italy in the group stage, he went even so far as to take a foul from Daniele De Rossi, which resulted in blood and stitches. De Rossi, incidentally, was punished and sat out multiple games, along with a fine. Of course, Italy went on to win this World Cup. For US soccer, it will be forever known as a journey to forget, seeing as the team finished last in group E. Following 2006, McBride retired from the US team only to be lured back in 2008 as an overage player for the 2008 Olympics, in which he represented the US again as captain.

His pro career continued onward as he suited up with Fulham from 2004-08, and then with the Chicago Fire from 2008-10. He never completely left the USMNT as he became the general manager of the squad in 2020.

53 Chris Armas
USMNT: 1998-2005

Chris Armas played for the national team of Puerto Rico (1993-94) before joining the USMNT. He played collegiately for Adelphi University in Long Island, New York.

Armas started out with the Long Island Rough Riders (1994-95). From there he moved onto the LA Galaxy (1996-97) where he played in 50 games. Finally, he ended his pro playing career with the Chicago Fire (1998-2007), where he played in over 210 games, with eight goals.

He was part of the MLS Cup title run with Chicago in 1998. Armas made multiple All-Star teams during his time in MLS (1998, 1999, 2000, 2001, 2003, and 2004). He retired from MLS play in 2007.

During his years with the USMNT, he played in 66 matches, with two goals. He got a knee injury in the early 2000s which precluded him from playing in the 2002 FIFA World Cup, which he likely would've been a part of.

He was honored with the US Soccer Player of the Year award (2000).

As a defensive center mid, Armas cruised the pitch, looking for tackles as he kept the fort clear of danger. He was relentless in getting stuck in. His prompt distribution was relied upon for transition play. Not much of a fancy dribbler or goal-scorer, he stuck to what he did best which was the aforementioned defensive work. A hard worker, Armas led by example and motivated teammates forward. For the USMNT, he quietly represented perseverance and fortitude.

During his time on the national team, he was part of the CONCACAF Gold Cup championship runs in 2002 and 2005.

Following his time as a player, Armas took on an interesting coaching career that has seen him land with Chicago Fire (assistant), Adelphi Panthers (women's side), New York Red Bulls (assistant and head coach), Toronto FC (head coach), Manchester United (assistant), Leeds United (assistant and co-interim coach), and Colorado Rapids (head coach in 2023). If anything, his experience as a coach represents a megalithic change in the view of

US soccer talent around the world. At what point in the pre-2000 era was a US player ever considered worthy enough to be an assistant coach at Manchester United? Other coaches that have joined Armas with overseas gigs include Bob Bradley and Jesse Marsch, to name a few. If anything shows progress, Armas's inclusion in the Manchester United coaching staff would be part of the equation.

54 Claudio Reyna USMNT: 1994-2006

Claudio Reyna—born in 1973—is the son of Miguel who had professional playing experience in his home country of Argentina. Claudio, who was born in New Jersey, kicked off his US soccer journey at Jonathan Dayton High School and eventually Saint Benedict's Preparatory School where he met fellow teammate, Gregg Berhalter. Once upon a time, there was a great bond there, but "a personal feud between the families threatens both men's careers and has thrown US soccer into turmoil just as the program enters a new World Cup cycle that will end with the tournament being played in the United States for the second time."[60]

The story seemed to be everywhere. While this feud, erupting over playing time for Reyna's son, Gio, was very much a noisy affair, it shouldn't be the sole focus of Claudio's life experience.

Claudio is the standard-bearer of US soccer. From an early age, Reyna distinguished himself with accolades that few can claim. He surged ahead in the midfield role and catapulted himself to *Parade* magazine's high school Player of the Year on two occasions, a unique achievement for a national award. What's more, he became the Gatorade National Player of the Year.

Reyna switched gears to collegiate soccer at University of Virginia (1991-93), and, with Bruce Arena as coach, won three NCAA championships. As a result, the Hermann Trophy went to Reyna in 1993. In addition, in 1991 and 1992, he was given the NCAA Men's Division I Offensive MOP Award[61] while playing for Virginia. *Soccer America* created an honor known as the Soccer America College Team of the Century,[62] which Reyna was part of. Not only that, he was also anointed Player of the Century![63]

Following his Virginia career, a unique three-championship run, he embarked on the pro game in Europe by joining Bayer Leverkusen from 1994-99. During that time, from 1997-99, he also was loaned to VfL Wolfsburg. Then from 1999-2001, he joined Rangers in Scotland. After that, he rounded things off with Sunderland (2001-03), Manchester City

(2003-07), and the New York Red Bulls (2007-08). Reyna was part of the 1992 and 1996 Olympic squads.

As for CONCACAF Gold Cups, in 1996, Reyna was part of the group that surged forward and attained a third-place finish. When the US placed second in 1998, Reyna was part of that run. The 2000 Gold Cup that saw the US get eliminated in the quarterfinals to Colombia was one Reyna joined. In the 2003 tournament, Reyna was a piece of the puzzle that saw the US earn third.

Then you have the FIFA World Cups. In 1994, because of an injury, Reyna didn't play in the loud and raucous World Cup that year. However, as a member of the team, he tallied up four World Cup experiences in total: 1994, 1998, 2002, and 2006. The 1998 tournament was a quick World Cup ride for the US. So too went Coach Steve Sampson. Replacing him would be Bruce Arena.

At the 2002 FIFA World Cup, under Coach Arena, the Virginia connection flourished as Reyna captained the USMNT to its furthest reach in modern times. Under Coach Bruce Arena, Reyna—a star pupil of his at Virginia—marched the team forward from center midfield. The team reached the quarterfinals, in which it lost to a talented German side, a great result at the time. This effort, which had inadvertent inspiration from the 1994 World Cup team, ushered in a new attitude within the ranks of US soccer; players were imbued with a feeling of possibility and triumph; it was a precedent that helped spur on future efforts. Somewhere down the road, when the US does when the World Cup, analysts will likely point to the 2002 effort, which Reyna oversaw from midfield, as a pivotal turning point in the right direction.

Reyna captained the group again at the 2006 FIFA World Cup, but the team couldn't escape its group. Very shortly after this tournament, Reyna announced his retirement from the national team.

Gregg Berhalter USMNT: 1994-2006

Gregg Berhalter—born in 1973—was a teammate of Claudio Reyna's in high school and with the USMNT. As a coach, Berhalter did quite well. He won the 2021 Gold Cup. Then he qualified for the 2022 FIFA World Cup. Then he got the USMNT into the round of 16. The soft-spoken man that offers steady gazes with, some might say, spurious utterances of wisdom, is charged with guiding the team further in a new age of US soccer. It's going to be viewed as a very historical time for the USMNT, and Berhalter is front and center a part of that ongoing story.

Once upon a time, this tall, lanky, defender emerged from North Carolina University and jumped into the arms of Zwolle (Netherlands), Sparta Rotterdam (Netherlands), Cambuur Leeuwarden (Netherlands), Crystal Palace (England), Energie Cottbus (Germany), 1860 Munich (Germany), and finally LA Galaxy.

Berhalter created a path of success for himself as a member of the USMNT. From 1994-2006, Berhalter amassed 44 caps—no slouch. He played in the 1995 Copa America, along with the 1999 FIFA Confederations Cup. As for the prominent 2002 FIFA World Cup, he played against Mexico and Germany as the team reached the quarterfinals. He was with the squad in spirit in the 2006 World Cup, but didn't contribute on the field.

His national team run ended in 2006, but his playing days professionally lingered into 2011 with LA Galaxy; in that final year of playing he also served as an assistant coach with the Galaxy. Thereafter, Berhalter began coaching as the lead with Swedish side Hammarby IF (2011-13) and then with Columbus Crew (2013-18).

This, in turn, led to his appointment as the USMNT coach in 2018. As of this publication, his story is still growing with every roll of the ball. With each day, week, month, and presumably year, he'll be met with both optimism and pessimism as he was supposed to take the dreams of US soccer fans into a familiar place—a quick exit in the World Cup—or something else altogether–a World Cup championship. Yet that changed. In 2024 he took over as coach of the Chicago Fire. A new coach, Mauricio Pochettino, took over for the USMNT. Whatever the outcome may be, he's one of a select few coaches that have led this team.

56 Steve Ralston USMNT: 1997-2007

Steve Ralston, who had 36 caps and four goals for the USMNT, is one of the most under-the-radar players you'll probably come across. But, without doubt, this unassuming character from St. Louis, the heartbeat of soccer in the US since the beginning, quietly went about his business and when all was said and done, he became—to date—the second all-time in MLS assists. But even before that stat became cemented in the record books, coaches realized they had a quiet talent on their hands.

Ralston hails from the ever-talented—and ever-competitive—city of St. Louis soccer where he actually, believe it or not, had a hard time starting on his high school team.

Out of high school, he landed with the FIU Panthers, had a good college run, and eventually was drafted by the MLS franchise Tampa Bay Mutiny in 1996. This came after a short, lesser-known, stint with the St. Louis Ambush, a pro indoor team, in 1995—a squad crowded with St. Louis talent, including Daryl Doran, Mark Santel, and Mark Moser.

After playing with the Tampa Bay Mutiny, where Ralston somewhat quietly made 177 appearances with 34 goals, he made a move to New England Revolution where he played in over 200 games, with an impressive 42 goals. Ralston's strategy—to get the pass just right, to stay consistent, to wear opponents down—was part of what coaches saw in him. The other part was his ability to make assists.

Soccer diehards may be interested to know that, as of 2021, the top five all-time assist leaders in MLS history are (from first to fifth): (1) Landon Donovan, (2) Steve Ralston,[‡‡‡‡‡] (3) Brad Davis,[§§§§§] (4) Carlos Valderrama,[¶¶¶¶¶] and (5) Preki. Two of those record holders, Ralston and Davis, are from St. Louis: the

‡‡‡‡‡ A Scott Gallagher alum.

§§§§§ A Scott Gallagher alum.

¶¶¶¶¶ Perhaps Colombia's best player ever.

US' first soccer capitol. Ralston exudes practically everything St. Louis soccer stands for: If you put him in, he'll do the right thing at the right moment and do it with quality.

According to a 1994 St. Louis Post-Dispatch story by Joe Lyons: "Ralston, 5 feet 9 and 150 pounds, got only minor recruiting interest before deciding on Forest Park Community College. He earned All-American honors there, with 17 goals and seven assists."[64] From there, he moved to Florida International University, quietly turning heads with perseverance. As mentioned earlier, he eventually played with the St. Louis Ambush during the 1995–96 season.

Then came MLS in the form of Tampa Bay Mutiny where he did well. This led to the New England Revolution and over time he became second only to Landon Donovan—perhaps the best US player of all time—on the MLS all-time assist list. Pretty incredible. Coaches saw his unique, but subtle, qualities: technique, passing, team orientation, a high soccer IQ, a strong work rate, with a will to win. Ralston made the list of MLS's top 25 players (for its first 25 years in existence).

Despite not playing in a World Cup, Ralston was a steady force for the USMNT between 1997–2007 as he attained 36 caps and four goals. In 2005, he scored a big goal in World Cup qualifications that helped defeat Mexico. In all likelihood, an injury led to him not attending the 2006 World Cup.

He was part of the 2005 and 2007 CONCACAF Gold Cup championship squads. In 2005, the US won its third Gold Cup title and 2007 marked its fourth.

In all, Ralston had a very interesting run. He was a soccer sabermetrics dream come true for coaches. Somehow his passes lined up, his possession was beyond solid, he got assists. Maybe Ralston, compared with Landon Donovan and Clint Dempsey, is one you haven't heard of as much, but alongside other St. Louis standouts from his era—Brad Davis and Pat Noonan, for example—he was a major contributor to both MLS and the USMNT.

57 Frankie Hejduk USMNT: 1996-2009

Frankie Hejduk was mainly known in MLS for his time with the Columbus Crew, where he was captain. After his playing days concluded, he became the Brand Ambassador for the Crew which has taken him to various parts of the city promoting the team. *The Columbus Dispatch* wrote: "During home games, fans might see Hejduk leading cheers in the stands of Crew Stadium, presenting honors during halftime or drinking a cold one in the beer tent."[65] It added, "Another sign of his affection for the city: Hejduk won an MLS Cup with the Galaxy in 2011 but rarely wears the ring. His Crew championship ring, however, he wears 24/7."[66] If there's someone proud to represent the Columbus Crew, it's him. "The seventh-graders at Medina Middle School stared wide-eyed at Hejduk as he described playing in Olympic soccer games in 1996 and 2000, and World Cups in 1998 and 2002."[67] He embraced the role and represented soccer in the Midwest like few others.

Born in 1974 in La Mesa, California, Hejduk played for the Nomads—a powerhouse club team in the San Diego area. He attended UCLA and played defense for the Bruins from 1992-94.

Frankie went to the MLS and first suited up for Tampa Bay Mutiny at the beginning of the league's existence (1996-98). He asserted himself there and played in over 55 games, with a few goals.

From there it was off to Bayer Leverkusen (1999-2003). He had a brief spell at St. Gallen (Switzerland) on loan and it was back to the US where he joined the Columbus Crew for the majority of his pro career (2003-10).

With the Crew he was a team leader and helped the squad earn a MLS Cup championship in 2008. Following his time with the Crew, he spent one season with LA Galaxy whereby he won another MLS Cup in 2011.

Frankie was part of the 1996 and 2000 Olympics representing the United States soccer team.

With the USMNT, he was predominately associated with the 2000s as a wild outside back, soaring up and down the line, looking for any tackle he could get his foot on.

He was part of three CONCACAF Gold Cup titles (2002, 2005, and 2007), and was included in the World Cup squads of 1998 and 2002. In the 2002 World Cup, he was a prominent figure for the US team. He suffered an injury in 2006.

His last goal for the USMNT arrived in 2009 against El Salvador. When he closed shop with the national team, he had acquired 85 caps, with seven goals. His pro career ended just a few years later in 2011.

He might have a rocking attitude that's all about fun but, as of late, the southern California native—who is also a talented surfer—has remained passionate about the Columbus Crew where he delivered an MLS Cup.

58 Eddie Lewis USMNT: 1996-2008

Eddie Lewis—born in 1974—competed for the USMNT in the 2002 and 2006 FIFA World Cups.

As a winger he brought speed, endurance, a stellar work ethic, and perseverance. Like a marathon runner, Lewis seemed to get better as time went on. Oftentimes, sprinters aren't good long-distance runners, but Lewis was both. Raised in California, he was recruited by the powerhouse soccer-factory, UCLA (1992-95).

In 1996, MLS launched, and so too did the career of Lewis who joined the San Jose squad (1996-99). With San Jose, he played in over 110 games, with a handful of goals. In 1999, he was an MLS All-Star.

He was another one of those players that were creating a path in Europe for future US talent to enjoy. So Lewis is that rare player who both enjoyed MLS in the early years and opened doors in Europe. Lewis had stops at Fulham, Preston North End, Leeds United, and Derby County, before landing back in the US with the LA Galaxy in 2008 at the end of his career.

In his time with the USMNT, he played in over 80 matches, with ten goals. For part of that run he won the 2002 CONCACAF Gold Cup. The US started out in group B defeating South Korea, 2-1, and then took down Cuba 1-0. In the quarters against El Salvador, in which Brian McBride scored a hat trick in the 4-0 rout, Eddie Lewis was a starter alongside Kasey Keller, Jeff Agoos, Carlos Bocanegra, Cobi Jones, and Landon Donovan. Lewis started in the semis against Canada and also the final where the US defeated Costa Rica by 2-0. That was the USMNT's second title in the Gold Cup. Lewis was emblematic of the strong, athletic lineup Bruce Arena fielded for that tournament.

He was a winger's winger. If you were a coach and you needed a true outside wing, he'd be top of the list. There have been some reliable greats over the years: Graeme Le Saux, Marc Overmars, Bruno Conti...guys who just dominated the wing. Lewis had a job: own that wing. And that he did.

Classy, professional, and statesmanlike, Lewis embodied the attributes that go hand in hand with a national team player.

59 Jovan Kirovski USMNT: 1994-2004

Jovan Kirovski—born in 1976 in Escondido, California—was a 6'1" forward that got picked up early by Manchester United, spending time in its youth program, circa 1992, and, eventually, in 1996, he suited up with Borussia Dortmund (1996-2000). This was during the time Borussia won the UEFA Champions League (1996-97) over Juventus in the final. Kirovski was part of the 1997 Intercontinental Cup that Borussia Dortmund won over a talented Cruzeiro side from Brazil that started Bebeto.

Kirovski had the dream of all dreams come true when playing in the San Diego area for the well-regarded Nomads. In 1992, he set sail for Manchester United and began an amazing journey that led to the 1997 experience of a lifetime with Borussia Dortmund.

During the late 90s he was on loan with Fortuna Koln, then wound up with a handful of top teams: Sporting CP (2000-02), Crystal Palace (2001-02), Birmingham City (2002-04), LA Galaxy (2004-05), Colorado Rapids (2005-08), San Jose Earthquakes (2008), and back again with LA Galaxy (2009-11). That's a remarkable run for a US player during the New Dawn period—1994-2010—when US talent slowly began seeing time with European clubs. As a result, Kirovski got a chance at the senior national team quite early in life.

He kicked off his first USMNT game against Saudi Arabia, which is definitely not a CONCACAF opponent.

Kirovski was part of the 1996 Olympics team, hosted by the United States. He started the first game against Argentina, a 3-1 loss in which Claudio Reyna scored. Incidentally, one of the scorers for Argentina was Hernan Crespo—one of the greats in the long history of strikers from Argentina. A few of Kirovski's teammates that game included Kasey Keller, Alexi Lalas, Frankie Hejduk, Brian Maisonneuve. The coach? Bruce Arena. In the next match against Tunisia, Kirovski started and got a goal in the 2-0 victory. Kirovski started in the last game against Portugal but the score was 1-1 and it wasn't enough to see the US squad through to the next round.

He also suited up in the 1999 FIFA Confederations Cup and the 2003 FIFA Confederations Cup. Beginning with the 1999 FIFA Confederations Cup, Kirovski got off to an early start with a goal against New Zealand for a 2-1 victory. Next, the US lost 1-0 to Brazil, thanks to a goal from Ronaldinho. In the last group game, Ben Olsen and Joe-Max Moore scored to defeat Germany. The US ended up losing in the semis to Mexico, leading to a third place finish overall. The US didn't fair too well in the 2003 FIFA Confederations Cup as it placed last in group B that also consisted of Cameroon, Turkey, and Brazil.

Kirovski was playing for Birmingham City around that time and soon was on his way to the Los Angeles Galaxy. The Galaxy won the MLS Cup in 2005 and 2011, along with the Lamar Hunt US Open Cup in 2005, during the time Jovan was listed with the club.

This was also toward the end of his tenure with the USMNT. As a forward that could distribute to teammates in the attack, with his back to goal, laying off passes, keeping things moving, Kirovski tallied up 62 caps and nine goals for the United States. Those strikes came against: Jamaica, Honduras, Guatemala, Israel, Germany, New Zealand, Haiti, Venezuela, and New Zealand again.

In 2012, with the approval of Bruce Arena, Kirovski became an assistant coach with the Galaxy. In years that followed, he became the team's technical director.

Jovan Kirovski, perhaps overshadowed in the history of US strikers by the likes of Brian McBride and Eric Wynalda, is still one that had a significant impact on the sport and was a trendsetter in many ways. His efforts in European soccer were opening doors for future talents like Pulisic and Sargent. While Jovan went under the radar a bit, it was largely due to time and circumstance. In total, his 60-plus caps and nine goals are pretty good for a guy sometimes lost in the shuffle of US soccer stars from yesterday.

60 Clint Mathis USMNT: 1998-2005

February 28, 2001. US vs. Mexico. In the second half, after a touch from Joe-Max Moore, **Clint Mathis** brilliantly—in an instant—trapped the ball deep in his half of the field with the right foot, then a swift long-distance half-volley with the outside of the same foot into space, just behind the bewildered defense, for the speedy Josh Wolff who took it by Mexican keeper, Campos, for a goal. The ingenuity for this pass was next level. This is exactly who top-level coaches look for.

After winning a state championship representing Heritage High School in Georgia, Mathis set his sights on South Carolina University, the land of the Gamecocks. A formidable soccer school, he and future USMNT star Josh Wolff—also from Georgia—set a path of excellence. Mathis took All-American honors in 1995 and soon thereafter played for the Los Angeles Galaxy, MetroStars, Hannover 96, Real Salt Lake, Colorado Rapids, New York Red Bulls, Ergotelis, Real Salt Lake (part II), and the Galaxy (part II).

While it might seem like he was a journeyman player, during his time in MLS, he had some big moments, scoring five goals in one game (2000), and the Goal of the Year (2001). What's more, he won the 2009 MLS Cup with Real Salt Lake.

His first game for the US arrived in 1998 against Australia. It would be two years before his first US goal arrived against Barbados in a soaring 4-0 win.

2002. Mathis decided to bang in a goal during the World Cup—one of the hardest things to do—at the drop of a hat. South Korea felt the brunt of this goal, a fierce shot from a marksman that cleanly trapped the ball with the inside of the right foot, followed by a pure strike with the left foot—a line drive, low and steady—to the right corner.

By the end of his national team career, he scored 12 goals which came against the aforementioned Barbados and South Korea, along with Brazil,

Honduras, Germany, Mexico, Jamaica, Canada, and Colombia. In addition, he was part of the 2002 CONCACAF Gold Cup championship in which he scored a critical penalty-kick in a semifinal shootout against Canada.

He was cool, he had swagger, and a knack for scoring. An all-around standout for the US soccer program.

61 Josh Wolff USMNT: 1999-2008

Josh Wolff—a 5'8" forward with speed like turbo-boosters—was born in 1977 in Georgia and continues the down-south connection with Clint Mathis. In fact, Wolff and Mathis ended up starring together at South Carolina University, turning heads and making waves.

His speed was noticed, quite quickly, as he was drafted into MLS and joined the Chicago Fire (1998-2002), where he scored 32 goals. Following his stint in Chicago, he made stops with Kansas City Wizards (2003-06), 1860 Munich (2007-08), Kansas City Wizards again (2008-10), and finally, DC United (2011-12). He did well with Chicago, initially. What's more, he was highly productive during his two stops with Kansas City, as he scored over 40 goals in all.

He attained 52 caps for the USMNT, with nine goals that came against Mexico, Costa Rica, Jamaica, Grenada, and Scotland. With the US team, Wolff was part of the 2000 Olympics in Sydney, Australia. A few teammates included Brad Friedel, Landon Donovan, Ben Olsen, and Jeff Agoos. In this tournament, Wolff scored against Czech Republic and Japan en route to a fourth-place finish.

Wolff was listed on both rosters of the USMNT for the 2002 World Cup and 2006 World Cup. In 2002, he contributed with an assist in the defeat of Mexico in the round of 16. It was a snazzy play all around as Reyna made a good dribble down the line, played it into a guarded Wolff and the ball found its way back to McBride for a well-guided shot into the goal; pretty much a textbook play, with moments of ingenuity, that coaches only dream of.

In the 2002 CONCACAF Gold Cup, Wolff scored a goal in the 2-0 championship victory over regional rival, Costa Rica. This was the second Gold Cup title for the United States, a definite step in the right direction for CONCACAF dominance. As for the 2005 CONCACAF Gold Cup: Wolff was part of that important run as well. In the quarters, Wolff got a goal against Jamaica for a 3-1 victory. As for the final, Wolff was among the starters—

alongside Kasey Keller, Clint Dempsey, and Landon Donovan—against Panama. Following the penalty-kick shootout, which the US won, it marked the third Gold Cup title for the US program.

These two Gold Cup titles—2002 and 2005, along with the successful steps taken in the 2002 FIFA World Cup—were a critical aspect of the USMNT's momentum in the New Dawn period (1994-2010) that was playing out in US soccer. Wolff was front and center for that progress. His speed, dynamism on the ball, and awareness around goal made him an integral part of the teams that were fielded.

As for pro ranks, Wolff was part of numerous victories with different teams. With the Chicago Fire, he won the Lamar Hunt US Open Cup in 1998 and 2000; the MLS Cup in 1998; and, overall, he was a major threat in the lineup for Chicago, in the late 90s and early 2000s, under the leadership of Coach Bob Bradley.

Wolff was part of a Lamar Hunt US Open Cup championship in 2004 with the Kansas City Wizards.

As coach, Wolff has assisted with DC United, Columbus Crew, the USMNT (alongside Gregg Berhalter), and in 2021 he became head coach for Austin FC.

In the early 2000s, Wolff suffered a knee injury, as many players do, and it curtailed much of his potential. However, this speedy attacking threat from Georgia was one to watch in the long history of US soccer. When he was on the field, there was always a feeling that, at any moment, a big play might break open...a run down the line; a lead pass right through the heart of the defense for Wolff to pounce on; a gap between two defenders, and there he goes; anything and everything seemed possible.

62 Ben Olsen
USMNT: 1998-2007

Ben Olsen—born in Pennsylvania, in 1977—is one of those interesting players that wasn't built like a ton of bricks (all of 5'8" on a good day) yet epitomized a multi-talented soccer player. While other players might come to mind first, ones with flash and big speed, like Landon Donovan or Eddie Lewis, Olsen was a guy that was fast enough and quick enough but never one to overwhelm with either one. Rather, he was a crafty player, with good instincts, technique, and a will to win. In addition, he was one that Coach Bruce Arena, and other coaches, noticed early on.

Prior to attending Virginia, Olsen was awarded National High School Player of the Year in 1993 by *Parade* magazine. Thereafter, in 1995, he teamed up with top-level players at Virginia—following the university's amazing four-year championship conquest of the NCAA tournament (1991, 1992, 1993, 1994). During Olsen's time there, he earned the *Soccer America* Player of the Year Award in 1997.

Subsequently, Olsen was signed by DC United where he spent the vast majority of his playing career (1998-2009). For a time (2000-01), Olsen was on loan to Nottingham Forest, where he gathered 18 appearances and two goals.

As for DC United, his home base, he played in just over 220 games, with 29 goals. With United, he was part of the MLS Cup championship seasons of 1999 and 2004. He was MLS Rookie of the Year in 1998, and MLS All-Star selection in 1998 and 1999, the 1999 US Soccer Young Male Athlete of the Year, the MLS Cup MVP in 1999, and the MLS Humanitarian of the Year Award in 2003, along with making the MLS Best XI in 2007.

Olsen—a midfielder that could play out wide and in the middle—suited up with the USMNT on many occasions, 37 in all, with six goals to his credit. Early on, he made the 2000 Olympic squad—that placed fourth—with Chris Albright (Virginia alum), Landon Donovan, and Josh Wolff, to name a few.

Another early experience for Olsen with the national team came in the form of the 2000 Gold Cup effort. Unfortunately, the USMNT didn't place that year. Canada won it.

Olsen played a significant part in the 2005 Gold Cup championship, for the USMNT's third title.

In the wake of the 2006 FIFA World Cup, in which Olsen came on for Claudio Reyna in the Ghana game, it was near closing time for his run with the national team. In 2007 Olsen wrapped it up, though he continued with DC United until 2009.

This quickly turned into coaching as he assumed the assistant coach position with United in 2010. Soon thereafter, he became the head coach—which lasted through 2020. At the time, he was the youngest head coach, on a full-time basis, in league history. In 2014, Olsen earned the title of MLS Coach of the Year after a turnaround season that followed a dreadful 2013 result. As of 2022, he became head coach of Houston Dynamo.

From Rookie of the Year to Coach of the Year, an MLS Cup and Gold Cup champion, along with seeing time in a FIFA World Cup, Olsen has been a mainstay of US soccer for over 20 years, with certainly more to come. The next USMNT coach? Yet to be seen. If so, it was predicted here.

63 Tim Howard USMNT: 2002-17

Tim Howard—born in 1979 in New Jersey—was a power goalie that stood around 6'3" with muscles head to toe. Agile, athletic, and robust, he was a strong presence in goal, one you couldn't ignore.

From 1997 onward, Howard played for a number of teams, including North Jersey Imperials, MetroStars, Manchester United, Everton, and Colorado Rapids. For a US goalie to tend the net for Man United and Everton is a dream come true. That's the crème de la crème and he was invited in, a trusted hand. Yet as he began his climb upwards in the goalie ranks, he had to contend with perennial forces known as Brad Friedel and Kasey Keller. The US is always replete with goalkeeping talent, so therefore it was a challenge for Howard to distinguish himself as the next guy up.

In the late 90s, he was making the rounds as a young keeper on the rise. He played for the U20 national team in the 1999 FIFA World Youth Championship and then the U23 national team in the 1999 Pan American Games. Then, for the 2000 Olympics, Howard was a back-up for Brad Friedel as the team competed in Australia.

With some patience, Howard got his first USMNT appearance in 2002. Howard was named to the 2006 FIFA World Cup squad where he served as a back-up. It was still the Kasey Keller and Brad Friedel era, two greats. Howard had to quietly wait his turn.

In the 2007 CONCACAF Gold Cup, Howard was a key figure on the team and a starter in the big final against Mexico as the US won its fourth title. By then, Bob Bradley was coach. This tournament was critical; it marked the ushering in of the Tim Howard era.

During the 2009 Confederations Cup, Howard stood resilient in the net against Spain in the semis. Getting there wasn't so easy. The US had taken two major defeats in group play to Italy (1-3) and Brazil (0-3). The US defeated Egypt 3-0 in the final group match to advance on points. With Spain in the semis, the US held onto a 2-0 victory. This is the same Spain that eventually won the FIFA World Cup the following year. As for the final of the 2009 Confederations Cup, the US had a rematch with Brazil; Howard held down the fort, and got off to a good start but endured a 3-2 defeat for second place. All in all, it was a resounding victory for many US fans as the team had taken down a major world power—in Spain—and held its own against Brazil in the lesser-watched****** yet still illustrious final. For his efforts, Howard won the tournament's Golden Glove award (for best goalkeeper).

There was a big moment in the 2010 FIFA World Cup in which the USMNT grabbed a decisive victory over Algeria to escape its group. At a crucial moment in the game, Howard threw the ball out quickly, jumpstarting a transition play down the field that happened in a flash and eventually, after a pass across the mouth of the goal resulted in a loose ball, Donovan guided the ball into the net. Big moments like this from 2010 offer proof as to how current pro teams and the next generation of youth players should be taught. Caught in the middle as a symbolic figure that initiated the play, Howard was simply doing what any keeper should have done: release a counterattack with alert awareness and a well-placed throw.

2011 marked a significant milestone for Howard as he re-took the net for the CONCACAF Gold Cup. If not for a valiant Mexican effort in front of 93,000-plus fans packed with vigor inside the Rose Bowl, the US would've conquered the Confederation yet again. But, as it turned out, El Tri got the best of its northern neighbor by 4-2. For his efforts, Howard was ranked top of the list for Best Saves.

In the 2014 FIFA World Cup, and his last, Howard was big in the round of 16 loss to Belgium wherein he recorded 16 saves—a World Cup record. As FIFA pointed out on its website, as posted on October 21, 2023, "On this day in 2014, Tim Howard made an unprecedented sixteen saves against Belgium." In 2014, Kevin Baxter with the *Los Angeles Times* wrote, "Historic, in fact. His sixteen saves were the most recorded in a World Cup since FIFA began tracking that statistic."[68] News of the achievement was seemingly everywhere. A piece by Denver Nicks in *TIME* said, "The 35-year-

****** Compared to the FIFA World Cup final.

old goalkeeper made a heroic sixteen saves against Belgium, keeping the US national team alive into extra time. On social media, US fans called for everything from a Tim Howard presidency to the creation of a new award for Goalie Laureate of the United States."[69]

In the 2017 Gold Cup, Howard was present—and started in the final against Jamaica—as the USMNT won the championship, its sixth overall.

He acquired over 120 caps in a USMNT career that spanned into 2017 as one of the US' most trusted hands in net. Throughout his career, Howard earned a number of honors: MLS Goalkeeper of the Year (2001); MLS Humanitarian of the Year (2001); an MLS All-Star (2001, 2002, 2017); the US Soccer Player of the Year (2008, 2014); MLS All-Star MVP as a member of Everton (2009); and CONCACAF Men's Goalkeeper of the Year (2013, 2014, 2015), to name a few.

As one of many great keepers in the past, including the likes of Frank Borghi, Tony Meola, Kasey Keller, and Brad Friedel, Howard kept the high standard alive with great saves, a fierce competitive nature, and passion for US soccer.

64 Carlos Bocanegra USMNT: 2001-12

Carlos Bocanegra—born in Alta Loma, California, in 1979—was a UCLA Bruin in the late 90s as a defender. Eventually, in 2013, he entered the school's esteemed Athletics Hall of Fame.

He entered the pro ranks in 2000 as a member of the Chicago Fire in MLS. He played there from 2000-03, making over 85 appearances, with five goals.

He transitioned from MLS to Fulham, Rennes, Saint-Etienne, Rangers, Racing Santander, and finally Chivas USA. In total, his pro career spanned from 2000-14. For the USMNT, he played from 2001-12, amassing 110 caps with 14 goals. The last part is noticeable: as a defender he got 14 goals for the national team.

Where and how did this start? He represented his country during the 1999 FIFA World Youth Championship. Two short years later, perhaps an eternity for some, he received his first cap for the USMNT in 2001 versus South Korea, always a tough foe.

As an outside left defender and an inside defender, Bocanegra was part of the 2003 CONCACAF Gold Cup in which the US placed third.

Events began rolling forward in Bocanegra's fortune as he was named to the 2006 FIFA World Cup squad and started in two of the team's games. With the end of the 2006 World Cup, so too went Arena (for the time being, anyway). Next up as coach was Bob Bradley, who had played for and coached Princeton. Bradley, like his yacht-sailing predecessor, saw good things in Bocanegra and made him captain in 2007 as the US played China.

Things picked up by 2007 in which Bocs helped the USMNT win its fourth CONCACAF Gold Cup over Mexico, 2-1, in the final at Soldier Field in Chicago.

A big test arrived in 2009 during the FIFA Confederations Cup where the US defeated Spain—a big upset—in the semis and put up a good fight with Brazil in the final, a loss that went to the Samba beat.

There's a well-known photo, taken at the 2010 FIFA World Cup, that floated around of former President Bill Clinton, shirt and tie, with a shirtless Bocanegra, each holding a Budweiser bottle.

By 2011, Bocanegra broke 100 caps. By 2013 Bocanegra was at the end of his time with the national team. In 2014, he played his last professional game with Chivas USA. Many players–John Harkes, Tab Ramos, Peter Vermes, Dominic Kinnear, Brian McBride, and others–stay involved with coaching and overseeing various elements of teams. As such, Bocanegra joined ranks when, in 2015, he became the technical director of Atlanta United and subsequently vice president. A co-chair for the Technical Development Committee at US soccer? Sure, count him in. That occurred in 2018. Bocanegra was inducted into the National Soccer Hall of Fame in 2020.

65 Steve Cherundolo USMNT: 1999-2012

Born in 1979 in Rockford, Illinois, **Steve Cherundolo** was raised in San Diego, a southern Californian city known for the La Jolla Nomads club team, a powerhouse "...which won the California state championship six times with him."[70] San Diego, a soccer city a little smaller than LA and San Francisco, essentially allows for players to unite together on one club team: in this case, the Nomads. San Diego, in essence, has been a powerhouse soccer community for a long time.

Cherundolo is one of many talents to emerge from the southern California paradise. According to the Nomads website on October 23, 2023, under "Alumni" a list of players included Eric Wynalda (Nomads Pro Team), Marcelo Balboa (Nomads Pro Team), Paul Caliguiri (Nomads Pro Team), Frankie Hejduk (Nomads), Jovan Kirovski (Nomads), among others. So what path did Cherundolo take after playing for the Nomads?

First off, he played for Mt. Carmel High School. After winning the 1996-97 Gatorade State High School Player of the Year in California, Cherundolo straight away landed with the University of Portland where he did well in the late 90s and quickly made a move to join Hannover 96 in Germany.

Germany is an ideal landing place for soccer players around the world. For over 14 years (1999-2014), Cherundolo remained there, with Hannover 96. Along the way, despite a knee injury, he proved himself—among local and international talent—and became an integral part of the German club that dates back to 1896. As the 2000s progressed, he continued doing well at right back and was appointed captain of the team around 2010. In total, he played a little over 365 games.

The year 1999 marked his first cap with the USMNT against Jamaica. Despite hurdles with injuries, the next decade would see his gradual rise in the team as right back. He was included in the 2002 FIFA World Cup roster but didn't play. Despite an injury, Cherundolo was part of the 2005 CONCACAF Gold Cup championship run.

The World Cup of 2006 was hosted by Germany and it was Cherundolo's first opportunity for playing time in a Cup. As most know by now, the Cup that year, unfortunately, didn't go in the right direction for the US. No quarterfinals appearance, no round of 16 appearance. Call it "a learning experience." For Cherundolo, playing for Hannover 96, it was a great chance to participate in the biggest tournament in the world, on home turf so to speak.

In the next few competitions for the US, Cherundolo found himself injured and was unable to play in the 2007 CONCACAF Gold Cup, along with the 2009 FIFA Confederations Cup. However, he was present in the 2009 CONCACAF Gold Cup; the US placed second that year.

Cherundolo was a key figure in the US lineup for the exciting 2010 FIFA World Cup run in South Africa. In group C that consisted of England, Slovenia, and Algeria, Cherundolo got an assist in the Slovenia game—to Donovan—as the US eventually came out of the group in first place. He started in each group match. Cherundolo was present in the all-important round of 16 nail-biter against Ghana—a talented side that year—that saw the US lose a close one by a score of 2-1. He played a key role—as an experienced outside defender—in that 2010 tournament, despite not being a focal point up top.

In 2011, Cherundolo was part of the USMNT that again placed second in the Gold Cup. This was a big one that saw the US face off against Mexico in the final that was held in the Rose Bowl before approximately 93,000 fans. A few of Steve's starting teammates that game included Tim Howard, Carlos Bocanegra, Clint Dempsey, Michael Bradley, Freddy Adu, and Landon Donovan. Under Coach Bob Bradley, the US lost an exciting one, 4-2.

Cherundolo represented one of the most cherished positions in all of Brazil: the outside defender. He was one of those dependable forces back there, respected by coaches and teammates alike. The 5'6" right back—who some in Germany refer to as "Dolo"—could have stepped into a Brazilian starting 11 with speed, quickness, confidence, leadership, soccer IQ, ability, technique, awareness, and a willingness to win that lent his teammates the confidence needed to get optimal results.

When his playing days wrapped up in 2014, he quickly transitioned to coaching with the Hannover 96 system. By 2015, he was an assistant for the club's first team. In 2018, he assisted with VfB Stuttgart and the USMNT, where he worked with Dave Sarachan. Interestingly, he became an assistant for Germany's U15 squad from 2020–21. After a brief stint coaching the Las Vegas Lights in 2021, he took on the head coaching duties of LAFC in MLS in 2022. Retirement doesn't seem in the cards, as yet. There are a number of options for future coaches of the USMNT: Peter Vermes, John Harkes, Michael Bradley. Perhaps Cherundolo should toss his name into the hat.

66 Taylor Twellman USMNT: 2002-08

Taylor Twellman, to date, has been the only player from St. Louis to win the MLS MVP award. Considering the talent from the heart of US soccer, that's quite a feat.

Taylor Twellman has a unique story that sets him aside as one to watch. If you can believe it, he made this list despite never getting into a FIFA World Cup! How is that possible? Well, the enigma of Twellman is that he was the 2005 MLS MVP—rare territory—and the following year Bruce Arena chose, instead, **Brian Ching** as an auxiliary option at forward for the 2006 FIFA World Cup. En route to the infamous 2006 FIFA World Cup, there was much talk about the last positions on the roster and who was going to get the nod: Twellman or Ching? Despite Twellman scoring a hat trick against Norway, Ching was chosen. In totality, after tossing up his USMNT cleats, Ching amassed 45 caps, with 11 goals which indeed outdoes Twellman's run of 30 caps and six goals.

A lot of talent went to SLUH (St. Louis University High School, which dates to 1818): Bob Kehoe (USMNT captain and coach), Pat McBride (USMNT), Dan Flynn (CEO of the US Soccer Federation), Tim Twellman (USMNT), Ty Keough (USMNT), and Jeff Cacciatore (St. Louis Steamers), to name a few.

Taylor Twellman won the 1996-97 Gatorade State High School Player of the Year in Missouri. Taylor was raised in St. Louis, Missouri, and attended Saint Louis University High School (SLUH), where he was an all-star athlete in American football, basketball, soccer, and baseball, in which he was offered a contract by the Kansas City Royals. After graduating from SLUH in 1998, Twellman rejected the offer, electing to play soccer at Maryland on an athletic scholarship."[71]

Eventually, he joined the New England Revolution, won the MLS Golden Boot in 2002 and 2005, the 2005 MLS MVP, was part of the US Open Cup championship in 2007 (in which he scored a goal in the final), played in the North American SuperLiga in 2008, and joined the MLS 100 goals club (with the likes of Landon Donovan, Chris Wondolowski, Jason Kreis). With the USMNT, he was part of the 2007 CONCACAF Gold Cup championship, though perhaps most famously of all, he didn't make the 2006 FIFA World Cup squad at the peak of his powers.

Following his playing career, he entered broadcasting—like fellow St. Louisan Ty Keough had done—for a myriad of pro and international games on television that included the European Championships of 2012, 2016, and 2020, along with World Cup coverage in 2014. This run has included time with ESPN, ABC, and Apple. This post-career broadcasting move has put Twellman right in the middle of US soccer, as an influential voice, speaking to millions, which will set him apart from others for decades to come.

In addition, as one who suffered from concussions, he's had a lot to say about the matter. In fact, he has offered up his brain for scientific study in the field.

As a player, he was a prominent scoring threat. He had a presence around goal, with instincts, quick movement, decisive movement, an awareness of where to be, skill, technique, and a strong work ethic. Twellman has become more than just a player with a scoring touch. He's touched the lives of many in the realm of soccer by way of a TV set. With an eye for good play, he's pushed soccer forward just as his predecessor Ty Keough did.

67 Brad Davis
USMNT: 2005-14

The third all-time assist leader in MLS is none other than **Brad Davis**. In front of him are: #2, Steve Ralston and #1, Landon Donovan.

Tommy Howe—a former pro player with the groundbreaking St. Louis Stars of the NASL—noticed Davis at the age of 10. Within the Scott Gallagher system, arguably the top club program in the US, Howe and other coaches spotted his talent. Howe said, "We knew then that he was a special player. He had unbelievable skills. His soccer IQ was, you know, he played like a professional when he was 10 years old, as far as decision-making and stuff like that." In addition, "He had an incredible left foot. Unbelievable touch." Incidentally, Howe would coach Davis during his time at the club, from the age of 10 through U19.

An interesting connection on this list of top 100 USMNT is that Steve Ralston (born 1974), Taylor Twellman (born 1980), and Brad Davis (born 1981) are St. Louis Scott Gallagher products. Davis was a standout at Chaminade High School where he won the 1999-2000 Gatorade State High School Player of the Year in Missouri, and later went on to play for Saint Louis University. Still to this day, SLU is number one in the nation for NCAA Division I championships in men's soccer: 10. Davis was an immediate impact player, joining a long list of talent from SLU that dates back generations: Don Ceresia, Carl Gentile, Pat McBride, Gene Geimer, Bill McDermott, Gary Rensing, John Pisani, Jim Leeker, Al Trost, Mike Seerey, Dan Counce, Don Droege, Dan Flynn, Ty Keough, Larry Hulcer, Daryl Doran, Jim Kavanaugh, Mark Santel, Steve Kuntz, Mike Sorber, Brian McBride, to name a few.

Tom Timmermann, writing for the *St. Louis Post-Dispatch,* reported in May of 2020, "It was 2002, and the Chaminade grad was a sophomore at SLU. After that season, he turned pro, being taken third in MLS draft and embarking on a career that took him across the US, as well as the world in his time with the US national team."[72]

Davis was a six-time MLS All-Star, won the MLS Cup on two occasions with the Houston Dynamo (2006, 2007), MLS Best XI (2011), and the Houston Dynamo team MVP recipient on four occasions (2009, 2010, 2011, 2012).

With the USMNT, he was part of the CONCACAF Gold Cup championship in 2005. Additionally, he also played in the 2014 FIFA World Cup that was hosted by Brazil.

In recent years, Davis rejoined his former club team in St. Louis, Scott Gallagher, in a leadership role. There are many distinguished coaches there, such as former captain of the USMNT, Steve Pecher. Davis—an MLS champion, Gold Cup champion, and participant in a FIFA World Cup—has helped shape US soccer and will continue to do so. Perhaps most impressive of his time as a player were the large amount of assists gathered from MLS that placed him third all-time. This, in part, along with his stellar all-around quality, led to his valued time with the national team. It should go without saying, but when someone gets that many assists, they're doing something right.

68 Landon Donovan USMNT: 2000-14

Landon Donovan—born in 1982, in Ontario, California—immediately catches your eye. Darting past players with jets that are meant to run at high frequency, Donovan moved like a flash.

February 7, 2007: USMNT vs. Mexico. Donovan takes a pass from a teammate around the midfield line, sees an opening behind the last defenders, taps the ball into the open space, takes off toward the goalie with electric quickness, cuts the ball to the left of the outstretched, helpless keeper, and puts it away with his left foot for a goal! How on earth was it that easy for Donovan?! Speed kills. Plain and simple. There's no way around it. Donovan had it in spades. Give him an inch and he was gone.

Another dynamic moment came in the 2009 FIFA Confederations Cup final against Brazil. For a moment, when Donovan and Charlie Davies worked a two-man counterattack down the pitch, Brazilians were caught off guard. By this time, now in front of the goalie, the ball came from the left—across Donovan's body—and with his right foot he chopped it back across his body, to the left again, throwing the keeper off momentarily, and with his left foot hit the ball low and into the net. In the blink of an eye it was over: There's the ball in the back of the net. What just happened?

That's where Donovan thrived. He knew, deep down, he was just plain faster than other guys. All he needed was to tap the ball by them, and boom! It's over.

Following a stint at the IMG Academy in 1999, Donovan joined Bayer Leverkusen II (1999-2000) and Bayer Leverkusen (2000-05). As a youngster, still under 20, he struggled in Germany. In 2023, CBS | Soccer reflected: "Donovan also addressed his club career, which started with an unsuccessful stint at Bayer Leverkusen as a teenager. The retired player said his rough adjustment to life in Germany paved the way for his return to the US, first with the San Jose Earthquakes."[73] Before he returned to the US for more playing time, he was still sorting things out in Germany. "He also said he was not prepared for the struggle to fight for a spot on the team, and had no one around him to explain to him that he should not be playing every game from the moment he arrived in Germany."[74] Essentially, it came down to one strong factor: "MLS suited him, he said, because he wanted consistent playing time."[75]

Things began to shift with the San Jose Earthquakes as LD entered the mix from 2001-2004 and won the MLS Cup in 2001 and 2003. For the 2001 title, his first, Donovan got a goal in the final against LA Galaxy—his future team—for a 2-1 win. (The other scorers were Dwayne De Rosario with the Earthquakes and Luis Hernandez with the Galaxy.) As for 2003, the Earthquakes—which included Troy Dayak, Jeff Agoos, Richard Mulrooney, to name a few—took it to the Chicago Fire for a 4-2 championship win. Donovan got two goals that game, with two others from San Jose teammates Ronnie Ekelund and Mulrooney; Donovan's USMNT teammate, DaMarcus Beasley, got a goal for Chicago. Donovan was named the 2003 MLS Cup MVP.

A big move came in 2005 as he joined LA Galaxy, his hometown team, for a run that would last through 2014 and success was ushered in as the league was bursting with talent: Donovan, David Beckham, Mike Magee, Robbie Keane, Gregg Berhalter, Chris Klein, Frankie Hejduk, to name a few. During LD's run with the Galaxy, it won MLS Cups in 2005, 2011, 2012, and 2014, along with the Supporters' Shield in 2010 and 2011, and a Lamar Hunt US Open Cup in 2005. In 2011, Donovan got the game-winner over Houston in the final for a 1-0 result. As for 2012, Donovan joined the scoring with a goal over Houston in the final for a 3-1 victory. The 2014 MLS Cup championship marked the sixth of Donovan's career.

What may be lesser known during this time is that he went on loan to Bayern Munich (2009), Everton (2010), and Everton Part II (2012). Donovan made a comeback in 2016 with LA Galaxy that lasted six games.

Playing for the US Under 17 national team in the late 1990s, Donovan had a number of appearances, over 40, and amassed some 35 goals. At the 1999 FIFA U-17 World Championship, Donovan won the Golden Ball, which is the tournament's best player award. The team placed fourth. A few of Donovan's teammates were Oguchi Onyewu, DaMarcus Beasley, and Kyle Beckerman.

A young Donovan made an entrance off the bench in the 2000 Olympics. As it turned out, Donovan got a chance as a sub against Kuwait–in group C competition–and scored a goal, along with teammates Danny Califf and Chris Albright, as the US won 3-1. The US won its group and moved onto the quarterfinals and defeated Japan, as Donovan entered as a sub. He subsequently scored one of the penalty kicks in the shootout that secured advancement. In the 3-1 semifinal loss to Spain, Donovan entered as a sub. Ultimately, in the consolation match, which Donovan was subbed into, the US lost 2-0 to Chile and earned fourth place. For a young LD, it was validation for coaches that had scouted his talent that he was a player on the rise.

In the 2002 CONCACAF Gold Cup, Donovan scored in the opener against South Korea for a 2-1 win. The US went onto beat Cuba 1-0 and advanced to the quarterfinals. The US leveled El Salvador in the quarters, by 4-0. As for the semis, the US defeated Canada in penalties, with Donovan delivering as one of the shooters. Donovan was among the starters in the final match against Costa Rica that went in favor of the US, 2-0 (goals came from Josh Wolff and Jeff Agoos). This was the second Gold Cup title for the USMNT. Donovan made the Best XI squad, along with Jeff Agoos and Brian McBride.

The 2005 Gold Cup started off with a bang as the US disrupted the dreams of Cuba by 4-1 and Donovan gathered two goals. In the next game against Canada, Donovan got a late goal in what turned out to be a 2-0 victory. A 0-0 tie against Costa Rica still allowed the US to win group B. In the quarters, the US stepped past Jamaica 3-1 and found itself in a battle with Honduras in the semis. The US managed a 2-1 win and advanced to the final. Awaiting the squad was a determined Panama side that forced penalty kicks. In the shootout, Donovan was one of four to convert and the US won its third Gold Cup title. Donovan was among the tournament scoring leaders, with three goals. He was named to the All-Star team, along with Oguchi Onyewu and DaMarcus Beasley.

By 2007, after a few years of hard work, advertising, and marketing, the Gold Cups were starting to become more of a thing. Group B action saw the US defeat Guatemala—always feisty—by a narrow 1-0 margin. Following this was a 2-0 victory over T&T. For the last group game, the US administered a crushing 4-0 defeat to El Salvador in which Donovan got on the score sheet with one goal. The US didn't waste any time in defeating Panama 2-1 in the quarters, with Donovan converting a penalty kick. In the semis against Canada, Donovan got a goal—by way of a penalty kick—as the US earned a 2-1 win at Soldier Field in Chicago. The final went to the US as it defeated archrival Mexico, 2-1, with goals from Donovan—yet again, a penalty kick—and Benny Feilhaber. That's multiple PKs in a row—pretty consistent—and PKs are no joke, especially if you take them often. This was the fourth Gold Cup title for the USMNT. Carlos Pavon—of Honduras—finished the tournament as the leading scorer, with five, but Donovan was right behind him, with four.

For the following two Gold Cups of 2009 and 2011, the USMNT finished second to Mexico on both occasions. The 2011 championship against Mexico in the Rose Bowl was a raucous affair that saw Donovan get a goal—with buildup play from Freddy Adu and Clint Dempsey—in the 4-2 defeat suffered at the hands of El Tri. Despite Mexico's large contingent of fans, it was an exciting match on Donovan's home turf, LA—an event that was showing US fans just how popular soccer was getting from coast to coast.

The 2013 Gold Cup got off to a good start as Donovan scored a penalty kick against hopeful Belize in a 6-1 shellacking. Next up was Cuba and a similar result. Donovan got a PK as the team trounced Cuba 4-1. Last was a 1-0 victory over Costa Rica that saw the USMNT win group C. In the quarters, El Salvador met the fury of the US as Donovan scored in a 5-1 blowout. Donovan ended up scoring two goals in a 3-1 win over Honduras in the semis. The final was a tight game, in which Brek Shea got the only goal over Panama. This became the fifth Gold Cup title for the US. By tournament's end, Donovan, Chris Wondolowski, and Panama's Gabriel Torres were tournament leaders with five goals each. The Miller Lite Golden Ball was awarded to Donovan.

The next Gold Cup championship for the US would be in 2017, but by then Donovan had retired from the national team.

In the Donovan era, his optimistic view on the United States' chances at winning ushered in a new era of confidence for the USMNT. Speed, which keeps opponents off-balance, can do that. And that's what Donovan brought to the table. He was plotting big things for the US team...something that really hadn't been realistic before his time. Largely speaking, he was part of the New Dawn period (1994-2010) and things were about to change in a big way for the USMNT. As most know, Donovan was also part of the Breakthrough period (2010-15). His long career spanned these two periods, and one thing was clear: US soccer was being taken seriously by opponents around the world.

For starters, Gold Cups were becoming more attainable for the US team; something that hadn't been the case in terms of North American tournaments in past years. What's more is that US soccer was seeing itself as a worthy contender for the FIFA World Cup title.

The 2002 FIFA World Cup set out in exciting form for the US as it got out to a very auspicious start by defeating favorites Portugal. Next up was a tie with one of that year's co-hosts, South Korea. Then things went downhill as the US lost 3-1 to Poland. Nonetheless, Donovan scored that game. Despite the loss, given the team's win-tie-loss record, the US advanced to the next round where they faced a familiar foe, Mexico. With big goals from McBride and Donovan, the US advanced over El Tri by a score of 2-0. Donovan and company had flashes of brilliance in the quarters against Germany, but it wasn't meant to be as the Germans snuck out a 1-0 win. For his efforts, LD won the Best Young Player award.

The 2006 World Cup was a disaster all around. The US lost its opener 3-0 to Czech Republic. The second match was a 1-1 tie against Italy, the eventual champions. Finally, the US lost 2-1 to Ghana. The tie with Italy wasn't the worst disaster in the world, but the tournament is one most people care to forget.

In 2009 at the FIFA Confederations Cup, Donovan, Dempsey, Coach Bob Bradley, and company led the charge in group B with a loss to Italy, a loss to Brazil, and a 3-0 win over Egypt. This advanced the US to the semis in which it defeated Spain 2-0...a huge upset. In the final, a rematch against Brazil,

Donovan scored a fast break goal, as mentioned earlier, yet Brazil came back to win 3-2. However, the US placed second overall—a great result.

As 2010 came around the corner, things were looking up for the USMNT's prospects. The 2010 FIFA World Cup in South Africa was a new beginning for the squad. By this time, the transition of Bruce Arena to Bob Bradley had taken place. In group C—against England, Slovenia, and Algeria—the US placed first. In the opener against England, the US got a crucial 1-1 draw. The US would earn yet another draw against Slovenia, with goals from Donovan and Michael Bradley, that ended up 2-2. As for the final match against Algeria, in the final minutes of action Tim Howard sent Donovan downfield with a perfect throw and LD's speed took over as he made a beeline toward the box, laid the ball off to the right, the ball was played into the six-yard box area, a scrum with the keeper and a US player ensued, and Donovan pounced on the loose ball for a guided pass into the back of the net. And with that, the US secured a spot in the round of 16. Every World Cup has moments were everyone worldwide seems to stop what they're doing and take a look. That was one of them. The highlight went viral and the Cup got a well-deserved shot of adrenaline. Donovan scored in the showdown with Ghana, yet the US lost 2-1 in a tight match. The top scorers in the tournament had five goals; Donovan wound up with three. The World Cup has the ability to skyrocket players to the forefront of everyone's attention and Donovan became the symbol of US soccer more than ever before.

This World Cup run was followed by the 2011 CONCACAF Gold Cup—in which the US got second place after the exciting 4-2 defeat over Mexico in front of over 93,000 fans inside the Rose Bowl—and subsequently the big 2013 Gold Cup that Donovan and the US won in style.

This future National Soccer Hall of Fame inductee—class of 2023—was the centerpiece of US soccer. In other words, the economy of soccer, in large part, was revolving around him.

Eventually Donovan needed a break. As the undeniable leader of the US' soccer community, he had so many eyes on him, his every move. So what did he do? He went to, of all places, Cambodia. Josh Whisenhunt, writing for MLS in 2013, titled an essay: "Landon Donovan really is in Cambodia."[76]

It turns out that "thanks to a couple tweets that surfaced this morning from the editor of Thmey Thmey Online News, we now know that LD was casually getting his pick-up game on at an island just off the coast of Sihanoukville. Barefoot."[77] There he was, posing for a picture—wearing nothing but a black and red swimsuit—with local guys who were more than likely appreciative of a good game with LD.

In a 2013 story in *The Washington Post,* DC United midfielder **John Thorrington**, close friend and former teammate, shared these thoughts on Donovan's hiatus: "'Nobody can fault his service to his club or national team. He has played in big games, he has had to carry the weight of multiple teams at the same time. Off the field, he has been the face of US soccer. It's a lot to carry. Credit to him: He has done it well and been very successful. He is a hard-working guy.'"[78] Thorrington—who played four games for the USMNT from 2001-08—added, "'Nobody in the history of US soccer has had to deal with all the pressure he has—not one. He has been doing this since 1999: international games, international travel, World Cups, MLS.'"[79]

In 2013, Donovan was with the LA Galaxy—which had won the MLS Cup in 2011 and 2012—and he helped guide the USMNT to the 2013 CONCACAF Gold Cup title that year. Donovan was riding high with stellar performances. Yet, as World Cup qualifying turned into a final roster, USMNT Coach Jürgen Klinsmann left an aging Donovan off the team. At this point in his career, after over a decade of game after game, Donovan needed a little more recovery time between long training sessions and Klinsmann wasn't having it, apparently. According to *Wikipedia*: "In May 2014, Donovan was named in the preliminary squad for the 2014 World Cup and joined the team in training camp. However, on May 22, 2014, he was controversially omitted from the final US squad by manager Jürgen Klinsmann. Donovan's absence from the team even became the comedic subject of a PlayStation commercial where Donovan makes light of his newly found free time."[80]

In 2014, LD wrapped things up with the Galaxy but rejoined the team in 2016 for a handful of games.

After 2016, Donovan continued to plug away, here and there, including a six-game run in 2018 with Leon (Mexico), a brief stint with the legendary

San Diego Sockers (2018–19), and a last stand with the United States national arena soccer team†††††† in 2019. Despite moving at a slightly slower tempo, people were excited to have him on board as he was just wanting to play the game he loves, at the highest level possible, as long as he could.

Just a couple years later, in 2023, Donovan was inducted into the National Soccer Hall of Fame. As it currently stands, Donovan is first in the category of assists in MLS history (136). Not bad. As of April 9, 2025, he was ranked third as the leading scorer in MLS history (145). Other awards include LA Galaxy Player of the Year (multiple); LA Galaxy Golden Boot (multiple); MLS Player of the Month (multiple); MLS Best XI (multiple); MLS Cup MVP (2003, 2011); MLS All-Star (multiple); MLS All-Star Game MVP award (2001, 2014); MLS 100 goals club; MLS Golden Boot (2008); MLS All-Time Best XI (2005); Everton Player of the Month (January 2010 and January 2012); and the number one player on the *USA Today* Top 25 MLS players ever (published in 2020). Then there's the FIFA World Cup Best Young Player Award (2002); Best Male Soccer Player ESPY Award (2002); Best MLS Player ESPY Award (2006, 2007, 2009, 2010, 2011); Honda Player of the Year (2002, 2003, 2004, 2007, 2008, 2009, 2010); US Soccer Player of the Year (2003, 2004, 2009, 2010); CONCACAF Gold Cup MVP (2013); Premios Univision Deportes Lifetime Achievement Award (2014); Walt Chyzowych Fund Distinguished Playing Career Award (2017); and IFFHS (The International Federation of Football History & Statistics) Legends list.

Over time, the title of MVP of MLS changed from being called the Honda MLS Most Valuable Player (1996–2007) to the Volkswagen MLS Most Valuable Player (2007–14), and finally, in 2015, the award was renamed the Landon Donovan MVP Award. To refresh your memory, he won the award in 2009.

He had a long run. A very long run. Within the realm of the USMNT, Donovan ranks second all-time in appearances (157). The one player ahead of him is Cobi Jones (164).

†††††† Some refer to it as minifootball.

As for the all-time leading scorer in USMNT history? You may already know: There's a tie for first. Clint Dempsey (57) and Donovan (57) hold that distinct honor. Christian Pulisic may be knocking on the door very soon. In terms of the best all-time player in USMNT history? That's a tough call. For a brief moment, Pat McBride. For the 80s, Rick Davis. Then there's Tab Ramos and Eric Wynalda. One from Donovan's era, one with just about every intangible skill you can bestow upon a player, Clint Dempsey. And in the modern era: Christian Pulisic. Yet, many would hasten to say Donovan. However you view it, Donovan is top of the list for legions of fans that remember the burst of speed that captured the imagination like practically no other US player has. The argument gets tricky with time and players from different generations, but the bottom line is that he's a tough act to follow.

DaMarcus Beasley
USMNT: 2001-17

November 16, 2023, Austin, Texas: The USMNT vs. Trinidad and Tobago. The US wins 3-0. In the post-game show, from the sideline, announcers analyze what just happened. Kyle, one of the male commentators standing next to **DaMarcus Beasley**, seemed to have Lotto sneakers on. I thought: that's pretty cool. There was Beasley, to his left, who seemed to have Puma's on. I thought: wait a second. Maybe, just maybe, US soccer has been cool all this time. Who are those naysayers all along? Who said it wasn't cool? Lotto and Puma? What was going on? This was post-Beasley, his post-soccer playing career. A suit and tie...and sneakers. Let's rewind.

It's the early 2000s—"Beas," as he's called, is fresh on the scene. Critics, not referring to myself, mind you, said he didn't have a first touch.

DaMarcus Beasley: They said he was too small, too skinny...in fact, at one point, he weighed somewhere around 130 pounds and in the 140s at the most. They said his first touch was no good. Somehow, someway, with these obstacles he used his lightning quickness to make a difference.

A longtime member of the Houston Dynamo, DaMarcus Beasley also had 117 caps with the USMNT and 17 goals. He started out in Fort Wayne, Indiana, where he played for South Side High School. From there he made his way to Bradenton, Florida, to train at the IMG Academy—a new development at the time that featured Landon Donovan and Bobby Convey.

In 1999, he was a featured player at the 1999 FIFA U-17 World Cup, alongside teammates Landon Donovan, Oguchi Onyewu, and Kyle Beckerman. The team placed fourth. After some shuffling early on (1999-2000), Beasley was with the LA Galaxy and then Chicago Fire where he played from 2000–04, wherein he played in over 95 games and scored 14 goals. The Dutch team, PSV Eindhoven came knocking, looking for his quickness, and he remained in Holland from 2004–07, playing in over 55 games while adding 10 goals. During that time, interestingly, he was loaned to Manchester City for just over 15 games.

After these two stints, he moved north to play for the Rangers (2007–10) in the mighty top league of Scotland; that would be the red, white, and blue of the Rangers—as opposed to the white and green of its rival, Celtic. A brief stop with Hannover 96 (2010–11) followed before a move to Puebla (Mexico) that lasted a bit longer (2011–14). At Puebla, he played in over 90 games with just over ten goals.

But perhaps the team he became most well known playing for was Houston Dynamo, where he led the team with experience. With Houston, Beasley gained over 120 appearances in MLS and won the Lamar Hunt US Open Cup (2018), the Dynamo defensive player of the year award (2015, 2018), and Dynamo Players' Player of the Year award (2019), and was named an MLS All-Star on multiple occasions.

With the USMNT, he won the CONCACAF Gold Cup Golden Boot (2005); was named to the Gold Cup All-Tournament team (2005); was part of numerous USMNT Gold Cup championship squads (2002, 2005, 2007, 2013) and was captain of the 2013 run under Coach Klinsmann; and was part of the FIFA World Cup squads (2002, 2006, 2010, 2014).

After the disaster that was the 2006 World Cup, the 2010 World Cup was a different story. While Beasley came on as a sub, he was nearing the end of his USMNT career in terms of fresh legs. Given a decade under his belt, and a few injuries along the way, Beasley was wearing down. However, by 2014, Beasley wasn't done just yet. As a member of the squad, he joined a unique group—Claudio Reyna and Kasey Keller—that joined four FIFA World Cup rosters. He played more significant minutes in Brazil during the Cup as the US got to the round of 16, losing to Belgium.

When 2017 rolled around, Beasley was included in a June World Cup qualifying match against Mexico in which he "became the first US player to play in five World Cup qualifying cycles."[81] All told, he ended with 126 caps and 17 goals. As for caps, that ranked him seventh in the history of the US team. In 2023, the 17 goals placed him in the top tier of the program.

He ended his professional play in 2019, and just a few years later, Beasley was inducted into the 2023 National Soccer Hall of Fame. In his post-playing career, he has stepped into a broadcasting role as seen on TV, adding commentary to various games.

70 Kyle Beckerman USMNT: 2007-16

Kyle Beckerman—born in 1982 in Maryland—was a midfielder that specialized as a defensive mid. Beckerman went to the IMG Soccer Academy in Florida in the late 90s to receive, what was then, the highest soccer education in the US.

Beckerman played in the FIFA U-17 World Championship‡‡‡‡‡‡ in New Zealand, along with Landon Donovan and Bobby Convey. That team finished fourth overall.

Around that time, the senior Brazil team had placed second in the 1998 FIFA World Cup and first in the 1999 Copa America. Prior to those results, Brazil had scouted its youth pool of players and targeted standouts—like Roberto Carlos, Rivaldo, and Ronaldo—to build from. It relied on its youth system—training players, getting them ready for the next step—to produce results.

In its own way, with the IMG Soccer Academy, the US was doing much the same. These names Kyle Beckerman, Landon Donovan, and Bobby Convey—were a few projected leaders for the next decade or so, following that tournament in New Zealand. Developing youth talent has been one of the tenets of US soccer for generations. It's manifested in different forms in sort of a trial-and-error way, often with disparate parts around the nation. During the late 90s, the talk was the new IMG Soccer Academy. Since then it has shifted to MLS academies. Nonetheless, Beckerman was one of the chosen few to guide US soccer forward.

Right out of the gate, following the IMG Soccer Academy, Beckerman joined Miami Fusion of MLS in the early 2000s where he got minimal experience under his belt. From there he moved to the Colorado Rapids and played in a little over 150 games.

One could argue that his MLS life really began after that with Real Salt Lake where he played in over 375 games, with around 30 goals and

‡‡‡‡‡‡Aka, the FIFA U-17 World Cup.

established himself as a team and league leader—essentially the ironman of soccer. He could not be stopped. If there was a game, he was going to play in it. It seemed nothing could get in his way.

As for the USMNT, Beckerman played in the 2007 Copa America, won the 2013 CONCACAF Gold Cup, and played in the 2014 FIFA World Cup where the US faced Germany, Portugal, and Ghana.

Beckerman oversaw the winning of the 2009 MLS Cup with Real Salt Lake, the crowning achievement of his MLS career. He was an MLS All-Star on numerous occasions (2009, 2010, 2011, 2012, 2013, 2016). He also earned a place in what's called the MLS 400 Games Club which is for MLS players that have racked up an enormous amount of experience. As the title would suggest, he played in over 400 games in MLS.

As a steady operator for the USMNT (2007-16), he gathered over 55 caps. Following his retirement, Beckerman took up coaching. In 2021, he became the head coach for the soccer team at Utah Valley University.

71 Herculez Gomez USMNT: 2007-13

Herculez Gomez—born in 1982 in the Los Angeles area, California—was a 5'10" forward with a powerful shot that had a lengthy pro career and humble beginnings. He played for a lot of teams, including LA Galaxy, San Diego Sockers, Colorado Rapids, Kansas City Wizards, Puebla, Pachuca, Tecos, Santos Laguna, Tijuana, Tigres UANL, Puebla, Toronto FC, and Seattle Sounders. He was part of the MLS Cup with the Galaxy (2005) and the US Open Cup (2005).

He's been a lead scorer in the US Open Cup (2005), the Mexican Primera Division, and the Copa MX.

He was part of the MLS Cup with Seattle Sounders (2016). By that time he was all tapped out. It was the end of his career; that would be the last pro team he played for. Three years prior to that, he wrapped things up with the national team.

In the early 2000s, he injured his foot. After he recovered, he played with the San Diego Sockers and later rejoined the LA Galaxy.

As a guy that has roots in California and Las Vegas, Gomez is of the American Southwest. He is of Mexican-American background. I've always been a little jealous of Mexican-American players that go back to Mexico to play. Players are essentially viewed as Hollywood blockbuster A-list actors. In Mexico, there's nothing cooler than soccer players. On top of being a little jealous of Mexican-American players that suit up in Mexico, I've also been a little envious of the Mexican culture surrounding soccer. For the Mexican fans, it's like part of their way of life. I was in San Antonio, in 2015, and there was a huge pre-game festival-like atmosphere on the grounds outside of the arena. For Gomez to have excelled at pro soccer in Mexico—the land of soccer—is like a player's dream come true.

As for the USMNT, he had another dream come true experience. For starters, Gomez played in the 2007 Copa America hosted by Venezuela. That team was coached by Bob Bradley.

Gomez was part of the 2010 FIFA World Cup squad—coached by Bob Bradley—for the US and played. Kevin Baxter, of the *Los Angeles Times*, wrote: "Herculez Gomez wasn't invited to play in any World Cup qualifiers for the US in the run-up to the 2010 tournament. But six months later, in the shape of his life, he scored in the final game before the World Cup roster was chosen and found himself on the team that played in South Africa."[82] It was the chance of a lifetime. Incidentally, Baxter noted, "He was at the top of his game in 2010, scoring 10 times in 15 games in Mexico's Torneo Bicentenario to become the first US player to lead a foreign league in scoring. That earned the attention of US coach Bob Bradley, who took Gomez with him to South Africa."[83] Just going to a World Cup is the pinnacle for most players. To play on top of that is something else special.

Toward the end of his national team run, he was listed with the team during the 2013 Gold Cup championship.

On July 3, 2013, Mark Zeigler at *The San Diego Union-Tribune* wrote,

> "Herculez Gomez is sitting on a couch in the lobby of a downtown San Diego hotel, reminiscing about how he once slept on one. How a buddy coaxed him into attending an open tryout for a new minor-league pro team in San Diego 11 years ago, how he was sick and didn't want to go, how his buddy loaded him into the car anyway in the pre-dawn darkness of Las Vegas and drove through the desert while he slept in the passenger seat. How he was paid $500 a month and housed at a 'kind of foster home for players'—some nights sleeping on the living room couch, some nights in a bedroom if one was available. How he bounced in and out of Major League Soccer reserve teams, making $16,500 per year (not month). How his car was essentially his closet. How after being cut from MLS the first time he returned to San Diego and played for the indoor Sockers while working at the UTC mall in the mornings and coaching two youth teams in Chula Vista

> in the afternoons, only for the Sockers to fold after 10 games. And how surreal it all seems now, sitting in this hotel lobby a decade later, wearing US national soccer team gear. He's a 31-year-old forward, here for a friendly against Guatemala on Friday night at Qualcomm Stadium ahead of the CONCACAF Gold Cup."[84]

On July 17, 2013, MLS reported online that:

> "Herculez Gomez appears to be on his way out of US national team camp ahead of Sunday's CONCACAF Gold Cup quarterfinal match against El Salvador. The veteran forward tweeted on Wednesday that he was departing the group, bound for San Diego to connect with Mexican side Club Tijuana, which he joined in June. Mexico's Liga MX begins play this weekend, with Tijuana hosting Atlas on Friday. Gomez appeared in two of the team's three group stage matches in the Gold Cup and the team's tune-up against Guatemala. He came off the bench and played 13 minutes on Tuesday night in a 1-0 win against Costa Rica."[85]

Perhaps *The San Diego Union-Tribune* best explains this unlikely story with the following: "Gomez was a kid who was never supposed to make it. He never played for tony youth clubs. He wasn't part of US Soccer's Olympic Development Program because his family couldn't afford it. He didn't play in college. And when he washed out in Mexico's minor leagues after high school, he returned to Las Vegas, figuring his soccer dreams were extinguished. Reality beckoned."[86] With all that said, *The San Diego Union-Tribune* story pointed out "how surreal it all seems"[87] as Gomez overcame the odds and turned it around.

All in all, he's a USMNT forward that got into that five-plus goal realm: 24 caps, six goals. His goals arrived against Czech Republic, Australia, Brazil,

Antigua and Barbuda, Jamaica, and Guatemala. If you think six goals isn't that much, well, you may be right. But you should remember how challenging it was to make it there in the first place.

Gomez worked his way up from the ground level—indoor soccer with the respectable San Diego Sockers—all the way up. His story is intriguing, and he continues forward on his journey with soccer as a member of ESPN's team of pundits reflecting on various games. In addition, he's involved with numerous podcasts. A great post-career for a player that has a lot of experience to draw upon.

72 Clint Dempsey USMNT: 2004-17

He's a rapper, he's a fisher, he's a footballer; he might be the best US player of all time. Who's the top US scorer of all time? It couldn't be Landon Donovan, could it? It's Landon Donovan *and* **Clint Dempsey**. They're currently tied for first with 57 goals each, but that record may be overtaken someday. (Ahem, his name is Pulisic.) Neymar overtook the top scoring position for Brazil and finally conquered the record that Pelé had for so long. So who knows? Maybe Donovan and Dempsey will be surpassed too. For now though, they have the title. Dempsey, just a tad younger, was always the next guy up when it came to Donovan.

Around 2012–16ish, it could be argued that three players ruled the roost in CONCACAF: Bryan Ruiz (Costa Rica), Joseph Campbell (Costa Rica), and Clint Dempsey. Ruiz, Campbell, Dempsey, and Guardado were playmakers with scoring touch, and, with no disrespect to the others, Dempsey seemed like the best one. He had a way about him that always made a simple pass have meaning. That is: all his passes did something. Even the simplest of passes in the middle of the field to a player five yards away seemed like it was getting something going. That's a quality few players possess. When it came to speed, he would surprise you with bursts, here and there, but he was never accused of being fast like Donovan. But Dempsey had guile. He had smarts. He had skill. He had a fighting spirit. He had confidence. There was always something in the air when he had the ball.

Dempsey was born in Nacogdoches, Texas. As a kid, Dempsey was raised in a trailer park and played soccer with locals that included a large number of Hispanic residents. As it goes, after being spotted by coaches, he ended up playing for one of the top club teams in Dallas. Only problem was: it was a far drive and the Dempseys were balancing a lot for Clint's soccer ambitions. Writing for *Daily Mail*, Richard Alleyne pointed out in 2014 that, "Two or three times a week the family embarked on the six-hour round trip and his dad sold his boat and guns to pay for the gas money."[88] In addition, "his mother, a nurse, worked every overtime shift she could and the family forewent their annual holiday."[89] Most people assume that US soccer players come from a middle-class background, but Clint's situation was different. "Special occasions were spent in McDonald's, the five siblings sharing one meal between them."[90]

Then tragedy struck. "When he was 12, Dempsey's 16-year-old sister Jennifer, an excellent tennis player, died of a brain aneurysm. Dempsey decided he had to make the most out of life, her passing affected him so."[91] Clint was certainly determined with soccer.

Full of hope and aspiration, Dempsey worked his way through the realm of Texas soccer: one of the best soccer states in the nation. Small-town Dempsey was gifted with talent and motivated to make it in Dallas with club soccer, despite the lengthy drive, and with the support of family he was making progress in strides. The fact that he's from a small town should be taken as a point of pride. So many players, particularly in the US, come from large cities where coaches from the same area often give preferential treatment to those players; on top of that, most US players are from middle class—often upper-middle class—households. Thus, Dempsey's small-town trailer park upbringing only adds to his mystique.

From humble beginnings, he went to Furman University. Furman is a college in South Carolina that also boasts former students Ricardo Clark (USMNT), Walker Zimmerman (USMNT), David C. Garrett Jr. (a former CEO of Delta Air Lines), and Victoria Jackson (a former member of *Saturday Night Live*). Despite being at a smaller school, Dempsey worked his way up the ranks, as best he could, at a lesser-known outfit. His undeniable talents were being noticed.

In 2004, Dempsey—who stands around 6'1"—was drafted by the New England Revolution and got to work quickly as he tallied up 71 appearances and 25 goals in about two years.

He joined Fulham in 2007 and made the most of his time with over 185 appearances and 50 goals. In doing so, he was breaking the US soccer glass ceiling that really hadn't been done before in such a way that was unique all unto himself. A few players before him had made big strides in Europe: John Harkes, Joe-Max Moore, Brian McBride, for example. With the exception of Brian McBride, though, none had really captured the attention of the world like Dempsey did. Dempsey represented US soccer as a go-to guy in the EPL during 2007-12. For purposes of US soccer, this carried over from the New Dawn period—1994-2010—to the Breakthrough period—2010-15—which was a big deal for future US talent, such as Pulisic, who benefited from this hard work. As such, Dempsey was a trendsetter.

Dempsey and Donovan—despite their inner-squad competition on the USMNT—were influential in bringing about a new way of looking at US soccer abroad. Each player was full of confidence and desire, and each shifted the pendulum in a positive direction for US soccer players at large.

Persuasive evidence that Dempsey was deserving of worldwide acclaim arrived when he moved from legitimate club, Fulham, to premium club, Tottenham Hotspur. This adventure only lasted from 2012-13, yet he was one of the first US field players to join such a highly regarded club. "On August 31, 2012, Dempsey joined Tottenham Hotspur on a three-year contract for a fee believed to be in the region of $9 million,"[92] said *Wikipedia*. "The deal made Dempsey the highest salaried US soccer player of all time."[93]

Dempsey sparks big questions about the greater place of US players in the pantheon of world soccer elites. Matt Pentz, representing *The Guardian*, wrote: "Who was better, Dempsey or Landon Donovan, the man with whom he will be forever tied on the all-time US men's goal-scoring chart? How do you compare an outfield player with goalkeepers such as Kasey Keller, Brad Friedel and Tim Howard, each of whom also had successful club careers abroad?"[94] What's more, Pentz added, "Rather than setting Dempsey in some kind of fixed hierarchy, however, it's more helpful to think of him as a mile marker on the longer arc of the growth of soccer in the United States."[95] He added that: "Pre-Dempsey, the list of US difference-makers in top European leagues was short, and almost exclusively limited to guys standing between the posts. Along with fellow Fulham cult hero Brian McBride—and where his legacy starts to diverge with that of Donovan, with whom he was so often compared—Dempsey did more than just about anybody to alter that dynamic."[96]

The following point, one could argue, is spot on with respect to how many European soccer minds have viewed US talent in the past. "His wonder goal for Fulham in the 2010 Europa League quarterfinals against Juventus, an audacious chip from the very edge of the penalty box, was a counterpoint to the narrative of US soccer players as brutish, hustling grunt workers."[97] All the same, it wasn't just a goal that set him apart, it was his keen insight to build up play. Europeans had to accept that, even if begrudgingly, there was quality coming from a US field player. Without Dempsey's work and effort, Pulisic would likely have been a crafty attacking mid on the LA Galaxy's misfortunate teams of the early 2020s trying to recapture what it once had.

As all players wind down, so too did Dempsey. His pro career ended with the Seattle Sounders, from 2013–18. If you're searching for loud fans then look no further than Sounders supporters. These very well might be the loudest, most ferocious fans around MLS and they had a hero in Dempsey. He contributed significantly as he attained 115 appearances, with 47 goals. *The Guardian* highlighted his place in MLS history: "Dempsey altered perceptions closer to home, as well. His signing with the Seattle Sounders in the summer of 2013 remains second only to the arrival of David Beckham in terms of watershed moments in league history. The addition of the 30-year-old captain of the US national team arriving straight from Tottenham Hotspur was something close to unprecedented."[98]

For years, MLS was constantly searching for impact players, from home and abroad, to boost viewership, attendance, sales. This was one of those victory lap stories. "Commissioner Don Garber's sentiments shared with Sports Illustrated in the aftermath of Dempsey's arrival are slightly hyperbolic five years on, but the general message still rings true: 'This signing ranks right at the very top,' Garber told SI. 'We have been going through a process that started almost 10 years ago to try and find the players that could really make a statement about our league and our plan to be a legitimate player on the global stage...With Clint, it takes all of this to an even higher level.'"[99]

During Dempsey's time with Seattle, the team won the 2014 US Open Cup, the 2014 Supporters' Shield, and the 2016 MLS Cup. There were moments where things got feisty: "On June 16, 2015, in the fourth round of the Lamar Hunt US Open Cup against rivals the Portland Timbers, Dempsey was sent off for ripping up referee Daniel Radford's notebook in protest at the dismissal of Michael Azira. The Sounders finished the match with seven men through three dismissals and an injury, and lost 1-3 at home. For the incident, he was given a three-match MLS suspension and a fine, and banned from the Open Cup for two years in addition to a second fine,"[100] said *Wikipedia*. In 2016, there was news of Dempsey having an irregular heartbeat. Around this time, he ended his playing career and by 2018 the era of Dempsey was over.

Hold on. Let's go back to the beginning of his USMNT career. Dempsey started out on the US U20 national team and earned 13 appearances, with 21 goals circa 2002–03. In 2004, Dempsey debuted for the main USMNT against Jamaica, a qualifier for the 2006 FIFA World Cup. It was a 1–1 draw.

A few games in, Dempsey got his first goal in 2005 against powerhouse England. It took place in Chicago, at Soldier Field, and the US happened to lose 2–1.

Nonetheless, Dempsey was primed and ready for the 2005 CONCACAF Gold Cup in which the USMNT took the championship. Dempsey got a goal in the opener against ever-present Cuba and subsequently started in the final against Panama. This was the United States' third overall Gold Cup title.

As it turns out, Dempsey pulled quite a number on the Gold Cups. He was part of the championship side for three of them: 2005, 2007, and 2017.

In the 2007 Gold Cup, hosted by the United States, Dempsey got things cracking with a 1–0 game-winner over Guatemala in the opener. The US followed that up with two back-to-back shutouts over Trinidad and Tobago (2–0) and El Salvador (4–0). In doing so, the US won group B, edging out feisty Guatemala (who came in second). Next up, in the quarters, semis, and final, the US won each game 2–1. In the quarters, it defeated Panama; in the semis, it defeated Canada; and in the final, the US defeated mighty Mexico. Dempsey was among the starters in the final against Mexico that took place in Chicago at Soldier Field. Bob Bradley was coach. A few other starters included Tim Howard, Benny Feilhaber, and Landon Donovan. This became the fourth Gold Cup title for the USMNT.

Bruce Arena was back for the 2017 Gold Cup. Dempsey joined the action against El Salvador in the quarters, alongside Tim Howard, Michael Bradley, and Darlington Nagbe for a 2–0 win. In the semis against Costa Rica, it was another 2–0 victory for the US. Dempsey got one of them and that put the team in the final against Jamaica in which the US won 2-1. This was the sixth Gold Cup title for the USMNT.

Dempsey was part of the impressive FIFA Confederations Cup of 2009 where the US placed second. After two losses and a win in group B, the US found itself finishing in second place to Brazil. In the win, Dempsey got a goal over Egypt in which the US won 3–0. From there it was onto the semifinals against Spain. The US took it to the Spaniards on this occasion and won the match by 2–0 with Dempsey accounting for the second goal. You might be thinking: It's only the Confederations Cup. Sure, it's a smaller tournament, but that's big time. 2–0. The US dropped Spain, with Dempsey racking one of the goals. As for the final, the US got off to a great start against Brazil and who got the first goal? Dempsey. However, the squad ended up losing to the determined Brazilians by 3–2. Dempsey earned the tournament's Bronze Ball and made the FIFA.com Users' Top 11 as a midfielder.

Three World Cups for Dempsey, and he scored in all three. The first outing for Dempsey came in the form of the 2006 FIFA World Cup, hosted by Germany. Despite the team's poor showing, for his first appearance on the world's biggest stage, Dempsey got a goal against Ghana in group E.

The 2010 FIFA World Cup saw Dempsey score against England, a dribbler of a kick from around outside the box that rolled helplessly toward the Brit-keeper, who let the ball trickle by his reach into the goal. The game ended 1-1. In the big last-minute hurrah against Algeria to get the US into the round of 16, Dempsey went in with the keeper, bravely, reaching out, trying to get a goal, similar to how Rivaldo and Bryan Robson might, causing the ball to carom out in front for just a second where Donovan guided it home. This was a great moment in the history of US soccer, despite not getting past new foe Ghana in the round of 16.

The 2014 FIFA World Cup rolled around—hosted by Brazil—and finally the USMNT got revenge over Ghana with a 2-1 win of its own. Dempsey scored early as the team got the win. In the next game against Portugal, a 2-2 tie, Dempsey—yet again—produced a goal. The round of 16 loss to Belgium was to be Dempsey's last chance at World Cup glory.

Toward the end, he was tallying up goals left and right. As everyone knows by now, he ended up tied for first with Donovan, all time, with 57 goals.

One such goal at the tail end of his remarkable career arrived in 2015, in LA–the StubHub Center in Carson, California, to be exact. This was where the LA Galaxy played. The USMNT was in a friendly against mighty Panama. Michael Bradley was on the field with Dempsey. Eventually, as the US broke free, Dempsey scored a goal. The game ended 2–0. Dempsey's was a doozy. By way of a through pass, he broke free into the box and had a one-on-one with the keeper. He wasn't quicker than Donovan, but he was no slouch. He did a scissors-kick fake to the left, with his left foot, then moved the ball to the left with his right foot–thus dribbling past the keeper–and, with a defender on him, tapped it in with his right foot as he fell to the ground. It was one hell of a goal. Perhaps his best. It required timing, quick thinking, skill, and guile. It was a little of Bryan Robson–surging ahead for England–and Brazilian Ronaldo wrapped in one. Exquisite. Formidable. Dempsey.

Dempsey was unique. As the 2006 FIFA World Cup rolled around, his first, Dempsey was ready to make his mark. As an up-and-comer, he was receiving a wide range of attention. Writing for ESPN *soccernet*, Wayne Drehs featured an aspect of Dempsey's story in 2006: "American soccer stars don't grow up in a trailer in their grandparents' backyard in East Texas, learning the game from the Hispanic kids in their neighborhood. They don't grow up playing on dirt fields, kicking rock-hard basketballs with their bare feet while using T-shirts and socks as the outline for goals. And if they do somehow, someway overcome all that to make it to the big time, they don't make a rap video when they get there, sharing their life story in a head-bobbing hip-hop tune for Nike that shows up on BET and becomes the soul of the shoe conglomerate's U.S. World Cup promotional campaign."[101] Welcome to the world of Clint Dempsey.

As of April 11, 2025, Dempsey ranks fourth in most appearances for the national team: 141. In those 141 appearances, he scored 57 goals, tied for first with Landon Donovan. For perspective, Donovan scored 57 goals in 157 appearances. Dempsey scored 57 goals in 141 appearances.

Dempsey was the MLS Rookie of the Year (2004); the Fulham Player of the Season (2010–11, 2011–12); top scorer for Fulham (2010–11, 2011–12); the CONCACAF Gold Cup Top Scorer (2015); US Soccer Player of the Year

(2007, 2011, 2012); Honda Player of the Year (2006, 2011, 2012); and MLS All-Star (2005, 2014, 2015, 2016); MLS Comeback Player of the Year (2017); and in 2022, he reached the National Soccer Hall of Fame.

Yet, all the same, one list may stand out a bit more. The IFFHS§§§§§§ listed the All-Time Men's Dream Team (2021). The top players of all time include:

Goalkeeper:
Lev Yashin (USSR)

Defenders:
Cafu (Brazil)
Franz Beckenbauer (W. Germany)
Franco Baresi (Italy)
Paolo Maldini (Italy)

Midfielders:
Xavi (Spain)
Diego Maradona (Argentina)
Johan Cruyff (Netherlands)

Forwards:
Cristiano Ronaldo (Portugal)
Pelé (Brazil)
Messi (Argentina)

There's also a list for Europe, South America, Africa, Asia, and even Oceania (a lot of New Zealand guys). Then there's the CONCACAF list of all-time greats. There's only one US player on that roster. The top CONCACAF players of all time include:

Goalkeeper:
Antonio Carbajal (Mexico)

Defenders:
Carlos Salcedo (Mexico)
Claudio Suarez (Mexico)
Rafael Marquez (Mexico)

Forwards:
Julio Dely Valdes (Panama)
Hugo Sanchez (Mexico)

Clint Dempsey (United States)

Midfielders:
Andres Guardado (Mexico)
Bryan Ruiz (Costa Rica)
Raul Cardenas (Mexico)
Luis de la Fuente (Mexico)

§§§§§§ International Federation of Football History & Statistics.

73 Chris Wondolowski USMNT: 2011-16

Chris Wondolowski is the most ridiculously underrated soccer forward EVER. While watching San Jose Earthquakes games on local TV, for a time, there was a duo that consisted of Wondolowski and Steven Lenhart. Lenhart—a larger built striker—would stir things up, bumping and grinding with opponents as he approached each game like a man determined to knock defenders around like bowling pins. His physical style of play created opportunities and loose balls around the box in abundance. It was an interesting combination. Regarding Wondo as an individual talent, he always seemed to be in the exact right place to score a goal.

The Athletic reported: "**Alan Gordon, former San Jose teammate:** To be honest, I thought he was the luckiest forward in the entire world. I was blown away by how fortunate the bounces came to him."[102] Coaches often talk of this quality in forwards: "They're always in the right place at the right time." It's a way of saying "the ball just lands right in front of them." Yet, with Wondo, it happened an uncanny amount of times. So how did it land right smack in front of Wondo so often?

First of all, he wasn't the fastest player in the world. In most circles, he'd probably be compared with a turtle. According to former teammates Jason Hernandez and Sam Cronin, *The Athletic* printed:

"**Dad bod Wondo**

Hernandez: On the other side of it, this guy in the gym is an embarrassment.

Cronin: You see him with his shirt off, he just looks like your buddy who's had a real job for 15 years.

Hernandez: This guy walks into the gym, would try to do one pull-up, maybe get half way, and walk out. He does zero. Guy can't touch his toes, he's not flexible, he's not pliable, he's not agile and he's not strong, but he can score."[103]

He had instincts and seized opportunities. As a slower player, he strategically maneuvered himself into those instinctual positions that only he—apparently—was privy to. Technically, coaches can teach positioning around the box, how to put yourself in good positions to succeed, but can they get a player to be as good as Wondo was? That, unfortunately, is something you can't teach. At around 6'0" tall, he had that intangible gift to seize on loose balls, find the right passing lane to receive a pass, and get on the end of crosses like few in the history of US soccer.

Perhaps this is why Wondolowski is still, to this day, the all-time MLS leader in scoring: 171. In second place is Kei Kamara: 146. In third is Landon Donovan: 145.

Born in 1983 in Danville, California, Wondolowski turned out to be the toast of the Bay. It makes sense that someone like Wondolowski emerged from that area as it has a big population with a strong outlet for competition; overall, it's a good soccer area. However, there's a drawback. The Bay Area is so vast, with so much traffic, that it's nearly impossible to play for your club team of choice. In other words, the Wondos of the world can't necessarily play for a club team in the South Bay or North Bay. This would explain why he evidently played for the clubs Diablo Valley Soccer Club and Danville Mustang Soccer Association in the Concord area in the East Bay.

Following a successful run at De La Salle High School in Concord, he played at Chico State before joining the Chico Rooks (2004) where his scoring efforts outweighed games played. He briefly joined the San Jose Earthquakes (2005) before moving to the Houston Dynamo (2006–09). During the time he was listed with the Dynamo, the team won the 2006 and 2007 MLS Cups, though while in Houston, he didn't have quite the goal-frenzy you might expect.

Then it was back to San Jose for part II with the Earthquakes (2009–21) as he went on a thunderous rampage and gathered the lion's share of his record-making MLS goal tally.

With the USMNT, Wondolowski was part of the 2013 CONCACAF Gold Cup championship in which he was a tournament leader with five goals.

He joined Landon Donovan and Gabriel Torres (Panama) who also had five goals each.

He was called up to the 2014 FIFA World Cup squad and contributed in multiple games.

He earned the MLS Golden Boot on two occasions (2010 and 2012), which is impressive in and of itself. In 2012, he won the MLS MVP award. He was an MLS All-Star on numerous occasions, and was part of the MLS 100 goals club.

As the all-time MLS leader in scoring, he gathered 35 caps for the USMNT and scored 11 goals. Not bad.

74 Eddie Johnson USMNT: 2004-14

Eddie Johnson—born in 1984 in Florida—was a 6'0" forward that trained at the IMG Soccer Academy (2000-01). Shortly thereafter, he joined FC Dallas (2001-05) where he played in more than 80 games, with over 15 goals. He moved from there to the Kansas City Wizards (2006-07), and got over 40 games under his belt, with a little over fifteen goals.

Like many US players, he found his way to the open embrace of Fulham (2008-11). In the EPL, he played in over 25 games and found difficulty scoring.

Eventually, after some shuffling around on loan, he landed with the Seattle Sounders (2012-13) in MLS. Back in the US, he registered over 45 games, with just over 20 goals. Johnson wrapped things up professionally with DC United (2014-15) as he played in a little over 35 games, with a handful of goals.

As for the national team, Johnson had success at the youth national level and eventually played his first game with the senior team in 2004 against El Salvador. He scored the first time out and set his sights on more goals. Shortly thereafter, he got a hat-trick against Panama. Over the course of about 10 years, he would score 19 in all. This placed him—as of the writing of this book—ninth in the all-time scoring position for the USMNT. Many of the goals came against fellow CONCACAF opponents. His time with the USMNT crossed over two periods: the New Dawn period and the Breakthrough period. Maybe you haven't heard of him? Well, he was a quieter player that was used during this 2004-14 timespan on some 63 occasions. As time has gone on, his name has somewhat been forgotten in the mix of players that have come since. For a while, he was touted as the next great forward threat for the United States. Yet, during his availability, he was competing with other attacking players that included the likes of McBride, Donovan, Dempsey, Altidore, Ching, and Wolff.

Johnson joined the team for the 2006 FIFA World Cup, hosted by Germany. A few teammates for that experience included Steve Cherundolo,

Eddie Lewis, Clint Dempsey, Claudio Reyna, Gregg Berhalter, Bobby Convey, Landon Donovan, and Brian McBride.

Johnson later competed in the 2007 Copa America. He got a goal against Argentina, a penalty kick.

He was part of the CONCACAF Gold Cup winning teams in 2007 and 2013. In the 2007 tournament, hosted by the United States, Johnson got a goal in the 2–0 victory over Trinidad and Tobago. As for the 2013 tournament, also hosted by the United States, Johnson got a goal in the 5–1 dismantling of El Salvador. In the semis, against Honduras, Johnson put away the first goal in the 3–1 victory; he finished the 2013 adventure with two goals.

All in all, as players go, Johnson earned a position on the scoring list with some of the top talent to wear a US uniform. As new players have been ushered in, he has been lost in the shuffle of mentions on TV, conversations, and the like. Whether you're talking about Brazilians, Argentineans, Germans, Italians, and so on, there's always a time-gap when newer generations take over. Then names like Bruce Murray, Roy Wegerle, Ante Razov, Jovan Kirovski, and Eddie Johnson start to fade. Yet, they still remain as part of this cycle that is the USMNT.

75 Stuart Holden USMNT: 2008-13

Stuart Holden—born in 1985 in Scotland—eventually moved to the Houston area of Texas as a kid and continued playing the world's most popular sport there. After showing early promise in Texas, he played college soccer at renowned Clemson University.

Holden only played at Clemson a short time before he pounced at the opportunity to play abroad, back on home turf, so to speak, for Sunderland in 2005. In the Newcastle area he was physically accosted outside a bar because of his association with Sunderland and damaged an eye socket, an injury that sidelined him for a time. Following this, he injured his ankle. Yikes. Rough start.

He eventually made his way back to the United States and played for Houston Dynamo (2006-09). Holden was one of the penalty kick shooters in the MLS Cup 2006 final against New England. That year, he teamed up with Dwayne De Rosario, Brad Davis, and Brian Ching to win the big one.

In the 2007 season, Holden was part of the crew yet again as the Dynamo won two years in a row.

Holden left Houston after 2009 to join English club Bolton, otherwise known as the Wanderers. From 2010-14, he remained there making quite a name for himself. He played in 30 games, scoring twice. Holden was a quick player, one that was tough, relentless, full of fight, and competitiveness. Due to a knee injury, he was limited in his overall performance. However, his impact on the team was evident as he earned Player of the Year for Bolton. He made a comeback only to have injury complications sideline him yet again.

Yet again, in 2013, when Holden played for the USMNT in World Cup qualifying and the coveted North American CONCACAF Gold Cup, he got injured! This time in the 2013 Gold Cup final "...it was confirmed that Holden had torn his anterior cruciate ligament in his right leg while playing for the United States in the CONCACAF Gold Cup final against Panama on June 29, 2013. In devastating news for Bolton Wanderers fans, it meant Holden would miss the majority of the 2013-14 season,"[104] said *Wikipedia*. However, he kept at it with Bolton: "After another comeback attempt, Holden returned to action in March 2014 in a reserve match vs Everton. In his first match back, his return from injury only lasted 23 minutes. It was later announced that Holden had re-injured the right knee and torn his anterior cruciate ligament for a second time. It required another surgery which would set him back for another six to nine months."[105]

After a brief stint with Sheffield Wednesday, he quit playing in 2014.

His USMNT run lasted from 2008-13. Amidst his series of injuries, he was a substantial help to the squad in midfield. Stu landed a 2008 Beijing Olympics gig that hoisted him up against some of the best in the world. A few teammates on that adventure were Benny Feilhaber, Charlie Davies, Freddy Adu, Maurice Edu, Dax McCarty, Michael Bradley. In group B, Holden scored against Japan for a 1-0 win. Yet, with a win, loss, and tie, the team wasn't moving forward.

Following an injury, Holden was able to join the US in the 2009 Gold Cup where he scored against Grenada in group B. He followed that up with a goal against Haiti. With wins over Grenada and Honduras, along with a tie to Haiti, the US won the group. The US managed to get by Panama in the quarters and Honduras in the semis, only to suffer a serious 5-0 defeat to Mexico in the final. Holden started in the 2009 final, along with Brian Ching and Kyle Beckerman, coached by Bob Bradley. Despite the tough loss, it was a second place finish—not bad at all. As a midfielder, Holden made the All-Tournament Team.

Holden joined the US squad in South Africa for the 2010 FIFA World Cup, earning time against England.

The 2013 Gold Cup was a monumental victory for the USMNT as Holden, Landon Donovan, Chris Wondolowski, and Brek Shea helped bring home the trophy. Along the way, Holden got a goal in the team's group C opening win over Belize—a destructive affair that saw our neighbor's to the south lose by 6-1. The US took it to Cuba in the following match with a score of 4-1. The US defeated Costa Rica by 1-0 to advance out of the group. In the quarters, the US walked all over El Salvador by 5-1. The US earned a 3-1 victory over Honduras in the semis. As for the final, against mighty Panama, the US walked away with a slim 1-0 victory that occurred in front of over 55,000 spectators at Soldier Field, Chicago. That was the fifth Gold Cup title for the US. During the final, he endured one of his multiple injuries. Holden was a piece of the puzzle as a midfielder, which was significant as 2013 would be his last hurrah with the national team.

He found new life after retirement in the press box as a TV broadcaster with ESPN, NBC, and Fox Sports. Typically in the role of color commentator, Holden has brought his wealth of experience to the analytical side of calling games. He and John Strong called the final for the 2018 FIFA World Cup between France and Croatia.

Interestingly, Holden and Steven Nash—the two-time NBA MVP—joined efforts to become owners of RCD Mallorca, the Spanish soccer team. Holden and Nash present their views on the podcast *2 Dads United* illustrating their entertaining ride. As Nash and Holden blend the worlds of basketball and soccer—a good match, in fact—the greater sports world should take notice. As a player that's had a ton of experience—from Scotland, to Houston, England, and the national team—Holden is no stranger to ups and downs. He has overcome injuries on the field, and, perhaps, it's led to an even more interesting life off it.

78 Maurice Edu
USMNT: 2007-14

Where do we start? How about, 46 caps, one goal? Why one goal? As a defensive midfielder, **Maurice Edu** was tasked with holding down the fort in the middle of the field and breaking up plays so that his side could counter and regain possession of the ball. That's what he was good at. Scoring? Ha! That's another man's game, like Wondolowski.

Maurice Edu was born in Fontana, California, and eventually joined the Maryland Terrapins for a college career that took place in the mid-2000s. He graduated to MLS's Toronto FC (2007-08) where he played in over 35 games, with five goals. In 2007, while at Toronto FC, he was the MLS Rookie of the Year. From there, he went to Rangers in Scotland (2008-12) and played many more games, a little over 95, with nine goals. Maurice was at Rangers during the years it took the Scottish Cup (2008-09), and the Scottish League Cup (2009-10, 2010-11). Next on the agenda were Stoke City, Bursaspor, Philadelphia Union, and lastly he was with Bethlehem Steel.

Maurice Edu debuted with the USMNT in 2007, against Switzerland. He was on the 2008 US Olympic squad that competed in China. A few teammates present were Brad Guzan, Michael Bradley, Stuart Holden, Freddy Adu, and Brian McBride. The team had a win, tie, and loss that ended chances to progress.

He was included in the 2010 FIFA World Cup squad. As such, he was part of a goal against Slovenia that was called back by the referee. That tournament was a so-close moment for the US as the team encountered major drama, excitement, and highlight reel fun in the big match against Algeria that turned out to be a 1-0 win. In many ways, that tournament was huge for US soccer at large. It was right around 14 years into MLS—still in its infancy, really. Having said that, the US was slowly warming up to MLS as a league, a thing to watch, something *not* to make fun of. With that momentum in the tank, the USMNT—always knocking on the door of international greatness—was raring to go. When group C concluded, lo and behold, the US found itself atop the group, over England, Slovenia, and Algeria. Then came Ghana in the round of 16 as things came crashing down all around the US squad in a close 2–1 loss. But the upside was that US soccer had received a shot of adrenaline that was felt nationwide.

He's spent time on TV as an analyst in his post-playing career for FOX Sports and Apple TV.

11 Charlie Davies USMNT: 2007-09

Charlie Davies—born in 1986 in New Hampshire—played at Boston College and as a forward he worked his way up the ranks to the USMNT. From 2006 to 2017, he had experience with Westchester Flames, Hammarby (Sweden), Sochaux (France), DC United, Randers (Denmark), New England Revolution, Philadelphia Union, and finally with Bethlehem Steel.

Davies played his first game for the senior USMNT in 2007. He played at the 2007 Copa America hosted by Venezuela. The squad that tournament was coached by Bob Bradley.

Davies was part of the US team at the 2008 Olympics. The group also included Michael Bradley, Maurice Edu, and Stuart Holden.

As for the 2009 FIFA Confederations Cup, in which the US defeated Spain and eventually placed second overall, Davies had a big moment. He and Donovan soared down field, like in a youth drill, with a couple quick passes, until Davies delivered one last pass to Donovan, around the top of the box, which allowed him to score. Sadly, though, Brazil came back to win that game 3-2.

However, the quality the USMNT had received, thanks to the implementation of MLS in 1996, was starting to show across the board by 2009. Bob Bradley, a coach with a keen eye for combination passing, was at the forefront of this progress. The quality of play was getting better, proven by the US defeat of Spain in the semis. So, the USMNT was moving in the right direction. Davies was at the forefront of a new and improved USMNT, as coached by Bob Bradley. It was a team with a confidence and swagger that players like Donovan and Dempsey pushed forward. It was a time when the national team program was substantially benefiting from the implementation of MLS in 1996 and more US players acquiring experience from European clubs.

In that 2009 semifinal defeat of Spain, Davies was among the starters. Davies also scored a goal against Egypt. He was part of a squad that was making noise around the world. Unfortunately, Davies was in an automobile accident around that time, 2009, though he made a comeback and continued playing professionally after that.

All in all, his time with the senior USMNT produced 17 caps, with four goals. Those goals arrived against Trinidad and Tobago, Egypt, Grenada, and Mexico.

After his playing career, Davies entered the realm of broadcasting. In 2023, WBZ News, part of CBS News Boston, wrote: "In addition to his color duties on Revolution radio broadcasts, Davies is now part of the crew on CBS Sports' Golazo Network, a free, 24-hour digital soccer network that officially launched Tuesday morning. It will bring soccer fans unprecedented coverage of soccer from around the world, highlighted by live morning and afternoon shows during the week and exclusive matches."[106] The article noted, "Davies will now spend his mornings on the network's flagship show Morning Footy, chatting about the game he loves with Susannah Collins, Nico Cantor, Alexis Guerreros and Jenny Chiu from 7–9 a.m."[107]

78 Graham Zusi
USMNT: 2012-17

Whatever happened to **Graham Zusi**? As of the writing of this book, he is soon-to-be coaching. A wily veteran, the hard-working, steady, technically sound, soccer smart outside mid player with Sporting Kansas City from 2009–2023.

Prior to joining MLS, the 5'10" winger and right-back—who was born in 1986—is from Longwood, Florida. In college he joined the renowned Maryland Terrapins (2005-08). During that time, Maryland won two NCAA Men's Division I Soccer Championships: 2005 and 2008. He won the NCAA Division I Men's Soccer Tournament Most Outstanding Player Award for Offense in 2008.

He was with the Central Florida Kraze, which didn't last terribly long. Yet, as he become a mainstay with Sporting KC, Zusi made quick work for himself and won the MLS Breakout Player of the Year in 2011. He was part of the MLS Best XI in 2012 and 2013. He's been an MLS All-Star on seven occasions. He won the Sporting Kansas City MVP Award in 2012 and 2013, the MLS top assist getter in 2012, and, perhaps best of all, he won the MLS Cup with Sporting KC in 2013. Under Coach Peter Vermes, Zusi and Matt Besler set Sporting KC apart from the league with stellar play that resulted in high-quality performances.

Not to mention, on three occasions, he's helped win the US Open Cup: 2012, 2015, and 2017.

When Zusi first joined the USMNT, it was in 2012. From that point onward, he gathered up 55 caps, with a substantial five goals to boot. His first cap was against Venezuela. Not long after that, also in 2012, he got his first goal for the US against mighty Panama. As he gathered some World Cup qualifying games under his belt in 2013, Zusi got another goal against Panama and by this time the US was a qualified team, yet the goal—with points as they are—was good news for Mexico. In turn, fans from Mexico supposedly created a plaque that essentially said "Saint Zusi."

In the 2014 FIFA World Cup, Zusi got a couple assists. That venture was coached by German World Cup champion, Jurgen Klinsmann. It was a move by the US to capture respect on the biggest stage in the world, despite its own coach saying the team probably wouldn't win the whole thing. With tension about, Zusi and teammates approached each game as pros working for a common goal: a World Cup trophy for the men. Instead of getting there and hoisting the Cup high into the air, Zusi was part of an effort that laid the groundwork for future generations.

Part of that process, becoming the best in world soccer, is dominating your own backyard. In the case of the United States, that would be the Gold Cup. As an integral part of the USMNT in the 2010s, Zusi helped to shape US soccer. He was part of the ill-fated 2015 CONCACAF Gold Cup. As the USMNT had won the 2013 Gold Cup, there was a chance to win two consecutive cups in a row. Yet, it didn't work out as planned and the result was a fourth-place finish.

And what about the 2017 CONCACAF Gold Cup? Coached by Bruce Arena again, Zusi was there along with teammates Matt Besler, Alejandro Bedoya, Darlington Nagbe, Joe Corona, Michael Bradley, Clint Dempsey, and Jordan Morris. When all was said and done, Zusi made the Gold Cup Best XI that year (alongside teammates Michael Bradley, Omar Gonzalez, Darlington Nagbe, Jozy Altidore, and Jordan Morris).

Things change with coaching. When Bruce Arena was dismissed from coaching the USMNT after not making the 2018 FIFA World Cup, that was essentially curtains for Zusi. Likely considering age, new coaches went in different directions, though, for a few years, he was a solid contributor and helped the team maintain a certain poise in possession. A smart, athletic player, Zusi had an eye for professional play in terms of making the right pass at the right moment.

79 Matt Besler USMNT: 2013-17

Matt Besler—born in 1987 in Overland Park, Kansas—attended Blue Valley West High School, in Kansas, and won a state championship with the team. From there, he went to the University of Notre Dame—one of the top schools in the Midwest—where he excelled as an All-American (and an Academic All-American).

Right down the road, so to speak, from the original headquarters of US soccer, St. Louis, Missouri, Kansas City has also perfected the art of soccer. Kansas City has rivaled St. Louis in high school soccer as the second-best area in the state, with Cape Girardeau coming in a respectable third. With that said, one has to remember that Kansas City has spawned a number of professional soccer teams over the years that include the likes of the Kansas City Spurs, Kansas City Comets, and the Kansas Wiz (later the Wizards and Sporting KC). These teams provided an outlet for young kids from the area, such as Besler, to emulate. In addition, the strong rivalry with St. Louis has only made Kanas City soccer, and for that matter, St. Louis soccer, better for both areas. The cross-state competition has benefited players like Besler over the years. As such, Besler took his talents to one of the elite universities in the Midwest and nation, at large.

Besler finished things up with Notre Dame in 2008. Shortly after Besler left campus, the soccer program won the coveted NCAA Division I men's soccer national championship in 2013. Despite Besler's group not winning the title, he was a standout player. In a team sport where individual players are not greater than the team, he has earned a place as the most noteworthy soccer alum to date. The website at Notre Dame wrote that Besler "has been named to the 2008 National Soccer Coaches Association of America (NSCAA)/adidas Division I All-America first team. Besler becomes the eighth All-American in program history and the fourth to garner first-team honors."[108] Besler distinguished himself there as a top student-athlete: "Last month, Besler copped Academic All-America honors from ESPN the Magazine and the College Sports Information Directors of America (CoSIDA). Besler is the first player in program history to be a first-team All-American and an Academic All-American. He is just the second student-athlete in the history of Notre Dame men's soccer to garner both All-America and Academic All-America honors in the same season."[109] That's saying a lot at Notre Dame, which is a powerhouse academic institution. Following his collegiate career, Besler was quickly gobbled up by MLS.

Where did he land? You guessed it, not far from home: Sporting KC where he'd spend the majority of his impressive professional career. At Kansas City he became teammates with Graham Zusi, thereby creating a firm friendship and working relationship that brought in much success. Not only did Sporting KC win the 2013 MLS Cup, it also won the US Open Cup three times: 2012, 2015, and 2017. All in all, Besler played for Sporting KC from 2009–2020, earning over 290 appearances. Besler wasn't much of a scorer for the light blue squad—many central defenders aren't. Nonetheless, he managed to acquire three goals. Toward the end of his career, he suited up with Austin FC for a bit.

In 2011, he was part of the MLS All-Star team (by way of a fan text message voting system). In 2012, he was honored as the MLS Defender of the Year. He also made the MLS Best XI. Around this time, there was interest from Birmingham City, Southampton, and Queens Park Rangers, yet the Midwest native opted to stay put. In 2013, he was included in the All-Star voting again, by way of fans.

In 2021, he retired from pro soccer after a brief stint with Austin FC.

2013 marked the first time Besler joined the senior USMNT on the field, at the request of Coach Jurgen Klinsmann, in a match against Canada. Baseball, hockey, basketball—Besler could've theoretically succeeded in all of the above. Klinsmann, who saw something special in the athletically built Midwest native, likely inserted Besler into the mix based on commonsense. With soccer, he fit in perfectly with the central defender position—at around 6'0"—as he was tall enough to fight off aerial assaults and low enough to the ground to contend with crafty dribblers trying to inflict damage. Often times, defenders that get over 6'2" are not fleet-footed. The ball skills—trapping, dribbling, passing—escape them, just a tad. Their reaction time isn't quite as succinct as someone like Fabio Cannavaro, who led Italy from defense to a 2006 FIFA World Cup championship with feisty, athletic, defensive ability combined with adept skill in possessing the ball. In terms of possessing the ball, Besler had that Cannavaro-esque quality: his skill was sound, good technique, poised on the ball, he didn't rush things, along with a strong soccer IQ. A perfect option for Klinsmann.

In his brief, yet significant run, Besler attained just over 45 caps, with a goal. He was there for the USMNT in many ways. First off, more often than not, no one marvels over central defenders. A few will make a list like this one, but there are so many midfielders and forwards that steal the show. Marcelo Balboa, Alexi Lalas, Carlos Bocanegra, Tim Ream, are but a few. Yet there's only room for a small handful. Besler was part of the efforts to help get the US into the 2014 FIFA World Cup and he played a crucial role in those qualifying matches.

En route to the 2014 World Cup was the 2013 CONCACAF Gold Cup where Besler was part of the championship run and started in the final against Panama, a 1–0 victory thanks to a goal from Brek Shea. A few other starters that game included Nick Rimando, Kyle Beckerman, Stuart Holden, Joe Corona, and Landon Donovan. Incidentally, 2013 was a huge year for Besler: an MLS Cup championship, a debut with the USMNT, and a Gold Cup championship.

The Midwest defensive stopper that decided to represent his hometown of Sporting KC was called up to the 2014 World Cup in Brazil to represent the US. His playing style and presence in defense led the squad to the round of 16 where it lost to Belgium. After strong performances, he reportedly was again sought by clubs—Freiburg (Germany), Fulham, Sunderland—and it made the news: "After a successful World Cup campaign with the United States national team, centre-back Matt Besler is a wanted man,"[110] said Bleacher Report. "According to Sam McDowell of *The Kansas City Star*, professional clubs from around the world are interested in obtaining the Sporting Kansas City player"[111] yet Besler opted to remain in the Midwest where he was raised.

That's saying something about MLS. Say what you will, and plenty have knocked the late to the party league that only took flight in 1996, but if a key player is opting to pass on the alluring glory of European soccer for MLS, then, on that front, good things are happening in US soccer. In fact, that's part of the light at the end of the tunnel that the USMNT needs to complete its quest to win a World Cup.

This is part of the two-sided argument. On one hand, a successful MLS will yield success with the national team, but on the other, you need top US players to compete with the best in Europe to come back home and make the national team stronger. Essentially both points of view are correct. You need a little of both. You need top US talent—marquee names—to maintain a domestic professional league. If everyone jumps ship for Europe then what are you left with? Besler staying with Sporting KC, when he had offers abroad, speaks volumes.

Good things came at the tail end of Besler's run with the USMNT as the 2017 CONCACAF Gold Cup rolled around. He got the start—alongside fellow Sporting KC teammate Graham Zusi—in the opening 1-1 draw with Panama. By the end of group play, Besler started again in the 3-0 knockout punch to notorious Nicaragua. The US stepped past El Salvador 2-0 in the quarters. That set up a semifinal encounter with Costa Rica whereby Besler started—alongside Paul Arriola, Darlington Nagbe, and Michael Bradley—as the US navigated a 2-0 victory. The final, against a talented Jamaican team, was played in Santa Clara before a little over 60,000 spectators. Besler started with teammates Graham Zusi, Michael Bradley, Darlington Nagbe, and Jordan Morris as Bruce Arena led from the sidelines. The referee? The great Walter Lopez of Guatemala. The result, a 2-1 triumph, was the sixth overall Gold Cup championship for the US.

A perfect sendoff tournament for the end of the road. Besler played his last soccer game for the USMNT in 2017.

80 Michael Bradley USMNT: 2006-19

Slate published a revealing piece in 2016 that goes through the cycles of **Michael Bradley's** career. At first it publicly flogged Michael Bradley—with critical analysis including "poor performance" and "nepotism"—while recanting, if you will, at the end by saying, "We love you no matter what."[112] It's not the first story about Michael Bradley, but it is symbolic of how people viewed him. Basically, what it revealed was that if you're the son of the national team coach you're going to be spoken down to but accepted. However you view it, the article illustrates some of the ups and downs Bradley went through as the coach's son. For starters, the title of the article was "Michael Bradley Will Always be the Coach's Son." Bob Bradley—a serious guy with an eye for the game—played at Princeton, and eventually (from 1981 onward) coached Ohio University, Virginia (as an assistant), Princeton, United States U23 (as an assistant), Chicago Fire, New York/New Jersey MetroStars, Chivas USA, United States U23, and then the USMNT (2006-11). The point here is pretty solid: that's the world Michael grew up in. The *Slate* piece focused on the 2016 Copa America which the US was in at the time. Michael was about ten years into his run with the national team.

"As has been the case for the past several years, the team's success depends on one man: central midfielder Michael Bradley."[113] It added, "Opponents know the easiest way to beat the U.S. is to take its captain out of the game."[114] That would be an appropriate strategy. "In the United States' first two games, a swarm of opposing midfielders and backchecking attackers harried Bradley every time he touched the ball. In the 2-0 loss to Colombia, he coped poorly with all that pressure. With Jermaine Jones tasked with providing defensive cover on the left flank, Bradley completed just 77 percent of his passes and turned the ball over in dangerous spots a couple of times, including in the build-up to the handball that led to Colombia's second goal. His poor performance set off a new round of hand-wringing over his partnership with Jones and his ability to handle that pressure."[115]

"This is hardly a new phenomenon. Bradley is our national coach's son, the player we attach our hopes and dreams to. That's how he entered the public consciousness, and that perception has colored his entire career, even as his role and our expectations for him have shifted."[116]

"Bradley was drafted out of high school by Major League Soccer's New York/New Jersey MetroStars, a team coached by his father, Bob Bradley. He earned his first start for the US men's national team in 2006 at age 19, again with Bob as the coach. You can't play high-level sports for your father even once without someone crying nepotism, but Michael played his way through doubts about his ability only to find doubts about his maturity arise in their place."[117]

The article goes on to point out his physical play and resulting cards, from time to time. One thing you can say about Bradley: he had an eye for tackles. Perhaps it wasn't as blatant as Vinnie Jones, but Bradley anticipated tackles well and got stuck in. That's the key: anticipation. A good tackler anticipates; a bad tackler reacts. His keen eye for seeing a play develop allowed him to anticipate tackles and break up plays. This, in part, was due to his dad's elaborate playing and coaching background, and, hence, Michael being raised in that world.

He might not have been the quickest or fastest on the field, but like Dempsey, he made up for it. Bradley was a physically fit player that, seemingly, could run all day. What's more, he had an eye for passing. In particular, short passing. He was a team player that relied on the passing game as opposed to dribbling. As for the latter, dribbling, he was never accused of being Garrincha. His dribbling was more like Pirlo's—side to side, in order to get another pass unleashed. One thing in his arsenal that was quite obvious was a cannon of a shot. He seemed to let it fly earlier in his time with the national team and as things progressed it was not used quite as often. Nonetheless, his shot was often kept low, about knee height, and it went straight with authority—a well-driven ball. The type a coach would be proud of.

Bradley—born in 1987—moved with the family based on his dad's coaching assignments, be it New Jersey when he coached Princeton or Chicago when he coached the Chicago Fire. Eventually, Michael went to the United States U-17 Men's National Team Residency Program that was located in Bradenton, Florida, in the early 2000s. That led to the MetroStars (2004–05), Heerenveen (2006–08), Borussia Monchengladbach (2008–11), Aston Villa (2011), Chievo (2011–12), Roma (2012–14), and lastly, Toronto FC (2014–23). At Toronto, he spent the most time and gathered over 255 appearances, with just over 15 goals. While at Heerenveen, in far fewer games, some 55, he evidently scored 15 goals. That would be proof that in his early years he was shooting for goal more and then later on, as he aged, he was seemingly going for goal less.

Bradley debuted with the USMNT in 2006 and in 2007 he was given the US Soccer Young Male Player of the Year award. From 2006–11, his dad was the USMNT coach. There were doubters early on, as the *Slate* article suggested, though Bradley earned some respect in a 2-0 defeat over Mexico—which took place in 2009 in Columbus, Ohio—where he scored both goals.

All in all, Bradley's US goals arrived against Switzerland, Barbados, Trinidad and Tobago, Mexico, Egypt, Costa Rica, Slovenia, Mexico, Scotland, Russia, Panama, Panama (two different occasions), Jamaica, Honduras, and Mexico (again).

Michael led the USMNT through two World Cups: 2010 and 2014. So where did his talent come from?

Michael comes from an athletic family. His dad, of course, played at Princeton. His dad's younger brother, Scott, was a Major League Baseball catcher for the New York Yankees, Chicago White Sox, Seattle Mariners (where he spent the majority of his career), and the Cincinnati Reds. Following his playing days, he ended up coaching the baseball team at Princeton (where brother Bob had previously coached the soccer team).

Michael was certainly a hard worker. He was always, so it would seem, in top shape. Another aspect of his game included his short passing prowess. It would seem that during the era of dominance that Barcelona, and, hence, Spain's national team, displayed (circa 2008–12), Michael and his father Bob were likely taking notes. Michael's attention to detail in passing was apparent around this time, and after, in little moments here and there where his unselfish team-oriented approach was on full display as he found moments to have simple interchanges with fellow players. Over the years, fans around the world, who enjoyed Spain's national team, coined this type of interchange *tiki-taka*. In essence, it's passing the ball right back to the player that just passed to you. It was, is, and always will be quite effective. After all, Spain won the 2008 Euro, 2010 FIFA World Cup, and 2012 Euro with that style of play. Teams must first master that style and then move onto free-flowing soccer if they really want to succeed. For the most part, Michael always had an idea with his passes. It was a well-coached approach to the game: always with an eye for passing and making others look better.

He won the MLS Cup with Toronto FC in 2017, along with the Supporters' Shield. He also won the Canadian Championship in 2016, 2017, 2018, and 2020. He was an MLS All-Star in 2014, 2015, and 2017.

Bradley was a member of the USMNT that won the CONCACAF Gold Cup in 2007 and 2017. In 2017, he won the Gold Cup Golden Ball award. He was named to the CONCACAF Men's Best XI in 2015 and 2018. The IFFHS put together a CONCACAF Team of the Decade (2011-2020) that included Bradley.

In 2015, Bradley was honored with the US Soccer Player of the Year award. Additionally, in 2015, which turned out to be a big year for Bradley, he won the Fútbol de Primera Player of the Year.

Though the FIFA World Cup championship was out of reach, the CONCACAF Gold Cup—North America's crème dele crème of talent—was captured on two occasions by Bradley. Bradley—who currently ranks third all time in caps, with 151—was such a player. A coach's son from the beginning that reached the highest levels of the game. Will he someday succeed his dad as the coach of the USMNT? There are many names in that pot, as of right now: Peter Vermes, Caleb Porter, Matt Besler, Shane Stay (just checking if you're paying attention—anything's possible), Graham Zusi, and maybe Jordan Morris, to name a few. Bradley's got a head start. As a former captain of the USMNT, he quickly became an assistant coach at Stabaek (Norway), under the auspices of head coach Bob Bradley.

81 Tim Ream USMNT: 2010-present

Tim Ream—born in 1987 in St. Louis, Missouri—has been used, to the team's detriment, at outside back. Center back is where he should be. What team, that is? The USMNT team, of course. To his credit, he could handle the outside back position. However, for ultimate usage, Ream is a perfect center back as he brings to the table notable traits: he's 6'0" tall (a preference for most coaches in that position to help fend off crosses and set pieces), he's highly skilled, he has a phenomenal soccer IQ, he reads the game well, he understands possession (yet another rarity in that position), and, perhaps most important of all, he wants the ball back after he passes it.

The body language of defenders, as to whether or not they actually want the ball back, is very telling. Often, if they have good technique, they'll want the ball back because *they have good technique*—pretty simple—and with this comes a liking of the ball because they want to show off their good technique.

As a defender, you have to want the ball back not just when you're wide open and no one's around you but also when you are tightly guarded! Possession in traffic is not for the weak. Only a few can survive under these harsh circumstances. It takes skill, knowledge, confidence, an idea of where to go with the ball, quick decision making.

What's more, in each game the players with the most touches on the ball are often defenders! One might think it would be center mids—and that makes total sense—but nope, the answer is defenders. This is why defenders are so important. They're not just there to stop the other team; they get the offense into gear.

Defenders are crucial in a team's development throughout the course of many games. Take, for instance, Spain winning the Triple: the 2008 Euro, the 2010 FIFA World Cup, and the 2012 Euro. Never been done before. Spain achieved this with a multitude of threats on the field, yet at its core there were defenders that had skill, great soccer IQ, and a desire to get the ball back after passing it off. Ream fits in. He's that guy. He's a solid player with any team.

In fact, Ream fits in so much that he's been captain of the USMNT and of Fulham. The captaining of the USMNT is impressive in and of itself, yet the other one might be more impressive, actually. A player from the US became captain of a major team in the EPL? Yes, Ream is so good that an English team (a place that has long dismissed US soccer players) appointed a Yank to be its captain. Absolutely amazing.

A knock on Ream would be he doesn't have out and out speed. Landon Donovan he is not. Yet he's fast enough. He leads a team with natural ability, skill, and a top-level knack for distribution.

His journey started in the very northside of St. Louis, northwest to be exact, where he attended St. Dominic High School (where he was part of a state championship), played for famed club Scott Gallagher (where he was part of two national club championships), and attended legendary St. Louis University (a college that, to date, is number one in the US for NCAA Division I championships in soccer: 10).

From SLU, the mighty mighty Billikens, he went to Chicago Fire Premier, New York Red Bulls, Bolton Wanderers, and Fulham. Fulham's been very friendly to US talent over years—Brian McBride, Clint Dempsey—so why should anyone think a move to this team is a big deal? Considering it's the EPL, considering the haughty way that Englishmen have looked at US players over the years: it's a big deal to land there and then become captain. What's more, Ream ingratiated himself to the fan base as a solid performer with over 275 games under his belt.

In 2010, Ream made his debut with the USMNT and saw his way through a somewhat long list of coaches—Bradley, Klinsmann, Arena, Berhalter, Pochettino—where he bounced around from outside back to center back and to the surprise of many, started in the opening match of the 2022 FIFA World Cup. Ream, in the opinion of many, should've been a perennial starter at center back yet found himself playing musical chairs with the latter and outside back. During qualifiers leading up to the 2022 FIFA World Cup, it was unclear if Ream, then a veteran, would be part of the team and he ends up being a starter?! To the relief of US fans that prefer to see a possession-oriented approach to the game, this finally happened. He started in all group B matches—versus Wales, England, and Iran—where the US placed second. For the most part, he was paired up with Walker Zimmerman. As for the round of 16 game against Netherlands, he and Zimmerman were the central defenders yet again, though things went south with a 3-1 loss in Khalifa International Stadium in front of over 44,000 fans.

Defenders often get overlooked. Ream has been in the role of starter, back-up, and team leader for quite a while, staying optimistic and resilient.

Ream's leadership as captain was on full display in a game against Trinidad and Tobago when teammate Dest went ballistic. According to *USA TODAY*, "Dest was shown a red card in the 39th minute after frustrations about officiating led to him kicking the ball towards the stands and shouting at the referee as his teammates desperately tried to calm the PSV defender down."[118] During moments like this, true character is tested. Ream was seen herding Dest on the field, ostensibly urging him to calm down. "Though the USMNT was already playing an uninspired match, the team was up 1-0 at the time. Being forced to play a man down changed the entire dynamic of the game, and Trinidad responded with two unanswered goals. While the USMNT did hold on to the aggregate advantage, the players were visibly livid with Dest after the match."[119] Typically, captains have natural statesmanlike qualities. "Captain Tim Ream didn't disclose what the players said to Dest in the locker room, but he didn't hold back on his disappointment with Dest in the postgame press conference. You almost never see a player speak about a teammate like this, and in Ream's case, he was totally justified for it."[120]

For a player that's been captain of the USMNT and Fulham, he's come a long way since Scott Gallagher in St. Louis. Additionally, he's been the Player of the Year for Bolton Wanderers (2013-14 and 2014-15); and the Player of the Year for Fulham (2017-18). As of 2024, he has joined MLS side Charlotte FC. As far as central defenders go: Ream is a guide stone for future US players in that position.

82 Freddy Adu USMNT: 2006-11

How can you not place **Freddy Adu** on this list? Sure, he fizzled out. Sure, his lofty USMNT expectations were not met. He didn't win a World Cup. He wasn't the lead player. He wasn't this, he wasn't that. But the point is: He earned a place on this list largely because of his unique story, the 14-year-old pro, his electric talent, and his presence in a big game back in 2011.

Freddy was a creative type whose defense was *not* something you'd call actively engaged. How about offense? If you saw Freddy Adu on the move you would probably ask, "Who's that?" Highlights of Adu are jaw-dropping. There are moments where you see why Pelé endorsed his rise to fame. In 2004, it was all the rage: the 14-year-old pro! Whoever heard of such a thing?

Inevitably, the conspiracy theory of his age came up. Reportedly, he was born in 1989. Some, like Mark Zeigler at *The San Diego Union-Tribune*, questioned his actual age. Some have suggested Adu's age was smoothed over when his family arrived in the US from Ghana. Some parents in the US do actually hold their kids back for sports like football, so they'll have a year advantage—physically—when it comes to competition, increasing the chances of potential scholarship offers. But there's never been any evidence that his birth certificate was altered, so it's all just rumors and conjecture.

He was lightning quick, fast, and, as a player, he always seemed a little wiser than your average 14-year-old. There was a maturity about him that had adult qualities—like he was just toying around with everyone.

Then as he got older, people began to suggest *he was not as dominant as people thought he might be*. Professionally, he went from team to team—his career was laughed at. Adu-mania, which began in 2004, seemed to be a thing of the past.

In 2010, the story was still going on, still being pursued. Mark Zeigler of *The San Diego Union-Tribune* wrote: "Maybe it is time to worry about why Adu hasn't become what he was supposed to be, or even close to it."[121] Many shared this sentiment. "He is 20 now and headed for his sixth pro club in seven years, meaning we can no longer pass off his rapidly spiraling career to mere youth and inexperience. Instead, we are left with two basic explanations: 1. He has crumbled under the weight of unrealistic expectations, or 2. he's not how old he says he is.

Of the two, sadly, the latter is becoming more plausible with each passing year. If Adu was indeed 14 when he made his MLS debut in 2004 (and became the youngest pro athlete in a US team sport in more than a century), he would hit a major growth spurt in his mid-teens. And if he was that good as a true 14-year-old, his natural arc of improvement in his late teens would propel him into the elite of global soccer,"[122] and then Zeigler said, "Neither happened."[123]

In my opinion, both of those assertions are flawed. For starters: You don't necessarily have to experience a rapid growth spurt in your mid-teens. Some people grow early and that's that. I knew players when I was around 14 that had grown early, were built like adults at around 5'7" and then when you saw them a few years later not much had changed. On top of that: the "natural arc of improvement" is misleading. A youth star doesn't necessarily keep improving with each year, scoring bicycle kicks each game like some goal-scoring superhero from another planet. There are plenty of youth players that have reached a ceiling of excellence early and cannot go past that later on when they're 25 because it is the ceiling.

Let's continue with *The San Diego Union-Tribune* piece. "A *Sports Illustrated* story from 2003, when Adu was 13, says he was 5-feet-8, 140 pounds. His current size at age 20 as listed on US soccer's website: 5–8, 140."[124] Zeigler pointed out: "Adu also hasn't appreciably improved as a soccer player, certainly not at the expected rate of someone with a birth certificate that says June 2, 1989. Forward Jozy Altidore plays in the English Premier League, commanded a $10 million transfer fee to Europe and is a projected U.S. starter at the 2010 World Cup, and is five months younger."[125] The Altidore comparison is key as, essentially, Adu lost out to Altidore as the top attacking choice—alongside Donovan and Dempsey—for the USMNT.

In terms of birth certificates, Zeigler added: "Adu was born in Ghana, among the nations most often accused of fudging birth certificates for international youth tournaments. Four times in the 1990s, Ghana reached the final of the under-17 World Cup with what opposing coaches insisted was closer to an under-27 roster. African players privately talk about having two ages—their real age and their considerably more youthful 'football age.' There never was any real proof, of course, except for the anecdotal evidence that came years later, when generations of youth stars never achieved the same success as pros,"[126] said Zeigler.

Personally, I always thought Freddy got a raw deal with the national team. The powers that be went with Altidore, a brick house, instead of the fleet-footed, creative-minded, Adu. The combination of Donovan, Dempsey, and Adu—which was showcased in 2011—could've and probably would've been a successful combination over the long haul.

The 2011 moment for Adu was quite epic: The CONCACAF Gold Cup final. He was part of the play leading up to two goals for the US against Mexico at the Rose Bowl, a packed house. The team lost 4-2 that day. Bob Bradley thought highly enough of his talents to include him on such a grand stage.

Outside of all his "age accusations" he was a quality player; one that was perhaps misunderstood by just about every team he bounced around with. It wasn't meant to be. His senior USMNT career (2006-11) amounted to 17 caps and two goals. Yet, Adu walked away as one of the most well-known USMNT players to wear a jersey, but maybe for all the wrong reasons.

83 Jozy Altidore USMNT: 2007-19

Jozy Altidore—born in 1989 in New Jersey—grew up in Florida and joined the IMG Soccer Academy (Bradenton, Florida) from approximately 2004-06. His training there helped lend to his arrival in MLS.

In 2006, Altidore signed with the New York Red Bulls and stayed with the team until 2008, playing just over 35 games with 15 goals. He hopped from MLS to Villarreal (2008-11) where he had nine games and one goal. There were a few loans, including to Hull City (2009-10), where he had 28 games and one goal; and Bursaspor (2011), 12 games, one goal. When he joined AZ (2011-13) things changed, abruptly, and he acquired just over 65 games with 39 goals. From there he made an ill-fated move to Sunderland (2013-15) that ended with 42 games, one goal.

He found a path back to MLS in the form of Toronto FC (2015-21). He played a little over 135 games, with just over 60 goals.

During 2022-23, he switched to the New England Revolution where he played just over 25 games, two goals. During that time, on loan, he had a short jaunt at Puebla where he gained some six appearances, two goals.

Altidore was never the fastest around. Instead, he used his frame to body opponents off the ball rather than speed by them. What else did he have? There was a cannon of a shot—displayed against Spain in the surprise 2009 FIFA Confederations Cup semifinal win—waiting to be unleashed. Essentially, if Altidore got a little room around the box, his shot was deadly.

Around the time he gathered up some 115 caps (2007-19), the USMNT overall passing structure had improved leaps and bounds from previous decades. This was thanks to the implementation of MLS in 1996 whereby USMNT players had a firm home base to operate from and hone their skills. In doing so, the gradual improvement of possession on the national team greatly improved. When Bob Bradley took office around 2007, as national team coach, the passing schemes improved even more. Hence, the quality of chances on goal improved significantly when Altidore took the field as a number 9 for the national team. Similar to AZ, where Eredivisie passing reigns supreme as an example around the world, the USMNT was clicking in the realm of passing like never before.

His 115 caps currently make him number nine all time for the USMNT. His 42 goals with the national team currently rank him third all time for the USMNT. He scored against 12 non-CONCACAF opponents, an impressive list that includes Spain, Turkey, Poland, Slovenia, Germany, Bosnia and Herzegovina, Nigeria, Colombia, Chile, Denmark, Peru, and Iceland. The rest were CONCACAF opponents.

During his time at AZ, the team won the KNVB Cup (2012–13). With Toronto FC, Altidore was part of the MLS Cup (2017) and Supporters' Shield (2017). During the 2017 MLS Cup title run, Altidore took home the MLS Cup MVP Award. In addition, he was part of the Canadian Championship runs (2016, 2017, and 2018). He won the US Soccer Young Male Player of the Year (2006). He won the US Soccer Player of the Year award (2013, 2016). He was an MLS All-Star (2015, 2017).

In World Cup competition, Altidore joined the US for the 2010 and 2014 tournaments. Altidore was part of the USMNT's 2017 CONCACAF Gold Cup championship conquest. As part of that experience, he was named to the CONCACAF Gold Cup Best XI.

Altidore, perhaps the greatest US forward ever or just a guy with big biceps? You be the judge. Whatever the case may be, he got very high in the USMNT goal count.

84 Darlington Nagbe USMNT: 2015-18

Darlington Nagbe: NCAA champion, Hermann Trophy winner, three-time MLS Cup champion, MLS All-Star, 2017 Gold Cup champion, 2017 Gold Cup Best XI, and one of the most technically sound midfielders in USMNT history!

When Berhalter took over as national team coach, it became noticeable to many people that a player was missing: Nagbe. Just one player won't win or lose a World Cup, Gold Cup, or any cup, right? In soccer, just one player makes a huge difference. Nagbe was the playmaker; he was never going to take over a game with pure explosiveness but he would set everything up, pass by pass—a possession master. The guy you can't get the ball from in keep-away drills.

Is Nagbe the best passing midfielder the USMNT has ever had? It's hard to argue against that. And he wasn't on the 2022 World Cup roster?! He wasn't even on the qualification roster! Just like when Taylor Twellman, who won the 2005 MLS MVP award, was mysteriously left off the US roster for the 2006 FIFA World Cup, Nagbe was excluded from the 2022 World Cup.

Darlington Nagbe—born in 1990 in Liberia—is the son of Joe Nagbe (a soccer player from Liberia). Eventually, with strife in the nation, his family moved to the Cleveland, Ohio, area. With youth success in the ODP developmental program of US soccer, Nagbe found his way to the University of Akron (Ohio)—a little known soccer powerhouse. Nagbe, who was coached by Caleb Porter at the University of Akron, won the NCAA Championship (2010). In the same year, he won the Hermann Trophy (aka, the best college player in the country).

This partnership proved successful. At both collegiate and pro levels it was almost unstoppable. Again with Caleb Porter as coach, Nagbe won the MLS Cup with the Portland Timbers (2015). Nagbe won an MLS Cup with Atlanta United (2018). Then, a short time later, he won another MLS Cup with Columbus Crew (2020). That cup, back in Ohio, he won with Caleb Porter—yet again. Nagbe won another MLS Cup with Columbus Crew in 2023.

Nage was honored with the MLS Goal of the Year on a couple occasions (2011 and 2020). He also won the MLS Fair Play Award (2013, 2015, and 2019). He was an MLS All-Star multiple times (2016, 2022, 2024).

His touch on the ball and soccer IQ—that is, who to pass to and when—were reminiscent of Chad Deering, without the perceived arrogance. Nagbe was mechanical and robotically elegant. When it comes to possession soccer, look no further—he was one of the best.

It seemed like he was destined for greatness with the USMNT—an all-time great. When he became a citizen in 2015, it looked like maybe his appointment with the national team was just getting started. And it was. He played his first game for the United States in 2015. For a time, he was one of the best center mids in CONCACAF, alongside Guardado and Herrera from Mexico. Then it ended, rather abruptly, one might say, in 2018.

With 25 caps and one goal, conjecture would suggest Berhalter went in another direction. There are reports that Nagbe declined call ups or perhaps Berhalter made it clear, somehow, someway, that Nagbe's time was up. Maybe Nagbe was tired of the travel and wanted to spend more time with his family. It seems like, if Berhalter really wanted Nagbe, he could've lured him in with the prospects of playing in the 2022 FIFA World Cup. Where did he go and why? It remains a mystery that has never been solved.

Berhalter had a stamp that he wanted to put on the game. No one was saying that Nagbe was going to singlehandedly drag the USMNT across the finish line and win the 2022 FIFA World Cup, in which the team finished with a disjointed loss in the round of 16. No one is saying that. There are always talented options for a national team. But when it comes to weird situations, and when you look on paper at everything that Nagbe accomplished before that World Cup, it brings up questions of why Berhalter and Nagbe did not unite to conquer the 2022 FIFA World Cup.

85 Brek Shea USMNT: 2010-15

When you come across as the offspring of Nordic Gods, sent down to earth—Texas, to be exact—for the purposes of soccer, chances are you might turn pro directly out of high school. That's what happened with the left mid and left-back, **Brek Shea**, from College Station, Texas. He went to Bolton. That's right, Bolton for soccer. From a stellar record in Texas, to the IMG Academy in Bradenton, Florida (2005-07), and Bolton, Shea excelled. "While in school in Texas, Shea won four consecutive state championships playing for the Texans SC youth soccer organization in Houston, Texas. He attended US Soccer's youth residency program, and later went to train with Bolton Wanderers in England in October 2007,"[127] said *Wikipedia*.

The 6'3" Brek Shea—born in 1990—had a knack. Plain and simple. There was something about that guy that gave you a feeling something on the field was going to happen. Born to play, Shea made good with his larger frame, long legs, and ballerina-like feet. He was coordinated as hell—a complete nightmare for wingers going against him. He was muscular and meant for a wide receiver position in football, the passion of his home state, but he chose otherwise. Instead of running up and down the gridiron, he floated back and forth with the best of them on a slightly larger pitch that became his home away from home.

The power of his arsenal of tricks lay in using **quickness** to overwhelm opponents offensively and defensively, **skill** to outwit them, **body presence** to gain advantages in one-v-one situations, **strength** to overpower forwards trying to get past him, and **soccer smarts** to connect with teammates in constructive ways to move the ball around in dangerous positions.

He joined FC Dallas in 2008 and ended up playing the majority of his professional games there. In total, he appeared in over 95 matches, with 19 goals. His time in Dallas ended in 2012 as he ventured overseas with brief stops at Stoke City, Barnsley, and Birmingham City. He returned to the US in 2015 as he joined Orlando City in a newfound effort at MLS competition.

He spent about two years in Orlando, playing alongside Kaka, before moving onto the Vancouver Whitecaps (2017-18). In 2019, he moved to Atlanta United and after a year he found a home with Inter Miami (2020-22).

He made the 2011 MLS All-Star team and MLS Best XI. In addition, he was named the US Soccer Young Male Player of the Year in 2011. After a year like that it was thought—by many—that Shea would be able to play on the senior USMNT at any time and place of his choosing. Shea's senior national team career began with playing time in 2010 and ran through 2015, where he gathered just over 30 caps, with four goals.

He had a legendary run at the 2013 CONCACAF Gold Cup where he put home the 1-0 game-winner in a critical match against Costa Rica for the last game in group C. The US won that group and moved into the quarters where it defeated El Salvador 5-1, a rout. Following a 2-1 US victory over Honduras in the semis, it was onward to the final match in Chicago. Awaiting the team was Panama and a little over 55,000 fans at Soldier Field. On July 28, 2013, Shea took center stage and put away the 1-0 game-winner for the title. That was the fifth Gold Cup title for the US.

These were two of his overall four goals for the team during his career—two big goals that came at the right time. Shea's goals for the USMNT came against Costa Rica, Panama, Chile, and Switzerland. For a defender, that's a pretty good result.

His first goal against Costa Rica, came off a brilliant assist from Landon Donovan. A through ball was sent down the line for Donovan, a little chip that bounced, and on his first touch he volleyed it across the field, right into space, at the top of the box, for Shea to run onto, trap it, and place it past the keeper.

The one against Chile was a cracker. In true Brek Shea top-level form, he took a bouncing ball down the left wing, which took him into the left side of the box and drilled a line-drive, about hip height, to the far corner—no chance for the keeper. Clinical, powerful, elite, forceful, first-rate.

His goal against Switzerland was a deadly direct free-kick with his left foot, taken a little ways outside the top right portion of the box. Basically, on a rope, the ball goes in. Just over the wall, well-driven, into the near right-hand corner. About midway up, just a bit under the bar, it smashed into the back of the net–the net makes a noise, that familiar noise of a ball crashing into the goal on a training ground...for a keeper, it's the sound of defeat.

Off the field, Shea has a passion for art as an avid painter. In terms of outside defenders that you'd want on your USMNT starting XI: how can you say no to Shea? He was one of a kind. As a defensive artist, he had the ability out wide to shut down any opponent and his offensive capability–skill and the ability to score–was phenomenal.

86 Bobby Wood
USMNT: 2013-18

Bobby Wood—born in 1992—emerged from an unlikely soccer-state: Hawaii. The 5'11" striker went against all odds, an island prospect, and shook the world with his ability. Another Hawaiian, Brian Ching, managed to get out of the Pacific realm as he surged forward on the USMNT (2003-10), earning 45 caps and 11 goals. Ching—born in 1978—helped pave the way for Bobby Wood. Hawaii, a laid-back place, better known for tennis, swimming, and surfing, is so far removed from the mainland—approximately 2,471 miles from Hawaii to California—that players often get overlooked.

When Wood moved from Hawaii to California—circa 2005—it was a good move. Still in his teens, Wood joined the youth club of 1860 Munich in Germany and made his debut in 2011. He'd eventually play for the German team from 2011-15, attaining around 50 appearances, with three goals. He made a switch in 2015 to Union Berlin where his goal-scoring touch was more prominent with a little over 15 to his name. Wood was picked up by Hamburger SV and played in over 70 games with eight goals. During his time with Hamburger SV (2016-21) he was on loan to Hannover 96.

He eventually flew back to the States for a uniform with Real Salt Lake (2021-22), before a transfer to the New England Revolution (2023).

Wood arrived in a USMNT senior kit in 2013. In 2015, his first goal on the big stage arrived in the first of a unique pair of victories. The US turned a lot of heads on a European tour in which it defeated Netherlands 4-3 and Wood got the game-winner. Shortly thereafter, Wood got another game-winner against Germany in a 2-1 upset. The pair of wins—over Netherlands and Germany—came one after the other, like dominoes. People were taking the US seriously, after all. When Wood led the charge with the back-to-back winners over top world powers, pulling the rug out from under them, it was a nice reminder that US soccer was lurking behind every corner of every match-up, even every World Cup, with a breakout moment just waiting in the wings. Wood was the game-winning scorer in both matches—a feat that can hardly be claimed by many forwards, if any. Were those two games friendlies? Sure, but those were two games, taken seriously by both sides, against Netherlands and Germany. On the scale of elite forces in world soccer it doesn't get much better than those two. As such, on an individual level, Wood has the distinct honor of toppling them both.

Wood's 45 caps and 13 goals put him near the top of the list for US players in terms of individual accomplishments. His 13 goals arrived against Netherlands, Germany, Mexico, the ever-present Saint Vincent and the Grenadines, Puerto Rico, Costa Rica, Saint Vincent and the Grenadines (again), Mexico (again), Honduras, Panama, Paraguay, Ireland, and Colombia.

A forward forgotten by some, Wood is one of the top strikers to carry the weight of expectations on his shoulders for the USMNT.

87 Sebastian Lletget USMNT: 2017-21

Sebastian Lletget—born in 1992 in San Francisco, California—has gathered up over 30 caps with eight goals to date as a member of the USMNT. So quickly, from 2017 onward, he became a veteran with the team as a midfielder to rely on. For steady play, rock solid defense, call Lletget. He'll get you there.

In his late teens, the 5'10"-ish Lletget—who likely impressed with his muscular build—signed with West Ham United in 2010. After testing the waters there, he returned to MLS and featured with the LA Galaxy (2015-21) where he gathered over 155 appearances and a little over 20 goals.

He was also an MLS All-Star (2021).

Lletget shifted gears, briefly, and headed over to the New England Revolution (2022). Following that, he shifted gears yet again and landed with FC Dallas (2022).

He's won a CONCACAF Nations League (2019-20), and the CONCACAF Gold Cup (2021) where he was captain against Haiti in the group stage and Qatar in the semis; that was the seventh Gold Cup title for the US.

To date, his goals for the USMNT have come against Honduras, Costa Rica, Panama, El Salvador, Jamaica, Switzerland, and Honduras (again).

Whether scoring goals on the field or making headlines off it, Lletget has proven to be something of interest for fans around the nation.

88 Walker Zimmerman USMNT: 2017-present

Walker Zimmerman—born in 1993 in Lawrenceville, Georgia—started playing college ball at Furman University in Greenville, South Carolina, and appeared with the team from 2011-12. The 6'3" center-back emerged onto the MLS scene with FC Dallas in 2013, where he appeared over 85 times, then transitioned to LAFC in 2018, with over 50 appearances. While at LAFC, he was an assistant coach for UCLA.

Every kid who aspires to play college soccer will likely have UCLA on their map of ultimate destinations. The storied program—winning multiple NCAA championships thus far in 1985, 1990, 1997, and 2002—is one of the best in US history. For Zimmerman, who went to a smaller college by comparison, to be an assistant coach must've been outstandingly surreal. In particular, to assume such a role simply for being him—that is to say, an accomplished player from a smaller neck of the woods—it was, certainly, gratifying.

In 2020, he made the next step in his formidable career as he signed with Nashville SC, a passionate hub of MLS's Midwest lineup. Zimmerman marked a spot in MLS history as the first scorer for the club.

In 2017, "Walker Zimmerman made his US National Team debut on Friday night in a 1-0 win over Jamaica, and did so in resounding fashion,"[128] reported Carter Baum at *FCDallas.com*. Not only that, Zimmerman had a hell of a showing: "Named Player of the Match by the FS1 crew, Zimmerman played a full 90 minutes in his Senior Team debut"[129] and this was a sign of things to come. This USMNT debut happened to be under the auspices of Bruce Arena and shortly thereafter, in the shift from Arena to Gregg Berhalter, Zimmerman became a strong member of the USMNT and subsequently was seen as a starter for the team during qualifiers for the 2022 FIFA World Cup and eventually the World Cup in Qatar.

At the actual FIFA World Cup in Qatar, Zimmerman was a featured starter for the US team that made its way through group B against Wales (1-1), England (0-0), and Iran (1-0). The team finished second in its group, just behind England. Despite the 3–1 loss the US endured from Netherlands in the round of 16, the US had ventured back into primetime. That is, the FIFA World Cup.

Every team, every country, in the world strives for the World Cup. To get in changes the economy of your given country; it changes the landscape of history for soccer in your given country; it alters individual careers of players, usually in a positive way. On top of that, the US broke into the coveted round of 16. That alone, depending who you ask, was an utter success. Zimmerman was a team leader, one of the anchors of defense. It was a huge moment in time for him and the team.

In general, Zimmerman has a great feel for chipping the ball to diagonally running attacking players toward the top of the box; he can feed them with an accurate lead pass that is softly waiting for the player; this is crucial as it allows his teammate to run onto the ball and collect it for, hopefully, a dangerous opportunity. Without this soft pass, the play is dead. This skill is highly sought after. Many central defenders do not possess it. It takes field vision, touch, and placement to pull it off. Zimmerman has shown, time and time again, that he can deliver this important pass. It creates confidence among the team, while it also presses the opponent into awkward situations. Of course, this pass is not done all the time. Aside from these opportune moments, Zimmerman has much more to offer.

In the general flow of possession, he distributes the ball with calm confidence and strong technique. Defensively, he's dominant in the air with an eye for breaking up plays. These attributes have been demonstrated time and time again, and they're appreciated by fans, players, and coaches alike. His play on the field has earned him praise around MLS as one of the very best at his position.

He won the US Open Cup (2016) and Supporters' Shield (2016) with FC Dallas. With LAFC he won the Supporters' Shield (2019).

Still an active player during the writing of this book, Zimmerman has been an MLS All-Star on numerous occasions (2019, 2021, 2022, 2023) and has been named one of the MLS Best XI on different occasions. What's more significant, he won the MLS Defender of the Year two years in a row

(2020, 2021). Winning that award two years in a row was done previously by Carlos Bocanegra (2002, 2003), and Chad Marshall (2008, 2009). With the USMNT, he won the CONCACAF Gold Cup (2021) and the CONCACAF Nations League (2022–23).

89 Jordan Morris USMNT: 2014-present

Jordan Morris—born in 1994 in Seattle, Washington—is your average run-of-the-mill guy that took an offer from Stanford University and was part of the team that won the NCAA championship in 2015. *The Stanford Daily* reported, "Behind two goals from Jordan Morris and a staunch defensive effort, Stanford men's soccer (18-2-3) won its first national championship with a 4-0 rout over Clemson (17-3-4) Sunday afternoon at Sporting Park in Kansas City, Kansas."[130] In addition, he won the Hermann Trophy as the nation's best NCAA Division I soccer player. What's more, Jordan Morris was honored with the Soccer America Player of the Year Award in 2015. And he won the NCAA Division I Men's Soccer Tournament Most Outstanding Player Award for Offense in 2015.

But hold on a second. 2015? Stanford? Did Morris score his first USMNT goal while attending Stanford? According to *The Stanford Daily*:

> "Wednesday night was a good night for the US Men's National Team, which downed Mexico 2-0, but it was truly an unforgettable night for sophomore forward Jordan Morris of the Stanford men's soccer team. The Mercer Island, Washington native, making his third cap for the national team, scored his first career USMNT goal in the 49th minute of the friendly to put the US up 1-0. The US had been threatening Mexico immediately upon return from the halftime break, and in the 49th minute, Michael Bradley found DeAndre Yedlin just outside the penalty box, and Yedlin's pass deflected off Mexican midfielder Mario Osuna toward the goal. Morris beat Mexican defender Oswaldo Alanis to the ball on a dead sprint and eased the ball under the diving goalkeeper Cirilo Saucedo into the net for an easy score."[131]

Was I there? Yes, coincidently, I was in San Antonio—working on a different book—and I can tell you the place was rocking all game long like few things you can ever see in sports. The atmosphere was beyond electric. The indoor arena aspect captured the sound and energy in such a way that is not available at outdoor venues. On top of that, all the attention was on the field and the arena surrounding it only intensified the action down there.

In 2016, Morris joined his hometown team—the Seattle Sounders—and despite multiple knee injuries, he persevered by attaining over 195 caps, with over 65 goals. As of the writing of this book, he's still going and those stats are likely to increase. Yet the injuries are worth a look. The setbacks he endured were quite overwhelming. He had knee surgery in 2018, following an ACL, and then another knee surgery in 2021.

As MLS reported, "Don't expect Jordan Morris to appear for the Seattle Sounders in 2021, at least based on what general manager and president of soccer Garth Lagerwey told KJR's Sounders Weekly midweek."[132] The injury-prone Morris was up against it again. "Morris tore his left ACL in late February while on loan at English Championship side Swansea City, creating an abrupt end to his time overseas. The injury is pretty severe, too."[133] This was part of an ongoing saga. "Morris previously tore his right ACL ahead of the 2018 MLS season, causing him to miss that entire campaign. Thus the 26-year-old homegrown winger is used to the recovery road, as challenging as it may be."[134] For a soccer, basketball, or hockey player, the knee is not an injury you're wanting to deal with. Morris could've given up. Instead, he made a comeback. "On January 21, 2022, after a lengthy recovery from injury, Morris received his first World Cup qualifying call-up since September 2017.[135]

In spite of these knee surgeries, he was summoned to the USMNT by Coach Berhalter for services in the 2022 FIFA World Cup. It's hard to not select Morris. As MLS pointed out in 2021, "When healthy, Morris is among the most dangerous attacking players in MLS. He's recorded 35 goals and 20 assists in 105 matches, coupled by ten goals in 39 USMNT appearances."[136] Morris joined Sounders teammate and friend Cristian Roldan (winner of the High School 2012-13 Gatorade National Boys Soccer Player of the Year). After two knee surgeries you might think: This guy, Morris, could never play in a World Cup after that. But some can find that spirit that seems to exist out there, a way to get over that hurdle of nagging injuries. Morris persevered. Somehow, someway, with the belief of Berhalter, Morris got in against Wales. In addition, defying the odds, "Morris made an appearance as a substitute in the first group stage match against Wales on November 21, 2022."[137]

He was the 2016 MLS Rookie of the Year. As a member of the Sounders, he was part of the MLS Cup championship teams in 2016 and 2019. With the USMNT, he won the 2017 CONCACAF Gold Cup, scoring two goals against Martinique in a 3-2 victory, and the game-winner in the 2-1 dash to the finish line over Jamaica in the final. With three goals in the tournament, he was top scorer along with Alphonso Davies (Canada) and Kevin Parsemain (Martinique). In turn, he made the Gold Cup Best XI squad that year (with teammates Graham Zusi, Omar Gonzalez, Darlington Nagbe, Michael Bradley, and Jozy Altidore). That happened to be the sixth overall Gold Cup title for the US.

In 2019, Morris was honored as the MLS Comeback Player of the Year. He made the elite MLS Best XI in 2020. He was an MLS All-Star in 2022 and 2023. With the Sounders, Morris was part of the 2022 CONCACAF Champions League title, in which Seattle defeated UNAM (Mexico) for the honor. He made the 2022 CONCACAF Champions League Team of the Tournament.

Somewhat misunderstood, Morris—who has Type 1 Diabetes, who worked on his online degree at Stanford during an injury, whose dad, Dr. Michael Morris, is the medical director for the Seattle Sounders—is quite a unique character. His accomplishments, along with the struggles he endured along the way, aren't something you hear about every day.

90 Matt Turner
USMNT: 2021-present

Matt Turner hasn't been on the team long but he's already impressed with strong performances in goal for the USMNT in the Gold Cup and World Cup.

Turner—who was born in 1994 in Park Ridge, New Jersey—stands about 6'3" with slight pigeon-toed movement as he shifts side to side, blocking his net. With great aptitude he does just that: blocks the net from shots and frustrates the hell out of opponents that can't quite seem to get one in.

Without a doubt, Turner has stepped up as a standout US keeper. Before players in the modern era—such as Landon Donovan and Clint Dempsey—garnered worldwide respect for US field players, it was typically only goalies that foreigners respected. Our goalies have been taken seriously by the international community, therefore we take them seriously. Pride has definitely been on the line. Goalies have been one of our best exports.

Outstanding keepers embody a special un-teachable quality: skill, technique, awareness, fight, determination, grit. It's the best US goalies have to offer. I think that's what people appreciate about Turner. There's something there that you trust in a keeper and that you look forward to watching. He's gonna go for it and give all he's got. Those unavoidable moments when the offense breaks through are when Turner's flopping around, sprawling out to get a glove on the ball—he's determined to win.

After playing for Fairfield University in Connecticut (2012-15), he joined the Jersey Express, New England Revolution, Richmond Kickers, and, as of 2023, Nottingham Forest (a storied operation that won the European Cup under Coach Brian Clough's guidance in 1978-79, 1979-80).

Turner's pro and national team record so far is extraordinarily good. He won the CONCACAF Gold Cup and the Gold Cup Golden Glove (2021); the CONCACAF Nations League and the Nations League Golden Glove (2022-23, 2023-24); he's been an MLS All-Star (2021); MLS Goalkeeper of the Year (2021); MLS Best XI (2021); he was also part of the Supporters' Shield with New England Revolution (2021).

As for the 2022 FIFA World Cup, he maintained two clean sheets in the group stage as the team progressed to the round of 16. Will he go down as the US' best all-time keeper? That is, will he be thought of with higher regard than Tony Meola, Kasey Keller, Brad Friedel, Tim Howard? We'll have to wait and see!

91 Paul Arriola USMNT: 2016-23

Early on, **Paul Arriola**—born in 1995 in Chula Vista, California—gained valuable experience with the IMG Soccer Academy, Arsenal FC (CA), and LA Galaxy at the youth levels. His pro career journey has included Tijuana, DC United, Swansea City, and FC Dallas. After substantial field-time with US youth national teams, he was called up to the senior side in 2016 where he gained 50 caps. To that end, he's hit the ten-goal mark. At of the time of writing this book, he was only 30, so there still might be a game or two left for him with the national team.

In the 2017 CONCACAF Gold Cup, Arriola was along for the ride as he started the group B match against Martinique, a 3-2 victory. He then subbed in against Nicaragua, a 3-0 runaway win for the US. The US finished group B in the lead, ahead of Panama, Martinique, and Nicaragua. In the quarters against a valiant foe, El Salvador, Arriola started as the US waltzed away with a 2-0 winner. In the semis, the US got another 2-0 win over Costa Rica in Arlington, Texas, in front of around 45,000 spectators; Arriola was leaned on for another start with teammates Matt Besler, Darlington Nagbe, Michael Bradley, and Jordan Morris. The final was a close 2-1 championship-winning match for the US as it bested Jamaica in Santa Clara, California; Arriola started yet again as the US gained its sixth overall Gold Cup.

Arriola was back for the 2021 Gold Cup as the US kicked things off in group B against Haiti with a 1-0 sneaker. Joining Arriola in the start were Matt Turner and Walker Zimmerman, coached by Gregg Berhalter. The next game against Martinique, Dike—Deeks—got a brace as the team won 6-1. In the quarters, Arriola took the captain's band and led a group that some categorized as a B team—Lletget, Dike, Matthew Hoppe, and Matt Turner—to a 1-0 thriller over Jamaica with a goal from Hoppe. Arriola started in the semis against a well-disciplined passing side, Qatar; the US defeated the Middle East contender by 1-0. In the final, with Arriola as captain, the team went up against heavy foe Mexico and earned a 1-0 win; a few starters with

Arriola included Matt Turner, Lletget, and Matthew Hoppe; the fans that piled in the Las Vegas-area setting comprised of around 60,000. That would be the seventh Gold Cup for the US.

Despite a 2020 knee injury, Arriola forged ahead. He's been an MLS All-Star (2022) and also the MLS Player of the Month (May of 2022) with FC Dallas.

What kind of player is he? Arriola is a keep-away nightmare for anyone stuck trying to guard him. He's a perfect mold to replace an ailing outside back at Barcelona as his possession instincts match their style of play: short passes left and right, delivered with sound technique and a desire to get the ball right back. It's as if Arriola gets in a passing trance of sorts, total focus, fully concentrated on the task at hand which is essentially playing keep away. Defensively, he's very active and keeps within a strong framework of solid positioning which helps with overall team shape.

He's been a go-to performer for the national team, with ten goals to date that have been pocketed against Puerto Rico, Trinidad and Tobago, Costa Rica, Guyana, T&T (again), El Salvador, T&T (yet again), Panama, and Grenada.

92 Weston McKennie USMNT: 2017-present

Weston McKennie—born in 1998 in Fort Lewis, Washington—jumped around a bit in his youth, living in Little Elm, Texas, and Germany as well. In Germany, for a few years, he played soccer as a kid and gained some of the insight that he brings to the field as an adult. Why Germany? His dad was in the US Air Force which took the family to Europe.

Back in Texas, McKennie played with the youth system of FC Dallas before joining Schalke 04 in Germany. McKennie played with the team from approximately 2017-21; during that time he was on loan to Juventus—the mighty Italian giant—where he played from 2020-21. Following 2021, he extended with Juventus yet was on loan to Leeds United in 2023.

For his first game with the senior USMNT, McKennie entered the mix in 2017 against Portugal and since that point he's gained over 55 caps, with over ten goals. As of the writing of this book, he was in his mid-20s, so he'll probably add to that as time goes on.

McKennie earned a little place in hat-trick lore against the island-neighbor of Florida. "On October 12, 2019, McKennie scored the fastest hat trick in the US men's national team's history, scoring three goals in thirteen minutes in a CONCACAF Nations League game against Cuba,"[138] said *Wikipedia*. The first arrived in the beginning of the match, pretty much right after kickoff. Cuba's defense was scrambling, ball watching, ball chasing, and a cross traversed the box where McKennie trapped it and placed it in the near post. The second arrived from a cross into the six-yard box area where McKennie tapped it in. The third, similar to the other two, was a result of the ball being played into the box from the right wing, and from close range, where bodies converged; it seemed as though McKennie guided it into the back of the net.

In the 2021 CONCACAF Nations League final, held in Denver, Colorado, the US defeated Mexico by 3-2 where McKennie got a goal, along with teammates Gio Reyna and Christian Pulisic.

Prior to the 2022 FIFA World Cup, McKennie injured his foot which caused him to be sidelined in the build-up to the big tournament. In February of 2022, *The Athletic* reported, "Juventus midfielder Weston McKennie fractured the second and third metatarsals in his left foot in the 81st minute of the team's Champions League round of 16 match against Villarreal on Tuesday, a source confirmed to *The Athletic*. The US men's national team star is expected to miss eight to twelve weeks as he recovers."[139] By the time teams converged on Qatar to find out who's the best in the world, McKennie was back in action for Coach Berhalter as the end result reached no further than a 3-1 loss in the round of 16 to Netherlands.

From deep-lying positions in midfield, or out on the flank, McKennie distributes the ball to teammates which opens up the field of play for forward movement. He's been noted for being able to play different positions. Though he's a midfielder, it would also be wise to regard him as a defensive mid that helps break up plays in order to facilitate an attack in the other direction. At around 6'0" tall, he's a good option during corner kicks with respect to both offensive and defensive options.

He likes Harry Potter. In fact, there's a Harry Potter tattoo—apparently a lightning bolt—on his person. What's more, he's been known to wave a "wand"—as if casting a spell—during goal celebrations. McKennie—whose guiding light apparently consists of magician prodigies riding around on broomsticks—represents a new generation of US players that have emerged in the post-2015 era.

To date, McKennie's goals have arrived against Portugal, Curacao, Jamaica, Cuba, Mexico, Mexico (again), Honduras, and Grenada. Overall, he's been part of a Coppa Italia (2020-21, 2023-24), Supercoppa Italiana (2020), the CONCACAF Nations League championship run (2019-20, 2022-23, 2023-24), and he won the US Soccer Player of the Year award (2020).

93 Tyler Adams USMNT: 2017-present

Tyler Adams—born in 1999 in Wappinger, New York—joined the New York Red Bulls II when he was 16, technically as a pro player, and eventually joined the senior New York Red Bulls team about a year later.

As captain of the USMNT at the 2022 FIFA World Cup, Adams helped lead the squad out of its group and then into an immediate loss in the round of 16 to Netherlands—a stunning, quick, clinical defeat that caught fans off-guard. Why is this so critical as it pertains to Adams? Well, on paper he was captain which brings with it responsibility and a lot of the blame should things go wrong.

For all intents and purposes, his presence at this current juncture—the writing of this book—is paramount within the bigger picture of US soccer. As a member of the Big Money period, he and his cohorts are the latest extension of many years of work that came before. There'll be an expectation with each new generation to get one step closer to conquering the World Cup—the United States' last athletic frontier. So when the USMNT got no further than the round of 16 in the 2022 World Cup, people quickly second-guessed the captain, coach, and everyone on board. That's an aspect of the job that Adams had to adjust to.

If there's someone that moves like a soccer player, it's Adams. His natural soccer movements—technique on the ball—are quintessential midfielder movements. He's accomplished quite a bit during his brief time as a member of the USMNT. He won the US Soccer Player of the Year award in 2022; he won the MLS Supporters' Shield with the New York Red Bulls (2018); he won the DFB-Pokal with RB Leipzig (2021-22); he won the CONCACAF Nations League with the USMNT (2019-20, 2023-24).

It'll be interesting to see where the team goes as this is a crossroads of time, talent, and ambition for the US soccer program. How long Adams will last as a significant contributor is anyone's guess. From 2020 onward the squad has been in relatively—surprisingly—good standing ranking-wise:

on December 22, 2023, the FIFA men's world ranking had the United States at #12. With a new generation of players comes expectations, intrigue, and results. Will the results arrive? In such a short time with the team and quick rise to the top, Adams—who has gone over 40 caps as of 2025—will have a few more years to prove just how far the US team can proceed.

As a New York native born in 1999, who only recently endured hamstring surgery, he has perhaps a new life to prove that it can be done: the USMNT can win a World Cup title. "Just days after Tyler Adams made his comeback after six months out injured, the USMNT captain suffered a setback and underwent his second hamstring surgery of 2023,"[140] wrote Joe Prince-Wright and Andy Edwards. So if he can stay healthy, which is always a challenge for players after surgery, it will be an interesting ride for a player only in his mid-20s.

94 Sergino Dest USMNT: 2019-present

Sergino Dest—born in 2000 in Netherlands—was held back by teammates. He was reined in. He was cordoned off. He was told to calm down. If you'll remember, in 2023:

> "Sergino Dest had a meltdown of epic proportions during the first half of the USMNT's Nations League quarterfinal second-leg match against Trinidad & Tobago...During the 38th minute of the match—one the US somehow lost 2-1—Dest was shown back-to-back yellow cards after launching the ball in the stands before shouting at the referee and blowing him a kiss as he walked off the field...Teammates Gio Reyna and Yunus Musah were seen trying to calm Dest down before the second yellow was handed out. After being shown a red card, that help from teammates immediately turned into frustration with Matt Turner and Tim Ream essentially telling Dest to get off the pitch. Turner even gave Dest a gentle shove off the field after the two continued to jaw back and forth."[141]

Dest—who has more years left in the tank—is significant because he's a USMNT player that suited up for Barcelona. That's saying something as Barcelona is one of the best club teams in the history of club. Period. For a US player to be a significant contributor, as Dest has, it's a huge step forward for US players in terms of respect worldwide.

Even though Dest was born and raised in Netherlands, he's still regarded as a US player that took the field with Barcelona. To have someone on Barcelona that can bring its inner-passing qualities to the USMNT is tantamount with a budding astronaut program in India having one of its proto-astronauts training on the Space Station with NASA, then returning to share his newfound expertise.

If you're looking for a new generation of US players that have experience with high-end European clubs, then Dest is the paramount example. He started out with Jong Ajax (2018–20), and from there he gained experience with Ajax (2019–20), Barcelona (2020–24), AC Milan (2022–23), and PSV (where he landed in 2023). That's top shelf. For those who think US players should be shunned from the rest of the world, this is loudly suggesting otherwise.

Dest played for the US U17 and U20 teams before climbing the ranks to the senior side in 2019. That was just around the time Berhalter—who has experience playing in Netherlands—took over as the United States coach. To date, Dest has played in over 30 games for the USMNT; as such, he's turned into a regular for the USMNT. With more appearances around the corner, barring injury, Dest should be a starter in the 2026 FIFA World Cup hosted—in part—by the United States. What he brings to the outside back position is reminiscent of "Brazilian outside backs meet Barcelona possession-minded giants" at their best.

He's been part of a few triumphs, including the Johan Cruyff Shield with Ajax (2019), the Copa del Rey with Barcelona (2020–21), and the CONCACAF Nations League with the USMNT (2019–20, 2022–23, 2023–24). On an individual level, he's won the US Soccer Young Male Player of the Year award (2019), and the Ajax Talent of the Year, aka the Marco van Basten Award (2020).

Back to his outburst. *The Sporting News* pointed out: "The most frustrating aspect of Dest's behavior, for those wearing USMNT colors, was he once again demonstrated his value to the squad with the beautiful cross from near the right sideline that Jedi Robinson was able to drive into the goal. It was Dest's fifth assist in 32 caps, not bad for a right back."[142] But now he's known for losing his temper against Trinidad & Tobago. Will he ever shake loose this image? Whether you're a fan of players throwing tantrums or not, Dest brings unmistakable drama to the fray.

95 Brenden Aaronson USMNT: 2020-present

Brenden Aaronson—born in 2000 in New Jersey—is quiet, unassuming, and focused to a point where he's relentless on offense, pesky on defense, and just plain a winner. With him in the lineup, with the right chemistry around him, it's practically unstoppable. In the era of Aaronson, the best combination for the US up top would be Aaronson, Pulisic, and Weah. If that's the starting forward line for the US, which it should be, it's a powerful trio that's going to get high quality scoring chances, in bundles.

Aaronson, who stands about 5'10" and weighs 150 pounds, is more of a left wing type of forward, an outside mid meets forward that combines skill and relentless ambition with a New Jersey soccer know-how touch that makes him so dangerous.

At the writing of this book, he's still playing but when people look back at his time on the field they'll likely realize what a useful attacking threat he was. Aaronson went through the academy of the Philadelphia Union and from there played with Bethlehem Steel FC (2017-18). With quick work, he was called up to the Philadelphia Union (2019-20) where he played in over 50 games with seven goals. He joined Red Bull Salzburg (2021-22) before heading over to Leeds United and seeing time on loan with Union Berlin (2023).

During his time with the Philadelphia Union he was part of the Supporters' Shield (2020). He also made the MLS Best XI (2020). In turn, around his time with Red Bull Salzburg, the team was champion of the Austrian Bundesliga (2020-21, 2021-22); in addition, the team won the Austrian Cup (2020-21, 2021-22). In the final of the Austrian Cup in 2020-21, Aaronson scored a goal in the 3-0 victory over LASK.

After joining the senior USMNT in 2020, he was around for the CONCACAF Nations League title runs (2019-20, 2022-23, 2023-24) which is a newer accomplishment for the USMNT. His first cap for the USMNT arrived in 2020. Hidden in a world of COVID-19 and social unrest, Aaronson quietly began making a name for himself at the highest level of US soccer. Initially, he was brought into the fold for the 2019 CONCACAF Nations League games against Cuba and Canada, though, he didn't make it in. In the world of soccer, this is sometimes a formality as the honor of sitting on the sideline alone is used as a learning tool for the player in question to take it all in—the crowd, the reality of representing your nation, the expectations, and the confidence derived from seeing it up close and personal. His debut, which turns out to be 2020, was against Costa Rica. His first goal would come against El Salvador in 2020, a 6–0 all-out destruction win for the US.

As Tom Brady says, the process of tryouts in pre-season moves fast. A lot of times players have but a weekend or, if lucky, a week to impress coaches. Decisions have to be made fast with guys that are tantamount in strength and quality with one another, so who is picked? Who makes the cut? Often it comes down to gut instincts. Coaches have a feeling about a guy based on his results, which match competitors, and also his vibe—whatever that intangible essence can be. What set Aaronson apart from the run-of-the-mill guy at the same tryout? A quicker step, a faster stride, a feistier demeanor over the long stretch. All there. Then there's an aura, a vibe: it's all there. It's something coaches are guilty of looking for, be it consciously or unconsciously. You can see it with Aaronson, where you see a guy on the left wing that Pat McBride, Al Trost, and Gene Geimer would've loved to have played a ball to, for him to pierce through the openings with a thundering shot on goal, roofing the upper net. Balls get to goal with Aaronson, bottom line. He's a gamer, and one you want to watch in his prime.

96 Timothy Weah USMNT: 2018-present

Timothy Weah—born in 2000—is the son of George Weah, world player of the year in the mid-90s, a star with AC Milan, and now president of Liberia. From time to time, great players have kids that might be good players in their own right but never step up to the elite neighborhood their dad was in. In the case of Timothy, with the training he got from his dad, it's pretty easy to determine rather quickly—with his first touch on the ball—that he belongs at the top.

For starters, his first touch is deadly. He pushes it in just the right way, with just the right technique, out in front into dangerous positions that keep defenders on their heels. Anson Dorrance—legendary coach of the North Carolina Tarheels and USWNT—has said to hit your first three touches of the ball with intent, going somewhere. This outlook is embodied in spades by Tim Weah who creates something interesting with that first touch.

He kind of scoots along, much faster than you think, with dynamite quickness coupled with a fierce shot that thunders toward goal. Out on the wing, he's an offensive weapon that has proven formidable for the US.

Born in Brooklyn, New York, he eventually lived in Florida before moving back to New York. Then it was off to France where he played with the Paris Saint-Germain Academy. Weah scored a goal for Paris Saint-Germain in the final of the 2018 Trophée des Champions, and PSG defeated Monaco 4–0.

He went on loan to Celtic in 2019 where he had a handful of games and a few goals. He went to Lille after that (2019–23) and gathered over 85 appearances with six goals. While at Lille, he was part of the 2021 Trophée des Champions. It ended up being a 1–0 win over his former team, PSG.

As of 2023, he joined powerhouse Juventus in Serie A.

He played with numerous US youth national teams before getting his senior team debut in 2018. With the USMNT he's acquired over 40 caps and a handful of goals. Since the time he joined the USMNT, it has won the 2019–20, 2022–23, and 2023–24 CONCACAF Nations league championships.

At the 2022 FIFA World Cup, Weah was a featured player for the US scoring a goal against Wales in the group stage. The team would go onto enter the round of 16 only to lose out to Netherlands.

As time goes on, he'll likely increase these numbers and come World Cup 2026, which the US is tri-hosting, he'll probably be a featured player. He's been a strong focal point of the squad in his first few years wearing a US kit, and this trend should continue.

As is the case with Aaronson and Pulisic, the only thing that might get in the way would be an injury. On November 9, 2023, *USA Today* reported, "US men's national team head coach Gregg Berhalter said Christian Pulisic and Tim Weah have hamstring injuries that 'aren't too serious,' but prevented them from making the USMNT's November roster."[143] Injuries are part of the process, and as such, "The Italy-based duo was omitted from the 24-man squad that will face Trinidad and Tobago in a two-leg CONCACAF Nations League quarterfinal on Nov. 16 and 20."[144]

Depending how things work out with the 2026 World Cup, including but not limited to coaching decisions, arguably the best trio up top in USMNT history might just be Aaronson, Pulisic, and Weah

97 Jesus Ferreira USMNT: 2020-present

No matter what, he'll always be the first US player to score a hat trick in two consecutive games. In 2023, **Jesus Ferreira** reached a milestone: two games in a row with a hat trick. No US player had done it before. The pair of hat tricks came against Saint Kitts and Nevis, along with Trinidad and Tobago. That was according to a story at ESPN online. It added, "Ferreira also became just the second player in USMNT history with three career hat tricks, joining the team's joint all-time leading scorer Landon Donovan."[145] "No other player, regardless of country, has multiple career Gold Cup hat tricks, according to ESPN Stats & Information research."[146]

Ferreira was born in 2000 in Colombia. According to US Soccer, "he earned his US citizenship in December 2019 and declared his intention to represent the USMNT the following month earning his first cap in the 1-0 win vs. Costa Rica on Feb. 1, 2020 in Carson, Calif." What's more, he "scored a USMNT record-tying four goals that propelled the side to a 5-0 rout of Grenada in front of a sold-out crowd of 20,500 on June 10, 2022, at Q2 Stadium as the US began defense of its Concacaf Nations League title. His four goals tie a USMNT record for most goals in a game, the fifth time the mark has been achieved and the first since Landon Donovan scored four against Cuba in 2003."

In 2022, "Ferreira became the first FC Dallas player to ever play in a FIFA World Cup match by starting the United States' round of 16 game against the Netherlands on Saturday, Dec. 3."[147] "Although he was an unused substitute in the USMNT's three group stage games, Ferreira was entrusted with a starting role in the opening knockout match that saw the US fall 3-1 to the Netherlands. Ferreira's outing lasted 45 minutes before being withdrawn at halftime for midfielder Gio Reyna."[148]

Many fans think that Ferreira is too frail to be the leading USMNT center forward. He's certainly not built like Jozy Altidore, Chris Wondolowski, Brian Ching, or Brian McBride. Ferreira is demanding that the US consider a Romario-like forward—one that is smaller in build that demands less crossing of the ball and more interplay in and around the box to supplement his skillset. He represents that type of player: The undersized forward that uses other means to score goals and create chances for teammates. This, according to 99% of Brazilians, is the best type of forward because it causes teammates to plan around skill, guile, and improvisation around the box. This is where Ferreira is a very interesting player. Therefore, Ferreira is confounding, he isn't the right vibe for fans—he's too skinny, frail, undersized, and so on. Yet, maybe at this juncture, that is, during the writing of this book, perhaps that's what US soccer needs to put it over the top, once and for all.

Most FIFA World Cup champion teams had a key forward under six feet tall:

1970: Pelé (5'5")
1974: Gerd Müller (5'9")
1978: Mario Kempes (6'0"), an exception
1982: Paolo Rossi (5'9")
1986: Joge Valdano (6'2"), an exception; Maradona (5'4"ish)
1990: Rudi Völler (5'11"ish); Jurgen Klinsmann (5'11")
1994: Romario (5'5"); Bebeto (5'9")
1998: Stéphane Pierre Yves Guivarc'h (5'10")
2002: Ronaldo (5'11" ish)
2006: Totti (5'11" ish); Luca Toni (6'4"), an exception
2010: David Villa (5'9")
2014: Miroslav Klose (6'0"), an exception; Thomas Müller (6'1"), an exception
2018: Olivier Giroud (6'4"), an exception
2022: Julián Álvarez (5'7"ish); Messi (5'7"ish)

Has Ferreira's presence brought forth a change in US soccer? Every once in a while someone comes along that will completely alter the way a team plays... the all-important style.

To date, Ferreira's USMNT goals have arrived against Trinidad and Tobago, Panama, Grenada, Mexico, Saint Kitts and Nevis, Trinidad and

Tobago (again), Panama (again). He's been an MLS All-Star (2022, 2023), the MLS Young Player of the Year (2022), the recipient of the CONCACAF Gold Cup Golden Boot (2023) and a member of the Gold Cup Best XI (2023). Ferreira soared to 15 goals—with a hat trick record—in a very short time. As things stand, it might be a long time before someone breaks his back-to-back hat trick.

98 Josh Sargent USMNT: 2018-present

Josh Sargent's strengths include finishing every move he makes like a clinical drill. He has pinpoint accuracy, the ability to see the game and read the field; he's unselfish, with natural athletic ability. He may lack Landon Donovan's speed and Denilson's maneuvering on the ball, but Sargent's dribbling ability is quite sound, and, in his own way, he's a very good constructive dribbler—one who gets things done, like someone that's task-oriented with good skill and technique.

Sargent hails from O'Fallon, Missouri, which is part of St. Louis, the heartbeat of US soccer, arguably the most competitive soccer area in the nation. He had experience with Scott Gallagher, St. Dominic High School, and eventually left for Bradenton, Florida, for the US Residency Program. In his late teens, he signed with Werder Bremer (Germany). According to ussoccer.com on January 9, 2024, "on December 7, 2018 he scored his first goal less than two minutes after coming on for his Bundesliga debut in a 3-1 win over Fortuna Dusseldorf, becoming the first player in the USMNT's modern era (1990-present) to score in both his international and professional league debuts." As per ussoccer.com, Sargent:

> "Earned his first cap and scored his first goal on May 28, 2018 in a friendly 3-0 win over Bolivia. At 18 years and 102 days he became the second youngest player to score for the USMNT in his debut game. He was named 2017 US Soccer Young Male Player of the Year. That November he was called up to the USMNT for a friendly against Portugal. Although he did not play, he became the first USA player called to camps with the U-17, U-20 and senior teams in the same calendar year."

To date, he's gone through doors opened by previous US players and has suited up with the aforementioned Werder Bremen. He's also played with Norwich City where he's gathered over 115 appearances and surpassed 40 goals. Not bad.

Since 2018, he's acquired over 25 caps and five goals to date. He was a starter in the 2019-20 CONCACAF Nations League final against Mexico, a 3-2 victory for the US.

Josh Sargent is on his way, theoretically, to more goals for the USMNT and potential record-setting accomplishments. He's done a bunch so far. Who's to say it's coming to a halt? Keep an eye out for Sargent as there's more around the corner.

99 Giovanni Reyna
USMNT: 2020-present

Giovanni Reyna—born in 2002 in Sunderland, England—is the son of Claudio, the former USMNT captain. How did Gio get so good? I think by now, everyone knows the story of his dad. Yet, his mom, Danielle, was quite a player in her own right. As a member of the North Carolina Tarheels, she has extensive experience around the great one's ideologies of the game. Who would the great one be? The guru of all women's soccer team gurus, Anson Dorrance. For Danielle to have been around his wisdom, combined with the prowess of North Carolina women's soccer and her stint with the USWNT in 1993, it would make sense that Gio grew up to be adept at dribbling, passing, knowing the game in general.

One might say he's a talent in his own right. When you compare him to his dad, Claudio, it's an interesting difference in style of play. Claudio had some subtle ways of dribbling around opponents, which were brilliant at times, yet he was much more of a connect-the-dots type of center mid. Gio, a creative attacking mid, on the other hand, is a steward of connecting the dots coupled with an innate ability to take guys on with the dribble in a daring way that, presumably, would make Anson Dorrance take a second look.

Gio Reyna joined Borussia Dortmund in 2020 and since then he's gained over 100 games, with over 10 goals. He was part of the DFB-Pokal championship (2020-21), scoring two goals in the semifinals.

He had extensive experience with US youth national teams before joining the senior side in 2020. In 2020, Gio won the US Soccer Young Male Player of the Year award. He was part of the CONCACAF Nations League championships (2019-20, 2022-23, 2023-24). He was also part of the 2022 FIFA World Cup squad that had a hint of drama. As things move along, he'll be a player to watch.

100 Christian Pulisic USMNT: 2016-present

The Top Five:

1. Christian Pulisic
2. Clint Dempsey
3. Landon Donovan
4. Ricky Davis
5. Claudio Reyna

If a scientist were in a lab, trying to make a perfect soccer player, and they put together combined elements of Landon Donovan, and Clint Dempsey, with a touch of George Best, you'd have **Christian Pulisic**. He's quick like Donovan, crafty like Dempsey, and shifty like Best. With the ability to stop and go on a dime, Pulisic can maneuver through traffic with relative ease, leaving opponents in the dust. His ability to score is sort of like Brazil's all-time leading scorer, Neymar: it just sort of happens. Pulisic uses craft and guile, chemistry with teammates, to get around the ever-pesky defenders to put the ball in the net. A head-balling giant? Not even close. And that's the beauty of having someone like him as your key threat in the attack. His height–which is about 5'8"–demands that you use other ways to score. With Pulisic in the attack, you're not going to see cross after cross–which is a good thing. Goals will arrive based on improvisation around the box, passing between teammates, with an opening here and there for him to use dynamic–and lighting quick–dribbling moves toward goal.

Born in 1998 in Hershey, Pennsylvania, Pulisic came from a soccer family as both parents played collegiately and his dad Mark actually played pro for the Harrisburg Heat, a quality indoor operation. Mark was quite a forward in his own right, scoring multiple goals while at George Mason University and with the Harrisburg Heat (in the 1990s).

Pulisic lived for a year in Tackley, Oxfordshire while is mother was on a teacher exchange in England. There, at the age of seven, he began playing for the youth team of Brackley Town. In the mid-2000s, Pulisic lived in Michigan and played for Michigan Rush. While there, he attended Workman Elementary School. He then moved to Germany just before his 16th birthday. Because his grandfather was Croatian, Pulisic was eligible for a European passport, which is how he was able to live and play in Europe at age 16, rather than age 18. In February 2015, Borussia Dortmund signed 16-year-old Pulisic and placed him first in their U17 squad, and then in their U19 squad later that summer. After he scored 10 goals and assisted 8 in just 15 games with Dortmund youth teams, he was called to join the first team over the winter break.[149]

Eventually, he was part of the DFB-Pokal (2016–17) with Borussia Dortmund. With Chelsea, he was part of the UEFA Champions League title (2020–21). History was made for US soccer. "On May 29, Pulisic won his first Champions League after Chelsea won 1–0 against Manchester City in the final at the Estádio do Dragão in Porto, becoming the first US player to play in a UEFA Champions League Final and the second to win it after Jovan Kirovski in 1997 with Borussia Dortmund."[150] Score wise, it was a tight game that Chelsea managed to win by 1–0.

The year 2021 proved monumental for Pulisic. He was also with Chelsea when it won the UEFA Super Cup (2021), and FIFA Club World Cup (2021). As of 2023, he joined Italian mega-club AC Milan where he scored goals and became Player of the Month in August, for example.

Pulisic received his first full senior USMNT cap in 2016 at the direction of Coach Klinsmann. According to *The Washington Post*: "He made his U.S. senior debut March 29, entering in the second half against Guatemala during a World Cup qualifier in Columbus, Ohio. With a rapid rise on Coach Jurgen Klinsmann's roster, Pulisic seems certain to join the U.S. squad for Copa America, a major 16-nation tournament to be staged in the United States next month."[151] In addition, "With the national team, he became the youngest player to represent the United States in a World Cup qualifier. Entry into that match tied him to the U.S. program."[152]

Unfortunately, the USMNT failed to qualify for the 2018 FIFA World Cup. Even Italy didn't make the 2018 and 2022 World Cup.

Pulisic was front and center for the 2022 FIFA World Cup and scored the game-winner against Iran, as the team earned a spot in the round of 16.

He helped push the USMNT in positive directions at the regional level as it won the CONCACAF Nations League (2019–20, 2022–23, 2023–24).

To start out, Pulisic was wearing Nike. But in 2021 Lucas Manfredi wrote, "Soccer star Christian Pulisic is trading in his Nike cleats for a fresh set of PUMAs after announcing a new brand partnership with the athletic sportswear giant on Monday."[153] Puma saw Pulisic as a leader for younger generations. "PUMA's global director of sports marketing, Johan Adamsson, said in a statement that Pulisic has 'paved the way for so many young US players who dream of playing in Europe for the world's biggest clubs.'"[154]

Shoe choices over the years are interesting to look at, like snapshots of the worldwide culture of soccer. A few players below wore more brands than the ones listed; for the most part, players will stay with one shoe brand as it provides a certain touch they can depend on. The brands listed reflect the main shoe choice by the players. Here are a few:

Pelé (Puma, Pony)
Maradona (Puma)
Platini (Adidas, Patrick)
Marco van Basten (Diadora)
Roberto Baggio (Diadora)
Donadoni (Diadora, Lotto)
Ruud Gullit (Lotto)
Rivaldo (Mizuno)
Ryan Giggs (Reebok)
Henry (Adidas, Nike, Reebok, Puma)
Pirlo (Nike)
Ronaldo (Nike)
Ronaldinho (Nike)
Neymar (Nike, Puma)
Zidane (Adidas)

David Beckham (Adidas)
Messi (Adidas)
Antoine Griezmann (Puma)
Gianluigi Buffon (Puma)
And, of course, Pulisic (Nike, Puma).

Pulisic won the US Soccer Young Male Player of the Year (2016), the US Soccer Player of the Year award (2017, 2019, 2021, 2023), and a standout in CONCACAF competitions. With his arrival, there was already talk. Who is the greatest USMNT player of all time? A Fab Five would be the following:

1. Christian Pulisic
2. Clint Dempsey
3. Landon Donovan
4. Ricky Davis
5. Claudio Reyna

You could easily switch Donovan and Dempsey. Or, perhaps, you could just have them tied for second. A list like that is never easy. It will always have opinion highly interlaced within the framework of the decision-making.

Other names fighting hard to get in that Fab Five would be: Pat McBride, Eric Wynalda, John Harkes, Tab Ramos, Thomas Dooley, Joe-Max Moore, Brian McBride, and a few others. As usual, attacking players get top billing.

When all is said and done, when he hangs up the cleats, don't be surprised to see the scoring record of Donovan and Dempsey demolished by Pulisic.

A NOTE FROM THE AUTHOR

There is a lot that goes into a book like this. The vast history of the USMNT is overwhelming. It goes way back, there are many players out there. But before I forget, special thanks to Seth Cullen for sharing knowledge on Texas soccer. Any players not listed, that you thought should be listed, are good players. You have to be a good player to reach the USMNT. All players, for the most part, that enter the USMNT camp are good players.

Having said that, I have been charged with the insane task of compiling the elite few. When you break down a list like this, 100 players, it gets tough. You quickly realize that such an endeavor is walking on treacherous ground. You start thinking of all the guys that could make the list. You start realizing that many players are extremely talented. But not everyone can be included in the top 100. **Jason Kreis**, for example. Man, was that guy good.

The great thing about soccer is that fans will disagree. Not everyone sees the best player in the world the same way. Some think Pelé, Maradona, and Messi, while others might say George Best.

If you have a player that *should've made the list* of the USMNT 100, with a little research, you may come to the conclusion that your list would look a lot like this one. Or not. That's soccer, after all. It is my hope that you take delight in reading about the players you have followed with great passion, discover new stories, then become agitated as to why your cherished players weren't included. This probably would be the best time to let you know that they were likely considered, weighed against others of similar stature, and a tough decision was made.

Let's get into a few players that didn't make this list, who could theoretically make the list.

Juli Veee was tough to leave out. The Hungarian immigrant was skillful, crafty, and flourished in the MISL. He played for the USMNT from 1976–82, only amassing four caps (with two goals). Not bad for an era in which fewer games were played. A great talent, but it just wasn't enough to place him on the list. Other talented players that deserve to be on the list: **Peter Millar**, **Tony Bellinger**, **Brian Quinn**, **David Vanole**, **Paul Krumpe**, **Roy Wegerle**, **Steve Trittschuh**, **Brian Bliss**, **Eric Eichmann**, **Mark Santel**, **Mark Chung**, **Jason Kreis**, **Ante Razov**, **Chris Klein**, **John O'Brien**, **Bobby Convey**, **Justin Mapp**, **Brad Guzan**, **Lee Nguyen**, **Cristian Roldan**, **Alejandro Zendejas**, **Luca de la Torre**, **Matthew Hoppe**, and **Cade Cowell**, to name a few.

What about **Dike**?! (Deeks!) There were a lot of players considered. Any which way you look at it: it's a competitive list to compile.

Lee Nguyen is a great example. I thought he was a super-talent. Yet, in the modern era, he was only allowed nine caps. He wasn't the coach; he couldn't pound his fists and demand to be put in. Before 1985, having nine caps was kind of normal. But in today's era, it's hard to force someone like that onto the list.

The elite talent of the USMNT represents a unique category in US sports. For those around the world that mocked US soccer long ago, those days are gone. As everyone knows, the United States is the athletic leader around the world. The United States is the leader in Olympic gold medals. It is *the* sports country. As for men's soccer, the USMNT will win the FIFA World Cup someday. Winning the FIFA World Cup for the men is the US' last athletic frontier. That's got a lot of people—Italians, Spaniards, Brazilians—nervous. They know, deep down, it'll happen. It's only a matter of time. When that time will arrive is yet to be seen. Until then, the US has produced world-class talent. This list represents the 100 top legends on that journey.

I'm glad you stopped by. There's much more around the corner.

ENDNOTES

1 By The Associated Press, "*Frank Borghi, U.S. Goalkeeper in a 1950 World Cup Stunner, Dies at 89,*" *The New York Times*, published February 4, 2015, accessed April 10, 2023, https://www.nytimes.com/2015/02/05/sports/soccer/frank-borghi-us-goalkeeper-in-a-1950-world-cup-stunner-dies-at-89.html

2 *Wikipedia, The Free Encyclopedia*, s.vv. "United States men's national soccer team," accessed April 8, 2023, https://en.wikipedia.org/wiki/United_States_men%27s_national_soccer_team

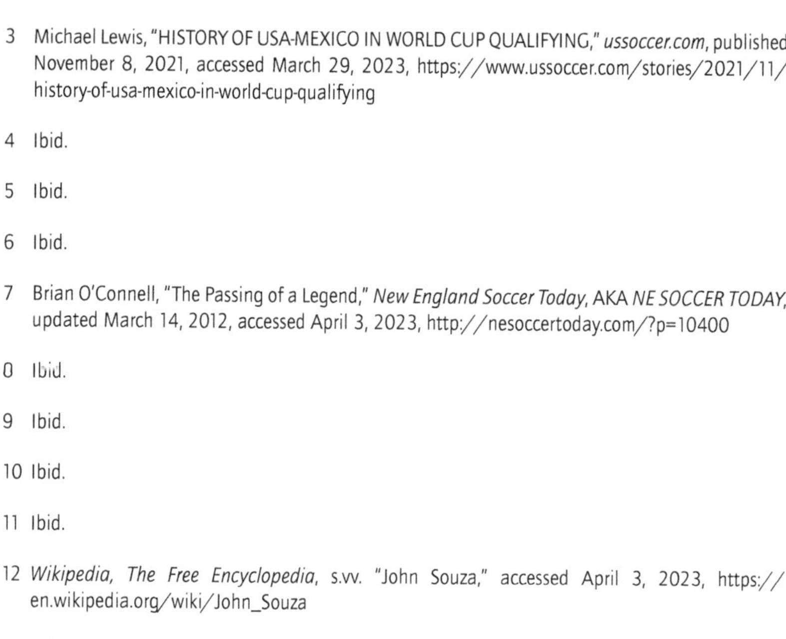

3 Michael Lewis, "HISTORY OF USA-MEXICO IN WORLD CUP QUALIFYING," *ussoccer.com*, published November 8, 2021, accessed March 29, 2023, https://www.ussoccer.com/stories/2021/11/history-of-usa-mexico-in-world-cup-qualifying

4 Ibid.

5 Ibid.

6 Ibid.

7 Brian O'Connell, "The Passing of a Legend," *New England Soccer Today*, AKA *NE SOCCER TODAY*, updated March 14, 2012, accessed April 3, 2023, http://nesoccertoday.com/?p=10400

8 Ibid.

9 Ibid.

10 Ibid.

11 Ibid.

12 *Wikipedia, The Free Encyclopedia*, s.vv. "John Souza," accessed April 3, 2023, https://en.wikipedia.org/wiki/John_Souza

13 *Wikipedia, The Free Encyclopedia*, s.vv. "Harry Keough," accessed January 29, 2021, https://en.wikipedia.org/wiki/Harry_Keough

14 Ibid.

15 *Wikipedia, The Free Encyclopedia*, s.vv. "Ed Murphy," accessed April 8, 2023, https://en.wikipedia.org/wiki/Ed_Murphy_(soccer)

16 *Wikipedia, The Free Encyclopedia*, s.vv. "Bill Looby," accessed April 6, 2023, https://en.wikipedia.org/wiki/Bill_Looby

17 Ibid.

18 (AP) *"Kicker-Victoria Team Wins U.S. Open Soccer Title, 2-0," The New York Times*, published June 22, 1964, accessed April 11, 2023, https://www.nytimes.com/1964/06/22/kickervictoria-team-wins-us-open-soccer-title-20.html

19 Ibid.

20 Ibid.

21 Ibid.

22 *Wikipedia, The Free Encyclopedia*, s.vv. "Al Zerhusen," accessed April 11, 2023, https://en.wikipedia.org/wiki/Al_Zerhusen#Biography

23 [No author] "Willy Roy," *Society for American Soccer History*, accessed April 12, 2023, https://www.ussoccerhistory.org/national-soccer-hall-of-fame-biographies/national-soccer-hall-of-fame-player-biographies/willy-roy/

24 Dan Caesar | *St. Louis Globe-Democrat*, "Pat McBride Comes Back To Save The Steamers," *Soccer Digest*, published Nov., 1985.

25 Ibid.

26 Ibid.

27 Dave Lange, *Soccer Made in St. Louis: A History of the Game in America's First Soccer Capitol* (St. Louis: Reedy Press, 2011).

28 Ibid.

29 Mike Kavanaugh | Editor, "THE PLAYERS," *St. Louis Steamers, 1981–1982 Media Guide*, Creative Printing Services, Inc., St. Louis, MO, published circa 1981–82, p. 22.

30 Gary Demuth, "Ellsworth Steakhouse owner is former Olympic soccer player," *Salina Journal*, published July 30, 2016 | updated July 30, 2016, accessed April 27, 2023, https://www.salina.com/story/lifestyle/2016/07/30/ellsworth-steakhouse-owner-is-former/21191666007/

31 Brian Trusdell, "The Express: The MISL's Most Vital Franchise," *Soccer Digest*, published Mar., 1987.

32 Ibid.

33 By Soccer America, "MLS: Perry Van Der Beck takes over Tampa Bay Mutiny," *Soccer America*, published July 13, 2001, accessed May 1, 2023, https://www.socceramerica.com/publications/article/11271/mls-perry-van-der-beck-takes-over-tampa-bay-mutin.html

34 *Wikipedia, The Free Encyclopedia*, s.vv. "Perry Van der Beck," accessed May 2, 2023, https://en.wikipedia.org/wiki/Perry_Van_der_Beck#National_Team

35 Bart Wright | *Tacoma News-Tribune*, "Preki: Tacoma's Rising Star," *Soccer Digest*, published Mar., 1987.

36 Ibid.

37 Ibid.

38 Ibid.

39 Dan Herbst, "Paul Caligiuri: The Great American Hope," *Soccer Digest*, published Nov., 1986.

40 Al Corona, "Does The U.S. Stand A Chance In Seoul?," *Soccer Digest*, published Aug./Sept., 1988.

41 *Wikipedia, The Free Encyclopedia*, s.vv. "Frank Klopas," accessed October 4, 2023, https://en.wikipedia.org/wiki/Frank_Klopas

42 Ibid.

43 Ibid.

44 *Wikipedia, The Free Encyclopedia*, s.vv. "Tony Meola," accessed May 23, 2023, https://en.wikipedia.org/wiki/Tony_Meola#Broadcasting

45 *Wikipedia, The Free Encyclopedia*, s.vv. "Jeff Agoos," accessed January 2, 2024, https://en.wikipedia.org/wiki/Jeff_Agoos

46 *Wikipedia, The Free Encyclopedia*, s.vv. "Kasey Keller," accessed July 9, 2023, https://en.wikipedia.org/wiki/Kasey_Keller

47 Ibid

48 *Wikipedia, The Free Encyclopedia*, s.vv. "Earnie Stewart," accessed June 9, 2023, https://en.wikipedia.org/wiki/Earnie_Stewart#See_also

49 Michael Lewis, "30 YEARS LATER: USMNT 1990 WORLD CUP ROSTER PLAYER CAPSULES," *ussoccer.com*, published June 23, 2020, accessed July 14, 2023, https://www.ussoccer.com/stories/2020/06/30-years-later-usmnt-1990-world-cup-roster-player-capsules

50 Ibid.

51 Ron Kantowski, "Eric Wynalda relives his dramatic goal in 1994 World Cup," *Las Vegas Review-Journal*, published June 22, 2019, accessed circa July 14, 2023, https://www.reviewjournal.com/sports/sports-columns/ron-kantowski/eric-wynalda-relives-his-dramatic-goal-in-1994-world-cup-1693104/

52 foxsports, "#OTD in 1996, Eric Wynalda scores first goal in MLS history," *Fox Sports*, published April 6, 2016, accessed July 13, 2023, https://www.foxsports.com/stories/soccer/otd-in-1996-eric-wynalda-scores-first-goal-in-mls-history

53 Ibid.

54 *Wikipedia, The Free Encyclopedia*, s.vv. "Cobi Jones," accessed July 25, 2023, https://en.wikipedia.org/wiki/Cobi_Jones

55 Michael Lewis, "30 YEARS LATER: USMNT 1990 WORLD CUP ROSTER PLAYER CAPSULES," *ussoccer.com*, published June 23, 2020, accessed July 14, 2023, https://www.ussoccer.com/stories/2020/06/30-years-later-usmnt-1990-world-cup-roster-player-capsules

56 *Wikipedia, The Free Encyclopedia*, s.vv. "Joe-Max Moore," accessed September 1, 2023, https://en.wikipedia.org/wiki/Joe-Max_Moore

57 Ibid.

58 *Wikipedia, The Free Encyclopedia*, s.vv. "Football at the Pan American Games," accessed September 1, 2023, https://en.wikipedia.org/wiki/Football_at_the_Pan_American_Games

59 *Wikipedia, The Free Encyclopedia*, s.vv. "1995 U.S. Cup," accessed September 7, 2023, https://en.wikipedia.org/wiki/1995_U.S._Cup#Champion

60 Ibid.

61 *Wikipedia, The Free Encyclopedia*, s.vv. "NCAA Division I Men's Soccer Tournament Most Outstanding Player," accessed July 25, 2023, https://en.wikipedia.org/wiki/NCAA_Division_I_Men%27s_Soccer_Tournament_Most_Outstanding_Player

62 *Wikipedia, The Free Encyclopedia*, s.vv. "Soccer America College Team of the Century," accessed September 5, 2023, https://en.wikipedia.org/wiki/Soccer_America_College_Team_of_the_Century

63 Ibid.

64 Joe Lyons | Post-Dispatch Special Correspondent, "U.S. OLYMPIC FESTIVAL '94," "Chance Sighting Leads Ralston To Festival," *St. Louis Post-Dispatch*, published July 2, 1994, p. 7C.

65 Staff Writer, "Former Crew player Frankie Hejduk revels in role as team and city ambassador," *The Columbus Dispatch*, published March 12, 2013, updated March 12, 2013, accessed January 3, 2024, https://www.dispatch.com/story/sports/mls/columbus-crew/2013/03/12/former-crew-player-frankie-hejduk/23760868007/

66 Ibid.

67 Ibid.

68 Kevin Baxter, "Tim Howard can't save U.S. at World Cup," *Los Angeles Times*, published July 1, 2014, accessed October 21, 2023, https://www.latimes.com/sports/soccer/worldcup/la-sp-us-belgium-world-cup-20140702-story.html

69 Denver Nicks, "U.S. Goalie Tim Howard's Heroic Effort in the World Cup," *TIME*, published July 1, 2014, accessed October 21, 2023, https://time.com/2947770/u-s-goalie-tim-howards-heroic-effort-in-the-world-cup/

70 *Wikipedia, The Free Encyclopedia*, s.vv. "Steve Cherundolo," accessed October 23, 2023, https://en.wikipedia.org/wiki/Steve_Cherundolo

71 *Wikipedia, The Free Encyclopedia*, s.vv. "Taylor Twellman," accessed May 22, 2020, https://en.wikipedia.org/wiki/Taylor_Twellman

72 Tom Timmermann, "Davis comes full circle," "St. Louisan returning to lead SLSG club here," *St. Louis Post-Dispatch*, STL TODAY SPORTS, published May 13, 2020, p. B1, B4.

73 Pardeep Cattry, "Landon Donovan opens up on USMNT time with Clint Dempsey: 'We loved winning and we were competitive as f–'," *CBS | Soccer*, published November 1, 2023, accessed November 2, 2023, https://www.cbssports.com/soccer/news/landon-donovan-opens-up-on-usmnt-time-with-clint-dempsey-we-loved-winning-and-we-were-competitive-as-f/

74 Ibid.

75 Ibid.

76 Josh Whisenhunt, "Landon Donovan really is in Cambodia," *MLS*, published February 28, 2013, accessed circa November 2, 2023, accessed April 9, 2025, https://www.mlssoccer.com/news/landon-donovan-really-cambodia

77 Ibid.

78 Steven Goff, "Landon Donovan offers thoughts about leave," *The Washington Post*, published February 21, 2013, accessed November 2, 2023, https://www.washingtonpost.com/news/soccer-insider/wp/2013/02/21/landon-donovan-offers-thoughts-about-leave/

79 Ibid.

80 *Wikipedia, The Free Encyclopedia*, s.vv. "Landon Donovan," accessed November 3, 2023, https://en.wikipedia.org/wiki/Landon_Donovan

81 Ibid.

82 Kevin Baxter, "Column: U.S. absence from World Cup draw shines a light on missed opportunities," *Los Angeles Times*, published December 2, 2017, accessed January 5, 2024, https://www.latimes.com/sports/soccer/la-sp-soccer-baxter-20171202-story.html

83 Ibid.

84 Mark Zeigler, "Herculez's soccer odyssey comes home," *The San Diego Union-Tribune*, published July 3, 2013, accessed January 5, 2024, https://www.sandiegouniontribune.com/sports/soccer/sdut-soccer-herculez-gomez-san-diego-xolos-2013jul03-story.html

85 MLSsoccer staff, "Gold Cup: Herculez Gomez leaves USMNT ahead of quarterfinals," *MLS | mlssoccer.com*, published July 17, 2013, accessed January 5, 2024, https://www.mlssoccer.com/news/gold-cup-herculez-gomez-leaves-usmnt-ahead-quarterfinals

86 Mark Zeigler, "Herculez's soccer odyssey comes home," *The San Diego Union-Tribune*, published July 3, 2013, accessed January 5, 2024, https://www.sandiegouniontribune.com/sports/soccer/sdut-soccer-herculez-gomez-san-diego-xolos-2013jul03-story.html

87 Ibid.

88 Richard Alleyne, "The secret heartbreak behind Clint Dempsey's goal celebration: Team USA's World Cup hero dedicates his career to sister and friend who each died tragically," *Daily Mail*,

published June 18, 2014, accessed November 11, 2023, https://www.dailymail.co.uk/news/article-2661342/With-fingers-sky-scoring-Team-USAs-World-Cup-hero-pays-tribute-sister-friend-died-tragically-Clint-Dempseys-secret-heartbreak-revealed.html

89 Ibid.

90 Ibid.

91 Michael Lewis, "CLINT DEMPSEY ELECTED TO NATIONAL SOCCER HALL OF FAME," *National Soccer Hall of Fame*, published January 30, 2022, accessed November 11, 2023, https://www.nationalsoccerhof.com/news/2022/01/clint-dempsey-elected-to-national-soccer-hall-of-fame.html

92 *Wikipedia, The Free Encyclopedia*, s.vv. "Clint Dempsey," accessed November 16, 2023, https://en.wikipedia.org/wiki/Clint_Dempsey

93 Ibid.

94 Matt Pentz, "Clint Dempsey was gritty as hell - but he could also conjure moments of inspiration," "The striker proved American outfield players could cut it in Europe and helped blaze a trail for the likes of Christian Pulisic," *The Guardian*, published August 30, 2018, accessed November 16, 2023, https://www.theguardian.com/football/2018/aug/30/clint-dempsey-seattle-sounders-fulham-retirement-usa-soccer

95 Ibid.

96 Ibid.

97 Ibid.

98 Ibid.

99 Ibid.

100 *Wikipedia, The Free Encyclopedia*, s.vv. "Clint Dempsey," accessed November 16, 2023, https://en.wikipedia.org/wiki/Clint_Dempsey

101 Wayne Drehs (Archive), "No ordinary background," *ESPN soccernet*, published June 8, 2006, accessed November 11, 2023, https://web.archive.org/web/20110629125514/http://soccernet.espn.go.com/columns/story?id=370300

102 *Christopher Kamrani, Matt Pentz and Sam Stejskal*, "Legend of Wondo: Untold stories about MLS' all-time leading scorer," *The Athletic*, published November 17, 2020, and November 7, 2021, accessed December 31, 2023, https://theathletic.com/2202333/2021/11/07/chris-wondolowski-untold-stories-mls-earthquakes/

103 Ibid.

104 *Wikipedia, The Free Encyclopedia*, s.vv. "Stuart Holden," accessed November 23, 2023, https://en.wikipedia.org/wiki/Stuart_Holden

105 Ibid.

106 WBZ-News Staff, "Charlie Davies excited to be a voice on CBS Sports Golazo Network," *WBZ News | CBS News Boston*, published April 11, 2023, accessed January 4, 2024, https://www.cbsnews.com/boston/news/charlie-davies-excited-to-be-a-voice-on-golazo-network-cbs-sports-24-hour-soccer-network/

107 Ibid.

108 *The University of Notre Dame* [no author], "Matt Besler Named First Team All-American By The NSCAA," *fightingirish.com*, published December 12, 2008, accessed November 29, 2023, https://fightingirish.com/matt-besler-named-first-team-all-american-by-the-nscaa/

109 Ibid.

110 Rob Goldberg, "Matt Besler Drawing 'Enormous Interest' According to Sporting Kansas City CEO," *Bleacher Report*, published July 3, 2014, accessed November 30, 2023, https://bleacherreport.com/articles/2118922-matt-besler-drawing-enormous-interest-according-to-sporting-kansas-city-ceo

111 Ibid.

112 Eric Betts, "Michael Bradley Will Always Be the Coach's Son," *Slate*, published June 10, 2016, accessed December 2, 2023, https://slate.com/culture/2016/06/michael-bradley-will-always-be-the-coachs-son.html

113 Ibid.

114 Ibid.

115 Ibid.

116 Ibid.

117 Ibid.

118 Andrew Joseph, "USMNT captain Tim Ream justifiably called out Sergiño Dest over his embarrassing tantrum and red card," *USA TODAY | SPORTS*, published November 21, 2023, accessed December 5, 2023, https://ftw.usatoday.com/lists/usmnt-tim-ream-comments-sergino-dest-tantrum-video-reaction-red-card

119 Ibid.

120 Ibid.

121 Mark Zeigler, "Adu's birth certificate worth questioning," *The San Diego Union-Tribune*, published January 6, 2010, accessed January 4, 2024, https://www.sandiegouniontribune.com/sdut-1s6socpage-2010jan06-story.html

122 Ibid.

123 Ibid.

124 Ibid.

125 Ibid.

126 Ibid.

127 *Wikipedia, The Free Encyclopedia*, s.vv. "Brek Shea," accessed December 9, 2023, https://en.wikipedia.org/wiki/Brek_Shea

128 Carter Baum, "FC Dallas Defender Walker Zimmerman Makes USMNT Debut, Named Player of the Match," *FC Dallas*, published February 3, 2017, accessed May 20, 2023, https://web.archive.org/web/20170204171043/http://www.fcdallas.com/post/2017/02/03/fc-dallas-defender-walker-zimmerman-makes-usmnt-debut-named-player-match

129 Ibid.

130 Alexa Philippou, "Men's soccer wins first-ever national title with dominant 4-0 win over Clemson," *The Stanford Daily*, published December 13, 2015, accessed December 15, 2023, https://stanforddaily.com/2015/12/13/champions-2/

131 Ibid.

132 Jonathan Sigal, "Jordan Morris injury "more serious" than last ACL tear," *MLS | mlssoccer.com*, published April 29, 2021, accessed December 18, 2023, https://www.mlssoccer.com/news/jordan-morris-injury-more-serious-than-last-acl-tear

133 Ibid.

134 Ibid.

135 *Wikipedia, The Free Encyclopedia*, s.vv. "Jordan Morris," accessed December 18, 2023, https://en.wikipedia.org/wiki/Jordan_Morris

136 Jonathan Sigal, "Jordan Morris injury "more serious" than last ACL tear," *MLS | mlssoccer.com*, published April 29, 2021, accessed December 18, 2023, https://www.mlssoccer.com/news/jordan-morris-injury-more-serious-than-last-acl-tear

137 *Wikipedia, The Free Encyclopedia*, s.vv. "Jordan Morris," accessed December 18, 2023, https://en.wikipedia.org/wiki/Jordan_Morris

138 *Wikipedia, The Free Encyclopedia*, s.vv. "Weston McKennie," accessed December 20, 2023, https://en.wikipedia.org/wiki/Weston_McKennie

139 By Paul Tenorio and The Athletic Staff, "USMNT player Weston McKennie fractures bones in foot, expected to miss 8–12 weeks: Source," *The Athletic*, published February 22, 2022, accessed December 21, 2023, https://theathletic.com/3510993/2022/02/22/usmnt-player-weston-mckennie-fractures-bones-in-foot-expected-to-miss-8-12-weeks-source/

140 Joe Prince-Wright, Andy Edwards, "Tyler Adams injury update: USMNT captain out until February after second surgery," *NBC Sports*, published October 20, 2023, accessed December 22, 2023, https://www.nbcsports.com/soccer/news/tyler-adams-injury-update

141 Mark Harris, "Sergino Dest rightfully gets called out by teammates, media after throwing tantrum against Trinidad & Tobago," *OutKick*, published November 21, 2023, updated November 21, 2023, accessed December 23, 2023, https://www.outkick.com/sergino-dest-red-card-trinidad-tobago-usmnt-reaction/

142 Mike DeCourcy, "Sergino Dest's petulance led to a red card that punished his USMNT teammates – now it's time for him to pay the penalty," *The Sporting News*, published November 20, 2023, accessed December 22, 2023, https://www.sportingnews.com/us/soccer/news/sergino-dests-red-card-punished-his-usmnt-teammates/ed64d79dfb14817cd14da3c3

143 Seth Vertelney, "Biggest stars left off USMNT Nations League roster. Latest injury update for Pulisic, Weah," *USA TODAY*, published November 9, 2023, updated November 9, 2023, accessed December 25, 2023, https://www.usatoday.com/story/sports/mls/2023/11/09/pulisic-weah-injury-news-berhalter-usmnt/71518658007/

144 Ibid.

145 Kyle Bonagura, ESPN Staff Writer, "Jesus Ferreira makes USMNT history with back-to-back hat tricks," *ESPN | Soccer*, published July 2, 2023, accessed December 25, 2023, https://www.espn.com/soccer/story/_/id/37951022/ferreira-makes-usmnt-history-back-back-hat-tricks

146 Ibid.

147 Garrett Melcer, "2022 Season," "Jesús Ferreira Becomes First FC Dallas Player to Feature in FIFA World Cup Match," *FC Dallas*, published December 5, 2022, accessed December 26, 2023, https://www.fcdallas.com/news/jesus-ferreira-becomes-first-fc-dallas-player-to-feature-in-fifa-world-cup-match

148 Ibid.

149 *Wikipedia, The Free Encyclopedia*, s.vv. "Christian Pulisic," accessed December 28, 2023, https://en.wikipedia.org/wiki/Christian_Pulisic

150 Ibid.

151 Stefan Bienkowski, "At 17, Christian Pulisic does what no one has with U.S. Soccer and in Bundesliga," *The Washington Post*, published May 3, 2016, accessed December 29, 2023, https://www.washingtonpost.com/news/soccer-insider/wp/2016/05/03/at-17-christian-pulisic-does-what-no-one-has-with-u-s-soccer-and-in-bundesliga/

152 Ibid.

153 Lucas Manfredi, "Nike loses Christian Pulisic to Puma," "PUMA will produce a pair of customized Pulisic ULTRA 1.3's, which will debut Aug. 11 at the Super Cup final," *FOX Business*, published August 9, 2021, accessed December 30, 2023, https://www.foxbusiness.com/sports/soccer-star-christian-pulisic-leaves-nike-for-puma-in-new-brand-partnership

154 Ibid.

ABOUT THE AUTHOR

SHANE STAY is a bestselling author whose books include *This Is Our CITY, THE World Cup 2022 Book, The Euro 2020 Book, European Soccer Leagues 2019, Major League Soccer 2019, THE Women's World Cup 2019 Book, THE World Cup 2018 Book, Why American Soccer Isn't There Yet*, and *The Cairo Project*. In 2008, he played professional soccer, co-authored a print book, published a magazine story, bottled Leaf Dressing, worked clubs as a comedian, was a restaurateur, and received a Master of Arts from Southern Illinois University. In 1999, he founded the first online Current Events Game (CE Game). He has appeared on TV and has featured on numerous radio broadcasts including ESPN and NPR.

Credits

Cover and interior design:	Anja Elsen
Layout:	DiTech Publishing Services, www.ditechpubs.com
Cover image:	© AdobeStock
Managing editor:	Elizabeth Evans
Copy editor:	Anne Rumery